KW-582-171

The rhetoric of historical representation

THE RHETORIC OF HISTORICAL REPRESENTATION

Three narrative histories of the French Revolution

ANN RIGNEY
Lecturer in Literary Theory, The University of Utrecht

The right of the University of Cambridge to print and sell all manner of books was granted by Henry VIII in 1534. The University has printed and published continuously since 1584.

CAMBRIDGE UNIVERSITY PRESS
Cambridge
New York Port Chester
Melbourne Sydney

Published by the Press Syndicate of the University of Cambridge
The Pitt Building, Trumpington Street, Cambridge CB2 1RP
40 West 20th Street, New York, NY 10011, USA
10 Stamford Road, Oakleigh, Melbourne 3166, Australia

First published 1990

Printed in Great Britain by
the University Press, Cambridge

British Library cataloguing in publication data
Rigney, Ann
The rhetoric of historical representation: three
narrative histories of the French Revolution.
1. French revolution, 1789–1799. Historiography
I. Title
944.04′1′072

Library of Congress cataloguing in publication data
Rigney, Ann
The rhetoric of historical representation : three narrative
histories of the French Revolution. / Ann Rigney.
p. cm.
Includes bibliographical references.
ISBN 0 521 38152 5
1. France – History – Revolution, 1789–1799 – Historiography,
2. France – History – Revolution, 1789–1799 – Literature and
revolution. 3. Literature and history – France. 4. French
literature – 19th century – History and criticism. I. Title.
DC147.8.R5 1990
944.04 – dc20 89-22330
CIP

ISBN 0 521 38152 5 hardback

For Joep

Contents

Preface

This is a literary study of historical writing. A few preliminary remarks on the relation between history-writing and 'literature' may therefore be in order. 'For a long time', as Lionel Gossman writes of pre-1800 discursive practice, 'the relation of history to literature was not notably problematic. History was a branch of literature' (1978:3). We might add that, for the best part of the last 150 years, the relationship between the writing of history and the writing of literature has been equally unproblematic – but for quite the opposite reason: history and literature being apparently of such separate orders, there was no common ground between them worth making an issue of. As a result, the literary or discursive dimension of history-writing has for long been ignored: on the one hand, by literary scholars, whose concern has been almost exclusively with the traditional 'literary' genres of prose fiction, drama, poetry; on the other hand, by historians, for whom the role of discourse in the constitution of historical knowledge has not been of particular theoretical importance.

The appearance of an essay such as Gossman's – pregnantly entitled 'History and Literature: Reproduction or Signification?' – indicates that the relationship between 'history' and 'literature' has become an issue again. The question raised in his title reflects recent developments in the concept and study of discourse (its extension beyond the confines of 'literary' works) and the growing interest, on the part of literary theorists as well as historians, in the role which discourse plays in historiographical practice.[1]

That the frontier between discourse and history is now open again is illustrated by the growing attention which historians are paying to the role of texts in their object of study and to their own role as interpreters of texts

[1] For a general survey of these diverse theoretical developments and the relations between them, see Struever 1985.

and decoders of signs. (Witness, for instance, Dominick LaCapra's insistence that intellectual historians should move away from a naively 'documentary' to a textual approach to their material; witness Carlo Ginzburg's self-consciousness in attempting to 'read' the semi-literate mind of a sixteenth-century miller in his *Il formaggio e i vermi*, 1976.[2]) Not only have historians been profiting from developments in semiotics and textual analysis to renew their own practices, but there has also been increasing interest in the role of the historian himself as a writer and producer of texts. What is or what should be – the difference is not always clearly drawn – the role of discourse and the role of narrative form in the constitution and communication of historical knowledge? In very different ways, works like Paul Veyne's *Comment on écrit l'histoire*, 1971/1978, Michel de Certeau's *L'Écriture de l'histoire*, 1975, and the collection edited by Jürgen Kocka and Thomas Nipperdey, *Theorie und Erzählung in der Geschichte*, 1979, have attempted to address these theoretical questions with a view to historiographical practice. Among those who have approached similar questions from a literary perspective, that is, with a view to a greater understanding of symbolic productions, we find above all the name of Roland Barthes and of Hayden White, whose 1973 *Metahistory* has played a key role in waking the sleeping dog (or sleeping beauty) of historical discourse after a century of positivist neglect.

In the first instance, those theorists approaching historical writing from a literary perspective concentrated on the referential function of historical discourse in an attempt to overcome what they perceived to be a general resistance on the part of historians to the very notion that historical writing involves 'signification' rather than 'reproduction'. Thus Barthes' seminal 'Le Discours de l'histoire' (1967) was implicitly based on a particular view of 'the historian' as someone who blithely ignores the discursive basis of his own representations, someone who naively (and erroneously) believes in his own power or the power of language to copy the past 'as it really was'.[3] In a similar way, the main thrust of Hayden White's early work was pitted against the 'reluctance to consider historical narratives as what they most manifestly are – verbal fictions' (1978:42).

[2] See also Schmid 1986 and its programme for an explicitly semiological *Geschichtswissenschaft*.

[3] Both in his 'Le Discours de l'histoire' (1982:20n; originally published 1967) and in his classic 'L'Effet de réel' (1968:88), Barthes exemplifies the 'naivety' of historians with a quote from Thiers: 'Etre simplement vrai, être ce que sont les choses elles-mêmes...' ('To be simply true, to be what things themselves are...'). See Bann (1984:8f) for a critical exploration of the mythical status of Ranke's infamous 'wie es eigentlich gewesen'.

Thanks in no small part to the critical endeavours of Barthes and White, it has now been generally recognised that historical works are not only documentary sources of information about the past, but also 'verbal artifacts' which may be legitimately studied as such. We can safely assume that the question 'reproduction or signification?' no longer needs to be asked.

But, having granted the theoretical point that there can be no discursive representation without signification, it seems time to go further in examining what sort of 'signification' it is that historians produce and how they actually go about producing it through the medium of discourse. Above all, it seems necessary to consider the discursive dimension of the historian's work more closely in the light of its specifically historiographical function, that is to say, its function in representing and explaining real events of collective significance. If we grant that all historical texts are signifying constructs, do we have no other option but to follow Hayden White in concluding that they are also 'verbal fictions'? These are the issues which concern me here.

Rather than address these questions in a purely theoretical manner, however, I shall proceed by way of the analysis of particular historiographical practices, using the insights of contemporary semiotics and narrative analysis – a body of critical discourse which, with the exception of Barthes' brief essay, has rarely been brought to bear on historical works. Through the close, sustained analysis of particular texts from the nineteenth century, I hope to be able to broaden the range of theoretical questions which might be asked of other historical discourses and to bring more clearly into focus the particular constraints involved in historical, as distinct from fictional, narration.

This interest in the relationship between discursive form and historiographical function prompted me to focus my analysis on three, roughly coeval narrative histories dealing with a common topic: namely, Lamartine's *Histoire des Girondins* (1847), Michelet's *Histoire de la Révolution française* (1847–53), and Blanc's *Histoire de la Révolution française* (1847–62). Three histories, written in a similar socio-cultural context, some 60 years after the Revolution to which they commonly refer.

The same concern with 'historiographical function' also dictated my way of proceeding with these works: rather than give primacy to the individual texts (by devoting one chapter to each work, for example), I have allowed the events to take centre field. More precisely, I have opted to organise my analyses around the different representations of certain core episodes or key figures in the Revolution – notably, the 'Journées d'octobre' (1789), the 'Massacre du Champ de Mars' (July 1791), 'Le 10 août' (1792), the judgement of Louis XVI (January 1793), the conflict between Danton and Robespierre. In adopting this comparative, event-based method, I aimed to bring into relief, against the background of a common event or a common figure, the discursive and narrative strategies actually deployed by the different writers in representing and giving meaning to events. While this event-based approach has enabled me to foreground the literary activity of the different historian-narrators, it has been equally important in helping to show up the constraints imposed on them by the nature of their historiographical role and the nature of the raw material with which they are dealing; the fact that they are not free to produce whatever meaning they choose; the fact that, unlike fiction-writers, they are not free to invent.

Some of the differences between the three writers in their view of the Revolution, and in their ideological presuppositions, do emerge in the course of my analysis; they are not, however, the immediate subject of the analysis itself. For my primary concern here is not to describe in detail the three interpretations of the Revolution and the ideologies which inform them, but to investigate the literary means through which those interpretations are established in the first place; the literary, and specifically narrative, means through which real events in the past can be symbolically reconstituted and invested with a particular significance for a latter-day public.

All quotations from foreign languages are given in translation and, except where otherwise indicated, all translations are my own. In certain cases, where the precise wording of the original seemed important, I have included both original and translation.

Acknowledgements

The preparation of this work has left me indebted to many different people in many different places. In particular, I would like to express my gratitude to Peter Nesselroth (who first suggested the project to me) and to Roland Le Huenen: their intellectual engagement with the enterprise stimulated my work, and their unfailing encouragement and support went a long way towards ensuring its completion.

I would also like to express my special thanks to a number of other scholars for their suggestions, criticisms and questions at various stages in the making of this book: to Claude Duchet, for helping me define the project; to Claudette Sarlet and Jacques Dubois, for the important role they played in helping me get it off the ground; to Linda Hutcheon, Mario Valdés, Graham Falconer, and Arthur Mitzman for their critical reading of the first completed version; to Linda Orr, for her intensive and generous reading of the whole, for her suggestions at various points, and for our heady discussion about Lamartine; finally, to Pieter de Meijer in Amsterdam, for offering his knowledge, time, and constructive criticisms towards the making of the final version. I am also endebted to Paul Viallaneix for his generosity in providing me with research material; and to the University of Toronto, the Ontario Government, and the French Community of Belgium, who made my research financially possible.

The combination of literature and history at the basis of this work reflects a long-standing debt to my parents. The work itself reflects throughout my debt to Joep, without whose partnership it now seems inconceivable.

Introduction

> Should we accept, as is, that differentiation between the main types of discourse, or between forms or genres, which sets science, literature, philosophy, religion, history, fiction, etc. against each other, turning each into some great historical individuality? We ourselves are not sure of the usage of these distinctions in our own discursive environment; let alone when it comes to analysing sets of statements which, at the time of their initial formulation, were grouped, classified and typified along quite different lines.
> Michel Foucault, *L'Archéologie du savoir* (1969)

In the preface to his *Histoire des Ducs de Bourgogne* (1824), Prosper de Barante deplored the 'artificial dignity' of French history as it had hitherto been written. The 'faithful representation of truth', he claimed, was foreign to eighteenth-century histories; 'the vivid impression produced on our minds by the spectacle of real events is nowhere to be found in them' (1838 edn, I:12). Barante's critique of his predecessors was echoed by Augustin Thierry who complained, in his *Dix ans d'études historiques* (1835), that French history as written until recently had been 'cold and monotonous', because 'false and contrived' (1851 edn, VI:258).

The nineteenth-century historians' rejection of their predecessors exemplifies what Michel de Certeau has recently described as historiography's tendency to carve out its own territory in a negative way, by setting itself up as different from the discourses it perceives as fictional or falsifying (1982:19). For it is above all through their rejection of the 'literary', artificial, false histories written in the eighteenth century by pseudo-historians[1] that Barante and Thierry credit themselves *a contrario* with the authority to speak for the 'real', to give – as Barante put it – 'a faithful representation of truth'.

What is of particular interest here, however, is the fact that Barante and Thierry, in setting themselves up against their predecessors, not only criticise earlier work for its inaccuracy or literariness, but also for its monotony, its coldness, and its lack of animation. In this way, the nineteenth-century historians imply that the *nouvelle histoire* which they

[1] Barante, for example, presents his predecessors as 'men of the literary profession, dedicated to making artificial compositions' (1838, I:8).

themselves are engaged in writing is (or should be) warm, alive, natural, as well as true: a 'spectacle' capable of producing a 'vivid impression' on its audience. Where modern theorists might work within the framework of the difference science/literature, the key terms for these nineteenth-century historians are 'animate' and 'inanimate' (viz. cold, monotonous, artificial). A faithful representation of the truth, they imply, is recognisable by its capacity to come *alive* for the reader, to provide him with 'that intimate knowledge which comes from seeing and hearing living beings' (Barante 1838, I:10).[2]

In this way, the new generation of early nineteenth-century historians set themselves up in opposition to the conventionality and artificiality of their predecessors in the eighteenth century. Yet, the very fact that the same cluster of concepts should regularly recur across the extensive metahistorical discourse of this period already suggests that, in turn, the 'new history' became itself conventional; that its programme of representing 'living' historical reality became codified and, hence, imitable.[3]

For us nowadays, what is almost as remarkable as the correlation 'vitality' and historical truth is the fact that the historians should have been so concerned with the problems involved in the discursive transmission of historical knowledge. According to Barthes, one of the characteristics of historical discourse is the fact that there are generally no signs of the addressee (1982:15): the theoretical writings of Thierry, Barante and their contemporaries seem to place a question mark beside this assumption since, in commenting on their own work, they show a

[2] See also Sismondi's *Histoire des Français* with its complaint that 'the principal cause of the coldness of French history lies in its lack of truth' (1821–44, I:iv); and its complaint that his predecessors had put enormous philosophical effort into their presentation of past events 'without our perceiving the animating principle [*le principe de vie*] which had made these events grow out of each other' (1821–44, I:iii).

[3] In their turn, the critical standards prevalent among historians in the first half of the nineteenth century were to be summed up, and with the same stone condemned as 'literary', by Charles-Victor Langlois and Charles Seignobos in their late-nineteenth-century positivist manual of historiography, *Introduction aux études historiques* (1898): 'Under the influence of the romantic movement, historians looked for expository techniques which would be more vivid than those of their predecessors, which would succeed in striking and in moving their public, and give the most poetical impression of lost realities... In the work of all the romantic historians, the way of proceeding and the choice of topic, of evidence, and of style were dictated by their concern to provoke an effect, a concern which is certainly not a scientific one. It is a literary concern' (1898:260–1). For the general background to the historiographical poetics of the first half of the nineteenth century, see Bann 1984, Reizov c.1962, Stadler 1958, Moreau 1935, Fueter 1911, Jullian 1897.

persistent concern with the effect which their representations would or should have on their latter-day readers.

Historical scholarship, as Thierry insisted in his 'Considérations sur l'histoire de France' (1840), is only one aspect of the historian's task; equally important is the way in which he communicates his findings. Thus, the work involved in researching and gathering facts has to be followed by the vital, complicated work of 'narration', requiring the interpretation, the collation, and the 'painting' of events. It is through the specifically literary work of narration that the historian actually re-presents past events for his contemporaries and makes manifest what is presumed to be their inherent, organic structure. It is only through narration that the historian can find 'the law of cause and effect which links facts to each other' and give to past events 'their significance, their character, and that liveliness which can never be absent from the spectacle of human affairs' (1851, VII:158). By implication, then, it is only through successful – vivid – narration that historical truth (by definition, vivid) can be encapsulated. The double task of the historian had been summed up earlier by J. Sarazin in his 1835 dissertation on modern historiography: after the historian had completed his research, Sarazin wrote, his power to resurrect the past as an organic whole must come into play:

> alors viendra le génie de l'histoire, avec sa puissance de création, féconder cette inerte matière, et commander ... à ces ossemens blanchis et épars de se redresser, de reprendre vie, de se rejoindre et de s'agencer de nouveau dans un corps harmonieux, et de reparaître aux regards de la postérité avec leur couleur, leur forme, leur mouvement d'autrefois.[4]
>
> [And then the genius of history will come with its creative power, fertilising this inert material, ordering ... these bleached and scattered bones to stand up, to come back to life again, to reunite and join together in a harmonious body, and to reappear before the eyes of posterity with the form, the colour and the movement which they had in former times.]

That these early nineteenth-century historians should have been so concerned with the literary work involved in conveying the character and significance of past events to a contemporary reader, that they should have grounded the historical authority of their work in its capacity to

[4] Sarazin 1835:22–3. The image of resuscitation or resurrection is also to be found throughout Michelet's writings; in the 1873 preface to his *Histoire du dix-neuvième siècle*, for example, he summed up his professional achievements in the following terms: 'I have given to many of the too long forgotten dead the assistance which I shall need myself. I exhumed them for a second life ... They now live with us and we feel they are our relatives, our friends. In this way, a family is formed, a federation [*une cité commune*] between the living and the dead' (1982:268).

'resurrect the past' for the reader, can be explained by the historical conjunction of a number of related theoretical and material factors:
(a) There was the persistent, albeit declining, influence of the rhetorical tradition, where the addressee figured as one of the primary concerns of all literary composition and where historiography figured as one of the more serious literary genres.[5]
(b) In the first half of the century, historiography was still generally practised by 'laymen' who wrote for the general reading public; the historical institution with its own clerisy of specially trained academic historians, its own objects and methods of research, and its own legitimising authorities, was beginning to be established; but it did not emerge fully until later in the century.[6]
(c) In the absence of an autonomous historiographical territory, and in the wake of Walter Scott (who was the original catalyst and model for the historians' emphasis on vivid narration), there was a certain degree of competition between novelists and historians for public attention and recognition.[7]
(d) Finally, the new poetics of history-writing, the new vivid manner of writing history based on narration, description, and details of local colour à la Scott, was regularly linked to, and as it were motivated by, the historian's new, explicitly *popular* subject-matter. If history as it had hitherto been written seemed cold, monotonous, artificial, and uninteresting, this was not only because of the philosophical, dignified, or formulaic style in which it had been written: its 'artificial solemnity' (Barante 1838, I:11) also stemmed from its exclusive concern with the activities of courts and kings, and with what Sarazin called 'those dry catalogues of political events in which the people played no part' (1835:25–6).

The 'new history', then, was not just a matter of writing the same 'history' in a different way. It involved, rather, writing in a new way the

[5] History was treated among the literary genres in Marmontel's *Eléments de littérature* (1787), for example, and in Mme de Staël's *De la littérature* (1800). Since then, it has not just happened that history ceased being 'literary'; literature itself had been something quite different when it was defined by Mme de Staël as 'everything which involves the exercise of thought through writing' (1820:200). For the emergence of the modern literary institution in France between 1830 and 1850, see Dubois 1983:19–30.

[6] For the emergence of history as an academic discipline in the course of the nineteenth century, see Keylor 1975, Den Boer 1987.

[7] Barante, for example, wrote that it was time to restore to history 'the attractions borrowed by the historical novel' (1838, I:16), while Macaulay urged that 'a truly great historian would reclaim those materials which the novelist has appropriated' (1906, VII:217). For the influence of Scott on historiographical practice, see Massmann 1972:81–9. For the changing status of the novel in France at this period, see Iknayan 1961.

real history, which had never yet been written about; what Thierry called 'l'histoire des citoyens, l'histoire des sujets, l'histoire du public, l'histoire de la masse' ('the history of citizens, the history of political subjects, the history of the public, the history of the majority'):

> cette histoire nous présenterait à la fois des exemples pratiques et cet intérêt humain que nous cherchons vainement dans les aventures bizarres d'un petit nombre de personnages prétendus seuls historiques. Nos âmes s'attacheraient au sort de ces hommes semblables en tout à nous mêmes, bien mieux qu'à la fortune des grands, la seule qu'on nous célèbre encore, et la seule qui ne nous importe point; leurs progrès nous sembleraient plus imposants que la marche des faiseurs de conquêtes, et leurs misères plus touchantes que celle des rois dépossédés.[8]
>
> [This history would offer at once practical models and that human interest which we look for in vain in the bizarre adventures of the few figures hitherto considered historical. Our hearts would become involved in the fate of men who are like ourselves in all respects, much more than they do in the fortunes of the great, which are as yet the only fortunes celebrated and the only ones to which we are indifferent; the progress of men like ourselves would seem more impressive than the advance of conquerors, and their miseries more touching than that of dispossessed kings.]

The history of 'citizens' or of 'the majority' was to be found, for example, in the struggles of the subject or conquered peoples, in the early history of the race,[9] in the history of customs, trades, technologies – all of which had hitherto received scant attention from the historians.[10]

[8] Letter to the *Courrier Français* (23 July 1820); quoted in Smithson 1973:82. See also the opening of Monteil's *Histoire des Français des divers états* (1828–44): 'If nowadays one were to write history for the first time in the way in which it was written in antiquity, in the way it is still being written, no one would fail to say: "That is the history of kings, of clerics, of military men... it is not the history of the different estates, it is not history"' (1843, I:5).

[9] In his study of historiographical practices during the *Restauration*, Stanley Mellon describes the popularity of ancient Gaul as a historical topic, and how the Frankish conquest was interpreted as an aristocratic one (1958:62). Augustin Thierry proposed that representing the struggle of our forefathers to gain their liberty would serve to remind today's generation of their debt to the past and to encourage them in their struggle to preserve that hard-won freedom in the future (1851, IV:95; V:365). On Thierry and this 'liberal historiography' see Gossman 1976.

[10] Monteil, in his *Les Français pour la première fois dans l'histoire de France ou poétique de l'histoire des divers états* (c.1840), set out clearly a historiographical programme which would get away from what he called the old 'histoire bataille' to 'what is truly history' (1841:5). This new *national* history would concentrate on such socio-cultural topics as agriculture, commerce, industry, institutions, village life, hospitals, language, and literature. It is interesting to note that, in the preface to his *Comédie humaine* (1842), Balzac also staked his claim to this socio-cultural

Since it not only took as its subject ordinary men or 'the people', but also presented these subjects in a vivid way, the new history would offer the public of today 'le vif intérêt d'un tableau de famille' ('the vivid interest of a family portrait', Capefigue 1829, I:ii).[11] Our interest and our natural, filial sympathies would be aroused by the representation of men who are at once 'like ourselves' and different: being men like ourselves as they lived and struggled at a different point in time. Who these 'men like ourselves' were – or indeed who 'we' might happen to be – is not raised as a particular issue here.

What is clear, however, is that the historian's claim to give a faithful or realistic representation of past actualities was regularly linked to his claim to take as his subject 'society as a whole' (however this might be defined in particular instances). For not everything in the past actually belonged to history, some topics being seen as more or less 'historical' than others. The 'historical' was thus recognised at once by the fact of its being 'real' and by the fact of its being *representative*, that is, by the fact that it represented the common past of the public, the adventures of society ('les aventures de la vie sociale', Thierry 1851, IV:95) rather than the bizarre adventures of some few, untypical, regal individuals.

In France, the project to write the 'history of the majority' was linked to the recent events of the Revolution, which had not only called upon the nation to play an active role in the making of history (Capefigue 1829, I:i-ii), but had also retrospectively brought to the light of day many, hitherto unrepresented, aspects of the past, 'which had been constantly left in the shadows although they were an essential part of the general life' (Sarazin 1835:7). The French Revolution inaugurated a democratic culture where the nation and public will are recognised as the source of political legitimacy, where power, therefore, belongs in theory to those who speak in the name of the people (Furet 1978:47, 85). The theoretical statements of Sarazin and his contemporaries show how the Revolution, in establishing the nation as the symbolic source of political legitimacy, also retroactively established the 'nation' – 'the men like ourselves' – as the

history, invoking Scott as his model and contending that social history ('l'histoire des moeurs') had simply been ignored by historians who had been too preoccupied with relating political events (1976–81, I:17).

L'historiographie se répète? Writing as recently as 1976, Carlo Ginzburg was still announcing history's breaking away from the narrow confines of political 'elite' history: 'In the past historians could be accused of wanting to know only about "the great deeds of kings", but today this is certainly no longer true. More and more they are turning toward what their predecessors passed over in silence...' (1981: viii).

[11] For the development of the moral and aesthetic category of 'the interesting' at the end of the eighteenth century, see Brooks 1985:13.

subject of history and, hence, as the proper subject of modern historiography.[12]

Since it marked the beginning of the modern age and, retrospectively, of the new history, the Revolution was itself the historical topic *par excellence.* Pascal Duprat wrote in *La Revue indépendante* in 1847, for example, that the Revolution had inaugurated a 'new life' and was, therefore, still the most 'living' of topics:

> Cette vie nouvelle... rend compte des oppositions et des sympathies que nos pères ont rencontrées dans leur laborieuse carrière; elle explique l'intérêt profond que leur oeuvre a suscité chez tous les peuples voisins. Elle justifie en même temps cette curiosité inquiète et passionnée que réveillent en nous les récits de leurs travaux. Nous serions tous moins ardents pour des choses mortes.[13]
>
> [This new life... accounts for the oppositions and sympathies which our fathers encountered in their laborious careers; it explains the profound interest which their work aroused among neighbouring peoples. At the same time, it explains the anxious and impassioned curiosity which every account of their work awakens in us. We would all be less ardent about dead things.]

However, if the French Revolution, as the event which had inaugurated the modern age, was the most interesting and vivid of historical topics, it was for that very reason also one of the most frequently treated ones – it was far indeed from being the history which had never yet been written. By 1847, for instance, when Duprat wrote the above lines, the French Revolution had already inspired – to name only the most prominent – Mignet's *Histoire de la Révolution française* (1824), Thiers' *Histoire de la Révolution française* (1823–8), Buchez and Roux's *Histoire parlementaire de la Révolution française* (1834–38), Lamartine's *Histoire des Girondins* (1847), Esquiros' *Histoire des Montagnards* (1847), and the first volumes of Michelet's *Histoire de la Révolution française* (1847–53) and Blanc's *Histoire de la Révolution française* (1847–62).

So many histories, so many 'French Revolutions' – each one claiming to represent 'the French Revolution' itself. The struggle between the different historians for what Furet has recently called 'the political

12 Linda Orr argues in her study of 'L'Autorité "populaire" de l'historiographie romantique' that the figure of the historian became theoretically eclipsed by that of the *peuple*: the public is both the 'author' of the history-to-be-represented and the addressee of the history-as-represented (1982:464).

13 Duprat 1847:62. Similarly, Etienne Cabet invoked the exemplary character of his topic in the 1839 preface to his *Histoire populaire de la Révolution française de 1789 à 1830*: 'Of all the revolutions whose memory has been preserved in history, there is none which presents, to the same degree as the French Revolution, such a majestic, dramatic spectacle, throbbing with interest, filled with instructive lessons, and deserving careful contemplation by all friends of humanity...' (1839–40, I:v).

administration of the revolutionary heritage' (1986:12) indicates the symbolic importance of 'the Revolutionary past' at each stage of the nation's development since 1789. At the same time, the multiplicity of different histories of the Revolution intimates the necessarily imaginary nature of any *single* 'national past' or single 'histoire de la masse'.

A survey of these different histories indicates the extent to which the (re)writing of history went together with the making of history in post-Revolutionary France.[14] The production of histories of the Revolution was closely linked to ongoing political developments: on the one hand, fresh political developments cast a different light on the events of 1789–94; on the other hand, new perspectives on those events served as a model or guide for future political action. Thus, Thiers' liberal history of the Revolution, produced in the final years of the *Restauration* and in opposition to the current regime, is considered to have played an important role in providing the ideological foundations for the Revolution of 1830 and the constitutional monarchy which it established.[15]

In a review essay written in 1850, Henri Baudrillart related how the Revolution of 1830 had completed and brought to fruition the work of the great Revolution, and how it had been influenced and inspired in this by Thiers' *Histoire de la Révolution française* (Baudrillart 1850:813). Baudrillart then turns his attention to the recent crop of new 'demagogic' histories (814) and complains that they had led to a betrayal of the true legacy of the French Revolution: they not only distorted the true (Liberal) Revolution by rehabilitating the 'demagogic' phase of 1793, but in doing so they in turn had influenced the events of February 1848 which led to the fall of the constitutional monarchy and initiated the establishment of a new, if shortlived, Republic (819). Clearly, for Baudrillart – though not for those whom he calls 'demagogic' historians – the history as well as the historiography of the Revolution ended or should have ended with 1830 and with Thiers' 'definitive' history.

As Baudrillart's critique suggests, the Revolution of 1848 (like the Revolution of 1830) had been prepared for by a new generation of histories of the Revolution. It is difficult to establish exactly how the new histories appearing in the last years of the July monarchy actually influenced the course of events, and who precisely read them; but there is no doubt that the revised image of the French Revolution which they

[14] See Mellon 1958 for a study of the period 1815–30 (when 'history was the language of politics', p.1). For general studies of the representations of the French Revolution during the Restoration and the July Monarchy (1830–48), see Gérard 1970, Geyl 1961, McManners 1965.

[15] Coornaert, for example, refers to the Revolution of 1830 as 'the historians' victory' (1977:26).

offered to the public reflected, at the same time as it contributed to, the growing perception that social change was needed or imminent; that the legacy of the first, of *the* Revolution had not yet been brought to fruition.[16] For the last years of the constitutional monarchy saw the production of a number of histories which challenged the by-now dominant history of Thiers in which the Revolution was defined by its pre-Republican, constitutional monarchy phases; in their different ways, these new histories sought to rehabilitate the Republican, democratic phases of the Revolution, presenting these as its true legacy and as a guide for future action.[17] Most prominent among these new histories were those written by Alphonse de Lamartine, Jules Michelet, and Louis Blanc – and it is these three works which shall be my particular concern here.

Lamartine's *Histoire des Girondins* appeared between March and June 1847 and, thanks to the prior reputation of the author and the prior publicity given it in the press, it was an immediate and immense commercial success; in July 1847, for example, a banquet was organised in Mâcon in honour of the poet-politician-historian and attended by more than 3,000 people.[18] Indeed, Lamartine's reputation as author of the *Girondins* contributed greatly to the writer's becoming minister in the provisional government of February 1848 as representative of the centre-left and to his being elected by no less than 10 *départements* in the April elections.[19]

[16] See Agulhon 1973:6–9.

[17] See Furet's discussion of the chronological displacement within the historiography of the Revolution from the '89-ism' of a Thiers to the '93-ism' of the new historians (1986:12f).

[18] According to Henri Guillemin, Lamartine had explicitly stated his desire to outdo Eugène Sue, the great popular success of *Les Mystères de Paris* (1842–3) having provided him with a model of what might be achieved with such a topical subject as the Girondins (1946:116n). And indeed he managed to sell the manuscript to the publisher for the phenomenal sum of 250,000 francs (cf. J.-P. Jacques' preface in Lamartine 1983, I:16n). Guillemin insists, however, that if Lamartine's motives were in part commercial (his personal finances were in a sorry mess), he was also motivated by his political commitment (1946:97f): having been aligned with the legitimist opposition in the early 1840s, he had grown increasingly aware that a return to the *status quo ante* was an impossibility; that radical social change was necessary and imminent; and that, this being the case, he should try to give direction to those changes (1948:6–7). Court 1985 (chap. 5) gives a detailed account of the reception of the *Girondins*: widely read and reviewed, it was highly acclaimed by many (particularly by women) as having shown the splendours and pathos of the Revolutionary period, while it provoked the anger of many others and, above all, of the legitimist opposition. See below, p.22.

[19] Having occupied a conciliatory position in the centre-left, Lamartine was soon outmanoeuvred by the right and had effectively fallen from power by the end of June 1848. For a detailed account of Lamartine's sudden rise and fall, see Guillemin 1948 and Agulhon 1973.

The first volumes of Blanc's *Histoire de la Révolution française* also appeared in 1847; and the socialist Blanc, like Lamartine, also went on to belong to the provisional government of the 1848 Republic where, as representative of the far left, he was active in organising the controversial *ateliers nationaux*. Having been forced into exile after the swing to the right on 15 May and the bloody suppression of the workers' demonstrations at the end of June, Blanc was to finish his history in exile in 1862.[20]

The first two volumes of Michelet's *Histoire de la Révolution française* likewise appeared in 1847. Although the professional historian, archivist, and university lecturer Michelet did not take a direct part in the Revolution of 1848, his rousing lectures at the Collège de France were considered so provocative in their republicanism that they were closed down by the authorities on 2 January 1848 (and opened again very soon after the declaration of the Republic on 24 February).[21] The next three volumes of his history appeared between 1849 and 1851, and the final volume appeared in 1853. By that time, Michelet had lost his official functions as professor at the Collège de France and as head of the national archives, for having refused in 1852 to take the oath of allegiance to the new empire of Louis Napoleon.[22]

It is against the background of these overlapping political, cultural, and metahistorical contexts that I propose to study the three histories of the Revolution written by Lamartine, Michelet, and Blanc.[23] Three histories

[20] Volumes 3 and 4 appeared in 1852, and the remaining eight volumes at yearly intervals over the next ten years. For the background to the writing of Blanc's history, see Godechot 1974:39–41; concerning his role in the events of 1848, see Agulhon 1973.

[21] For the background to the writing of Michelet's history, see Walter's introduction to the 1952 edition. For an account of his work at the Collège de France during the period 1847–8, see Viallaneix 1973. Walter suggests that, by the time the Revolution broke out, the historian had effectively withdrawn from direct political activity (1952:I, xviii).

[22] The opening volumes of Michelet's narrative, like those of Blanc's, received considerable attention (they were often reviewed together with Lamartine's *Girondins* – see Duprat 1847, *Le Charivari* 1847, Lerminier 1847, Baudrillart 1850). Due to the change in political climate after 1848, and to the protracted manner of publication, the remaining volumes of Michelet's history, like those of Blanc's, seem to have received relatively little public attention. Michelet's history was, however, later to be consecrated as a *lieu de mémoire* in the form of a 'national edition' voted by the Assembly of the Third Republic on the occasion of the first centenary of the Revolution in 1889 (see Ory 1984:527).

[23] Alphonse de Lamartine, *Histoire des Girondins* (Lamartine 1983); Jules Michelet, *Histoire de la Révolution française* (Michelet 1952); Louis Blanc, *Histoire de la Révolution française* (Blanc 1847–62a). Unless otherwise indicated, all references to

and three 'French Revolutions'. Unlike previous comparative studies of these histories, however, the primary concern of this work is not with situating the three narratives within the history of the historiography of the French Revolution. Nor is my primary concern with analysing the different political viewpoints of the historians as reflected in their accounts of the Revolution and as indicative of the intellectual debates of the 1840s.[24] Instead, as is already indicated, both by my title – 'The rhetoric of historical representation' – and by my approach to the historiography of the Revolution through the historiographical poetics of the first half of the nineteenth century, the particular focus of this study is the textual representation and transmission of past events.[25]

How, through the literary medium of a prose narrative, are the collective events of the Revolution represented – given 'life', as Thierry put it – and at the same time, invested with a new signification for a latter-day public? In other words: how do the three historians represent a common set of events so as to constitute a different Revolution? And how does each such representation establish its claim to portray 'our history', that is, to speak for the 'real' Revolution and 'the general life'?

We have seen above how Thierry and his contemporaries were concerned with the literary work of the historian, and with the importance of narration in the transmission of historical knowledge. This late-twentieth-century study of three nineteenth-century histories is also concerned with the role of historical narration. But, situated as it is in a different

these works will be from these editions and will be included parenthetically in the text (volume and page number, without repeated reference to the year of publication).

24 Earlier studies of these works are Godechot 1974, Gérard 1970, McManners 1965, Geyl 1961. The most comprehensive is Godechot's *Un Jury pour la Révolution* (1974): a close and useful study of the personal and professional backgrounds, the methods of research, the principal sources, of thirteen historians of the Revolution (including the works studied here) as well as of their treatment of certain key interpretative issues in the Revolution. Although the historians Gérard and Godechot recognise the existence of a 'literary dimension' in the works of Michelet, Lamartine, and Blanc, Gérard dismisses this as a question of 'verbalisme' (1970:44), while Godechot's analysis is restricted to pointing out the length of the texts, the presence or absence of footnotes, the recurrence of the same metaphors in Carlyle and Michelet, and to qualifying the 'style' of each writer as 'grandiloquent', 'brilliant', 'vivid', as the case may be (1974:73f).

25 A number of individual studies of Michelet as a writer/narrator do exist: notably, Barthes 1954, Orr 1976, Hughes 1984; but with the exception of Morse 1974, Gaspard 1985 and Orr 1989, there has been little detailed attention paid to his narrative of the Revolution. Among the individual studies of Lamartine to consider his historical writing are Reboul 1980 and Court 1985.

theoretical context, it does not presuppose that events have a natural, organic coherence or an intrinsic significance which is potentially reproducible or recoverable through the medium of a narrative discourse. Rather, it presupposes that the defining identity or significance of particular events, as well as the intelligible coherence between different events, are not inherent to historical actuality, but continuously come into existence as a product of the many different representations which are given of it – by participants as well as by later historians.

Historical discourse is defined by the fact that it deals with real events and not imaginary ones. Whereas fictional events are brought into being with the discourse which narrates them, historical events have by definition an existence prior to, outside of, the particular discourse in which they are represented: the historian is not, by definition, the author of the events he narrates. The Bastille was demolished, brick by brick, after 14 July 1789; a large crowd of women made their way to Versailles on 5 October 1789; Louis XVI was guillotined on 21 January 1793; Robespierre fell from power on 9 Thermidor *an* II and was executed the following day. These events really did take place: the blood on the guillotine was real and could be really seen by the attendant public in what is now the Place de la Concorde.

But while we recognise that these events actually took place, we must also recognise that they could never be recounted after the fact without being translated into another medium. Since language cannot reproduce non-verbal reality, but represents it through a limited number of verbal signs, every discursive account of these events is inevitably a form of shorthand *vis-à-vis* the totality of 'what happened' (leaving aside for the moment the problem of the speaker's access to information concerning those events). In being represented through a finite, linear discourse, 'what happened' becomes constituted as one sort of event, or set of events, rather than another, in the sense that it is made intelligible in one way rather than another. As Barthes puts it, 'le discours historique ne suit pas le réel, il ne fait que le signifier' ('historical discourse does not follow the real, it signifies it', 1982:20).

'To signify reality': the verb here is a transitive one. By this I mean that events are invested with significance, are constituted as signifiers, in the very act of being referred to and represented in discourse. But if it is the discourse which actually constitutes the events as signifiers, the authority of the discourse itself, as *historical* discourse, always remains grounded in the extra-textual events which it represents. (We can see this complex interaction between event and discourse, between representation and signification, at the basis of Thierry's claim that, through the work of narration, the historian could succeed in 'giving' to events 'their' significance and character (see above, p.3)).

To a certain extent, much of the above might also be applied to all forms of referential discourse. What is particular to historical writing, however, is the fact that its referent, the 'reality' to which it refers, is a bygone one. The events and states which it represents are not simply real vs. imaginary: they also belong to the *past*. They no longer exist except in the traces which they have left in the actual world and in the different symbolic representations which have been given of them 'after the fact'. Being no longer directly observable, the events of the Revolution are accessible to the historian and his public only through the mediation of records, traces, other representations. As Barthes puts it, historical discourse 'est sans doute le seul où le référent soit visé comme extérieur au discours, sans qu'il soit jamais possible de l'atteindre hors de ce discours' ('This type of discourse is surely the only one in which the target referent is envisaged as lying outside of discourse at the same time as it is impossible ever to reach it except through discourse').[26] Qualifying Barthes' statement, we can add that the historian's claim to speak with the authority of reality is paradoxically linked to his use of *other* discourses, and that since a historian is, by definition, dependent on source documents for his information about events, any reference to the targeted events must also involve, either implicitly or explicitly, a reference to another, intermediate text and, by extension, to the work of research and the situation of the utterance.[27]

For all the subtlety of Barthes' analysis of the complicated interrelation between reference and signification in historical representation, his approach to historical discourse is ultimately limited by the fact that he considers it from the perspective of its inevitable failure to 'reproduce' historical reality, and presents historians as generally attempting to 'suppress' all traces of their own activities as narrators and interpreters. His analysis seems to me not only to leave no room for any self-consciousness on the part of historians as to the real conditions of their own production, but to leave out a vital dimension of historical narration: namely, that it is a discourse written *for* a contemporary public *about*

[26] 1982:20. For history as 'knowledge through documents', see Veyne 1978:14–15. The past is 'simultaneously abolished and preserved in its traces', writes Ricoeur (1983–5, III:149), a paradoxical status which he sees as problematising the concept of 'reality' in its application to past events.

[27] I use the term 'utterance' here as a translation of the French *énonciation*, to indicate the 'act of uttering' or the discursive act as distinct from its product or *énoncé*. See Ducrot and Todorov 1972:405.

interrelated events in the *past*.[28] It is always both *discours* and *histoire*, a story told by someone at a different point in time; and as discourse it necessarily addresses itself, either implicitly or explicitly, to a latter-day public – be this other members of the profession or, as in the case of the writers considered here, the reading public at large.[29] And as we have seen, the contemporary 'addressee' of the historical text was far from being occulted in the metahistorical discourses of the early nineteenth century, but figured as an essential aspect of historiography as a representation of the collective past.

The temporal distance between the historiographical discourse and the past events it narrates 'after the fact' can be seen, moreover, as one of the very conditions for the emergence 'after the fact' of the specifically historical significance of those events. As Arthur C. Danto argues, when Newton was born on Christmas Day 1642, it could be apparent to no-one that this infant was 'Newton', the author of the Newtonian Revolution: it is only from a historical perspective that one can 'anachronistically' say that 'the author of *Principia* was born on Christmas Day 1642' (1985:158). Similarly, the crowd which set out in search of arms on the morning of 14 July 1789 could not know that this was to become 'Le 14 juillet' when the Bastille would be taken at 5.30 that afternoon, or that the Taking of the Bastille itself would be followed by 'Le 10 août', the *Terreur*, Napoleon, the *Restauration*, the Revolution of 1830 and the July monarchy, 1848... Each new, unforeseen development can cast new light on the original events (the historical signifiers) and retroactively change their significance.

In order to take into account its specifically historiographical function, then, historical discourse must be seen as 'anachronistically' situated with respect to its object: it represents past events at the same time as it considers them retrospectively from a particular distance and reveals their significance for a later public.[30] The particular complexity of historical writing as a representation/signification of events and states which are past is brought vividly into relief, as we shall see, by the texts to be considered here. On the one hand, in keeping with the 'vivid'

[28] See Greimas' comments to the effect that the 'presence' of historical events in a representation always remains 'a presence in the past' (1973:146).

[29] See Genette's discussion of the inseparability of 'discourse' and 'story' (1969:64–5).

[30] Thus Barante's comment that 'one has to be outside of the picture if one is really to see which are its most prominent and characteristic features' (1838, I:8); and, more recently, Braudel's: 'But what wouldn't the traveller through contemporary times give to be able to take that step back (or step forward) in time which would unmask and simplify life as it is now, which is confused and barely legible, because too cluttered up with minor acts and signs?' (1969:58).

historiographical poetics of the period, the narratives of Lamartine, Michelet, and Blanc are characterised by the primacy of the figurative representation of actors and incidents *in situ*: in extensive *tableaux*, they include details of appearances and settings which may have little or no relevance to the course of action as such, but which have a privileged role in making the reader 'an eye-witness' to former states, in providing the reader with an image of the 'men themselves' or of the 'events themselves' at the very moment of their occurrence. On the other hand, however, the historians' preference for scenic 're-presentation' goes together with an apparent lack of embarrassment about disclosing their own presence, and their own interpretative activity, at a later point in time.

Michelet, for example, opens his 2,000-page narrative of the events of 1789–94 with a definition of the Revolution taken as a whole: 'I define the Revolution: the advent of Law, the resurrection of Rights, the reaction of Justice' (I:51). From the outset, thus, the historian makes clear to his reader the double thrust of the work which is to follow: on the one hand, its referential function in narrating the different constituent events of the Revolution from the *états généraux* to the fall of Robespierre; on the other hand, its hermeneutic function in (re)defining the significance of 'the Revolution' for his contemporaries.[31] 'I define': from now on, this is what the words 'French Revolution' shall mean (for us). The very fact that the historian should present his interpretative role in this explicit fashion also makes clear to us that historical texts do not consist exclusively of narrative or representational statements, but may be woven through with interpretative comments serving to spell out the significance of the events represented.[32]

'I define the Revolution': as it stands at the head of Michelet's narrative, this may serve as a hermeneutic guide to his reader in posting the historian's interpretative agenda, but the definition itself has (as yet) no force or authority. 'The French Revolution' may perhaps be brought to signify the 'resurrection of Justice', but the name 'French Revolution' refers first, foremost, and in the last analysis, to the actual events of the Revolution, from the *journées révolutionnaires* of 1789 through to 10 August 1792 to the *Terreur* and the fall of Robespierre on 9 Thermidor. If Michelet's explicit interpretation of the Revolution is to acquire

[31] This recognition of the communicative and rhetorical (versus simply referential) function of historical discourse has benefited from recent work on fictional realism. Philippe Hamon, for example, has approached 'realist description' as a 'transfer of knowledge about' a certain object (1972, 1973, 1981), while Susan Suleiman has argued that there is a 'didactic tendency' at the root of the realist novel (1983:19).

[32] I have addressed the role of such interpretative commentary in greater detail in Rigney 1988.

historical authority, then, if it is to be more than simply an indication of the individual historian's desire to have the Revolution take on a particular meaning for his public, then it must be shown to be grounded in, and retroactively ratified by, the objective signifier it presupposes: the events themselves of 1789–94 – or, what in practice will come to the same thing, 'the events themselves' as narrated by the historian.

In a recent essay, 'The Value of Narrativity in the Representation of Reality', Hayden White argues that narrative historians have traditionally sought to give to historical reality the form of a story: to make the historical world 'speak itself as a story' (1987:2). Unfortunately, he does not investigate in any detail the ways in which historians actually go about investing real events with such a form; nor does he address the particular problems they might encounter in constructing a particular story from the disparate, inherited materials with which they must work. For the fact that historical events do not themselves take the form of an 'untold story' not merely has the epistemological implications Louis O. Mink refers to (1978:147); it also poses specific narratological problems which have hitherto received scant attention. For, unlike the traditional novelist, who organises his fictional narrative around the actions of a limited number of actors, the historian of the Revolution must deal with a complex *ensemble* of collective events which, lacking a figurative or actorial focus, are not 'naturally' narratable as a single, coherent story.[33] The collectivity or 'the general life', as Sarazin called it, may well be posited as the subject of the historical narrative; but the fact is that the particular events of the Revolution were carried out or experienced by great numbers of different individuals and groups, acting in many different places and – what is as important – often acting at the same time. How is the historian-narrator to go about representing this complex, collective event through the medium of a finite, linear narrative discourse? And what is even more problematic: how is he to render these different events as a coherent whole which has a particular significance?

[33] The difficulties involved in historical representation, i.e. the fact that historical events are not 'naturally' narratable, is made evident *a contrario* in Marcel Graner's study of the narrative incoherences which resulted from Alexandre Dumas' attempt to transpose the huge canvas of Michelet's representation of the Revolution directly to his novel *La Comtesse de Charny* (Graner 1984:70f). To the extent that historical novelists are also involved in representing collective, historical events, they face many of the representational problems encountered by the historian. However, unlike the historian, a historical novelist is free, on the one hand, *not* to submit to the 'authority of reality' and, on the other hand, to incorporate fictional elements into his narrative and organise his historical representation around a fictional plot focussed on a limited number of actors. See below, p.104n.

Yet, if the finiteness and linearity of the discursive medium limit the historian in his presentation of the complex historical event, these very limits must also be seen as providing the basic means through which he himself can give to that complex collective event a particular order and intelligibility. The discursive, specifically narrative medium both imposes constraints on the historian and provides him with specific technical tools for selecting and conjoining the particular actorial figures, actions and circumstances which are to represent the history of the collective subject across time.

The discursive medium, for example, not only makes the selection of representative actors and incidents necessary, but it also makes it possible to refer to the same incident in different ways; to refer to the same incident on more than one occasion; to refer to the same incident in more or less figurative detail; and to refer to different incidents in differing degrees of detail, whereby some incidents and actors are given greater prominence than others. Again: the linearity of discourse makes it impossible to relate more than one event at a time, even events which took place at the same time; but, by the same token, events may be presented and articulated in the narrative in a new order different from that of mere chronological sequence. Again: the discursive interventions of the retrospective narrator draw attention away from 'the events themselves' to the later act of representing them; but such interventions, as we have already seen, may play an important supplementary role in the narrative by guiding the reader in the interpretation of the events as they have been, or are about to be, represented.

But even then – and here we come back to the relationship signification-representation – it is not enough for the historian of the Revolution to succeed in constructing a coherent story, with a particular significance, from the diverse events which he chooses to present to the reader. If it is to be recognised as history, if it is to have authority as such, his narrative must also be seen to represent, in the sense of 'standing for', historical reality. At its simplest, this means that the historian-narrator must respect the conventions of historiographical discourse and, in one way or another, indicate the basis of his account in fact: the extent of his research and the trustworthiness or 'authority' of his source-texts (as we shall see in chapter 1 below, p.31, the use of specific bibliographical references apparently did not belong to the dominant historiographical conventions of the mid-nineteenth century). But if a representation of the Revolution is to gain authority, it must also be seen to refer to, or somehow take into account, all those elements which have been previously recognised as defining the topic, even if these are not directly related to the particular interpretation the historian wishes to give – even, indeed, if they seem to militate against it.

Thus, while the individual historian may *want* to represent the Revolution as signifying 'the advent of Justice', his interpretative programme can only be carried out against the resistance of the inherent lack of structure of the events themselves and, what is even more important in this context, against the resistance of certain undeniable events – such as the September massacres and the *Terreur* – which may not yield themselves easily to the interpretation being proposed, which may even appear to contradict it. These adverse elements must somehow be included in any account of the Revolution since they cannot be ignored with impunity by a discourse which lays claim to the authority of historical reality and which seeks to assert that authority over the claims of other historians and their rival interpretations of the common past.

As Lucien Febvre put it, the past is 'a reconstitution of the societies and human beings of former times' by and for persons who are 'involved in the network of human realities of their own time' (1948:viii). As I have been suggesting in the preceding pages, the 'reality' in whose name the historian claims to speak is paradoxically located between past and present: it is past actuality symbolically reconstituted for a later public caught up in 'the network of human realities of their own time'. The authority of the historical text as a representation of history is thus dependent on its being recognised as both 'unbiassed' and 'unfabricated' by the historian's public – a public which in the case of the French Revolution is already familiar with the outline of events and which has a number of different versions to choose from.

The 'rhetoric' of historical representation is to be understood here, then, in the broad sense of the discursive and narrative strategies actually used by Lamartine, Michelet, and Blanc in order to re-present and simultaneously give (their) meaning to past events; but also in the narrower sense, of the strategies available to them in order to persuade the public of the reality of the representation and hence of their own authority as spokesmen for the collective past.

1

Historical representation and discursive context

[History] is the only *articulate* communication ... which the Past can have with the Present, the Distant with what is Here.
Thomas Carlyle, 'On History Again' (1833)

Historical representation in context

Vergniaud's nephew

In Book 47 of his history of the Girondins (1847), Lamartine recounts how Vergniaud's brother-in-law, a certain M. Alluaud, came to Paris from Limoges in order to bring money to the imprisoned Girondin leader, who had already been stripped of his worldly possessions and was soon afterwards to die on the scaffold; how he was accompanied by his ten-year-old son who, terrified, hid from the sight of the famished, pale face of his uncle, with his torn and dirty clothes, his unkempt hair and his long beard; how the child clung to his father, but how Vergniaud took him up in his arms:

> 'Mon enfant, lui dit le prisonnier en le prenant dans ses bras, rassure-toi et regarde-moi bien; quand tu seras homme, tu diras que tu as vu Vergniaud, le fondateur de la République, dans le plus beau temps et dans le plus glorieux costume de sa vie: celui où il souffrait la persécution des scélérats, et où il se préparait à mourir pour les hommes libres'.
>
> L'enfant s'en souvint en effet, et le redit cinquante ans après à celui qui écrit ces lignes. (II:517)

> ['My child', said the prisoner to him as he took him into his arms, 'don't be frightened and take a good look at me. When you are a man, say that you saw Vergniaud, the founder of the Republic, at the most beautiful moment and in the most glorious costume of his life: the moment at which he was suffering the persecution of scoundrels and preparing to die for free men'.
>
> And indeed the child remembered, and fifty years later repeated these words to the man who writes these lines.]

In fact, as Antoine Court (1980) has recently shown in his detailed study of this episode, Vergniaud's nephew never gave any such account to the historian of the Girondins. Lamartine's source for this incident was indeed M. Alluaud *fils* who, in March 1845, had sent him a *résumé* of his *Notice sur Vergniaud* (1842); but in this document, the incident at La Force (which Lamartine locates at the Conciergerie, hence on the eve of Vergniaud's death rather than a couple of months before it) is only briefly mentioned and with few of the details which Lamartine included in his history. Moreover, in a letter of protest which M. Alluaud wrote to Lamartine in October 1847, he begged to correct the historian on a number of points, some of which had already been specified in his *Notice*: in 1793, he was fourteen years old, not ten; he did not go to the prison with his father, but had come directly from his boarding school with a valet; although Vergniaud's appearance was *négligé*, it was by no means as dilapidated and unkempt as Lamartine portrays it; instead, the boy's terror was due to the fact that it was his first visit to a prison; Vergniaud did not give him any speech to pass on to posterity, but asked, 'So, François, do they also want to kill me at your school?' (Alluaud does ironically allow that Lamartine may have penetrated to the spirit, if not to the letter, of his uncle's remarks.)

As it transpires from Alluaud's alternative account, then, Lamartine started from the fact of an encounter between the imprisoned Vergniaud and his young nephew, and proceeded to make the rest of it up. The message which Vergniaud sent to future generations via his nephew, who passed it on to Lamartine, who is now passing it on to the public, turns out to be simply an invention on the part of he 'who writes these lines'.

The fact that we now know that the prison visit was largely invented enables us to see all the more clearly the non-arbitrary nature of this historian's deviation from, and elaboration upon, the historical facts; the procedures whereby, in representing the actual encounter between Vergniaud and his nephew, the historian constitutes it as a highly significant scene. The very young boy through whom the scene is focalised (and Lamartine has exaggerated his youth) reacts strongly to the striking, memorable figure of Vergniaud, so strongly that he remembers the scene vividly even fifty years later; still under the impression of the imposing figure of Vergniaud, the nephew is witness to Vergniaud's final, eloquent 'last words', which are quoted directly in Lamartine's text (although the historian did not know the exact date of the prison visit, he chose to situate it close to Vergniaud's death). The content of this monumental 'deathbed' message to posterity is in effect both a transformation and an interpretation of the image of Vergniaud as hitherto perceived by his nephew, the fallen Girondin becoming transfigured: glorious instead of terrifying – 'say that you saw Vergniaud, the founder of the Republic, at the most beautiful moment and in the most glorious costume of his life...'

Lamartine's version of this episode *makes sense*: it invests the figure of Vergniaud with symbolic value according to the literary topos of the glorious, fallen hero, and makes the encounter 'readable' in terms of yet another topos, that of the deathbed scene. And unless the receiver of Lamartine's message happens to be Vergniaud's nephew himself or one of his acquaintances in Limoges, or unless he has access to Court's painstaking 1980 study of the episode, there is no way for him to know that many of the details of the scene have actually been fabricated.

Lamartine's representation of the encounter between Vergniaud and his nephew thus brings dramatically into relief the fact that historical events are represented through, and replaced by, a signifying construct: the historical text. At the same time, the fact that this particular historian should have actually invented some of the phenomena he is claiming to represent illustrates the way in which, like all semiotic systems in Umberto Eco's definition, historical discourse is capable of lying.[1]

Should we then conclude from Lamartine's mistreatment of Vergniaud's nephew that the referentiality of historical discourse (the fact that it claims to represent events which actually happened rather than fictional ones) is irrelevant to the study of historical texts as signifying constructs? Or, to use Eco's terms, to the 'conditions under which the message may be communicated and apprehended' (1979a:65)?

My answer is no. For all that Lamartine may have fabricated many of the details of the encounter between Vergniaud and his young nephew, his invention was not free. In the first place, the general outlines of his story were already drawn up (Vergniaud did exist, together with the other Girondins whose history is being told, and Vergniaud did meet his nephew in prison). Secondly – and this is perhaps the more important point here – the historian could not invent with impunity.

The licence which Lamartine granted himself to transform and embellish the facts was incompatible with the claim he made to be a historian, a claim underlying the very title of his work, *Histoire des Girondins* – not only a history, but a history of a group of men known to have really existed. As a historian, it was not enough that he should *seem* authoritative (an authority signalled in the text by his claim to have been in personal contact with the eyewitness); the understanding of the

[1] The statement 'your house has burned down', writes Eco, makes sense independently of the fact that it may be true or false (1979a:65): 'Every time there is signification there is the possibility of using it in order to lie', i.e. to signify and communicate something to which no real state of things corresponds (59–60).

historiographical contract is that he should also actually *be* so. As history, as the account of the collective past, his work implicitly claims verifiability and invites verification.

Now, unfortunately for Lamartine, he was simply not taken at his word, for he wrote in 1847 in a particular historical context where (as we have seen earlier) the French Revolution was still a hotly disputed issue. What is even more directly to the point is the fact that there were still survivors like Alluaud, and many sons and daughters of those who had participated in the Revolution, who were not only able, but more than willing, to point out the numerous freedoms Lamartine had taken with historical facts.[2] Alfred Nettement's 1848 'Etudes critiques sur les Girondins' consisted for a large part of letters written (by interested parties or relatives like M. Alluaud) in critical response to Lamartine and hot on the heels of the publication of his work. Madame Roland's daughter, for example, while expressing her appreciation for the historian's use of vivid, intimate details in the representation of other Revolutionaries, complained that, in the portrait of her father, Lamartine was guilty of misrepresentation; M. Roland was not so very uxorious, she insisted (Nettement 1848:159).

Moreover, as Court suggests (1980:766–7), and as the critique by the *légitimiste* Nettement exemplifies, complaints concerning Lamartine's untrustworthiness as a historian were closely linked to disagreement with his political views. Even where political issues were not directly related to the contested passages, the sin of inaccuracy provided his opponents with the critical ammunition with which to reject the work as a whole.

Apparently, M. Alluaud did not keep his criticisms to himself or to his correspondence with the errant historian. Another letter, quoted by Court, was written in September 1847 by one of Lamartine's well-wishers in Limoges and warned him of the rumours around town which undermined his credit as a historian:

> le bruit se propageant, voilà tous nos bourgeois criant à qui veut les écouter: l'histoire de Lamartine est un roman, une oeuvre de fantaisie; l'imagination de l'auteur y a plus de part que la vérité – jugez-en par l'épisode controuvé de l'entrevue de Vergniaud et de son beau-frère... (Court 1980:765)
>
> [Word having spread, all the *bourgeois* are now crying out to anyone who will listen to them: Lamartine's history is a novel, a work of fantasy; the author's imagination is given more room in it than the truth – you can judge this by the concocted episode of the encounter between Vergniaud and his brother-in-law.]

[2] For a study of Lamartine's methods of research, the many errors he committed and the freedoms he took, see Nettement 1848 and Court 1985:chap.4.

Because he is publicly seen to have violated the contract whereby a historian is to respect historical facts, Lamartine's history ceased to have any authority or significance *as history* for the bourgeois of Limoges who could denounce it as merely 'a novel, a work of fantasy'; indeed, more than simply fictional, it was mendacious.[3]

For those who do not have access to Alluaud's alternative version of this episode, the vision of Vergniaud in Lamartine's narrative might appear as both real and significant ('Vergniaud was glorious in his downfall', 'the French Revolution was full of sublime gestures and moments'). But, for those who do have access to the other account, the sublime scene loses all its aura as a real event, as a historical moment (the prestige of what Barthes calls the '*avoir-été-là* des choses' ('the having-been-there of things') 1968:88). It is shown to be an incident which in fact never pre-existed Lamartine's representation of it in 1847. The representation of the scene at the *Conciergerie* continues to make sense, then, but no longer as history: rather than representing 1793, it points to Lamartine's own literary and/or political desire in 1847 to present Vergniaud as a glorious fallen hero.

Thus, by its very failure in this case to 'make sense of' and, at the same time, to 'represent' the past (the Revolution, the Girondins...), Lamartine's work points to the fact that there are important differences as texts between historical and fictional works; that there is a complex interaction between the historical text (as *historical* text) and its particular historical and social context; and that this interaction must be seen as part of the conditions under which a given historical message 'may be communicated and apprehended', to recall Eco's phrase.

The particular historical context in which Lamartine, Michelet, and Blanc produced their narratives now belongs, like the events of the Revolution, to the past. In the following pages, I shall study the texts

[3] In the contemporary reviews of the different histories, appreciation or condemnation of their literary style is generally linked to agreement/disagreement with the historian's political views: in an 1849 review in *The British Quarterly Review*, for example, E. Edwards praised Lamartine unreservedly for his impartiality, his scholarship, and the art with which he represents events and generalises from them (182); the reviewer's focus on the representation of Robespierre suggests that his endorsement of Lamartine's account is linked to his appreciation of, and agreement with, the 'truthful', lifelike portrait of the *Incorruptible*. See also the 1847 review written by the liberal Lerminier, who condemns Blanc's work for its monotonous straining after literary effects (1054), Lamartine's work for its preoccupation with producing 'novelistic effects' rather than historical truth (1061), and Michelet's work for the 'the audaciousness of its expressions, the motley character of its colours, and the slovenly shape of its sentences [*l'allure débraillée de ses phrases*]' (1059).

which they produced in that context and attempt to disengage the different discursive and semiotic conditions created for these narrators of the French Revolution by their claim to represent historical (versus imaginary) events – historical events belonging, moreover, to the comparatively recent and controversial past of their public.

The discourse in history

Historical discourse, as I suggested in my Introduction, must be seen in the first instance as a discourse in the present about real events in the past. There is always an implied historical connection between past and present, between the events of the Revolution which are narrated and the historical context in which the act of narrating them takes place – whether this be 1823, 1847, 1930, or 1958. The revolutionary events of 1789 to 1794 and the discursive events constituted by the writing of the different histories of that Revolution together belong to French History, Modern History, or simply History (depending on what your frame of reference is). Although the French Revolution may have begun with the Bastille and ended with Thermidor, French History (to which the Revolution belongs) neither began nor ended with these events. Instead, History went on after Thermidor to produce the *Directoire*, the regime of Napoleon, the *Restauration*, the July monarchy, the writing of the various histories...

The historical *fabula* which the historian of the Revolution relates must be seen, then, as both closed and open.[4] It is 'closed' in the sense that it involves a series of events taking place between two fixed dates; let us say, 1789 and 1794. It is open in the sense that the events taking place between 1789 and 1794 have historical antecedents and later historical consequences which, although they lie outside the chronological framework of 'the French Revolution', may nevertheless be presented as belonging to the narrative of that event to the extent that it belongs to History.

The post-revolutionary history of France entered in a particularly direct, indeed disruptive, way into the writing of Michelet and Louis Blanc. In the first place, the publication of their works was literally interrupted by the events of 1848, which eventually carried Michelet and Blanc into exile, in Nantes and London respectively.[5] In the later sections

[4] I use the word *fabula* here in the Russian Formalist meaning of 'the basic story stuff' (the set of events to be related in the narrative) as distinct from the *sjužet* (the way in which the story is actually told and the different events linked together). See Erlich 1981:240.

[5] The two volumes of Blanc's history published before the events of 1848 included his long introduction to the 'Origins and Causes' of the Revolution (with its historical survey of the growth of bourgeois individualism and its theory of 'the two revolutions', I:185f), and his narrative of the early bourgeois phase of the

of their histories of the first Revolution, moreover, the two exiled historians refer to the historical events which have occurred since the publication of the first volumes of their work. By the time Blanc reaches his account of the insurrection of Prairial (May 1795) in the final volume of his work (1862), he can draw a parallel between what happened in 1795 and on 'that too famous day', 15 May 1848, when the expulsion of demonstrators from the Assembly initiated a reactionary backlash (III:205). By the time Michelet reaches the *Terreur* in a history whose first volume was published in 1847, it is 1853 and the historian is exiled in Nantes:

> Je plonge avec mon sujet dans la nuit et dans l'hiver. Les vents acharnés de tempêtes qui battent mes vitres depuis deux mois sur ces collines de Nantes, accompagnent de leurs voix, tantôt graves, tantôt déchirantes, mon *Dies irae* de 93. Légitimes harmonies! je dois les remercier. Bien des choses qui me restaient incomprises m'ont apparu claires ici dans la révélation de ces voix de l'Océan (janvier 1853).[6]

> [I plunge with my subject into the night and into the winter. The relentless gales, which for two months past have been beating against my windows on the hills of Nantes, accompany my *Dies irae* of 93 with their cries – sombre one moment, heartrending the next. A fitting chorus! I owe them my thanks. Many things which used to be incomprehensible have become clear to me in the revelations of these voices from the Ocean (January 1853).]

The new circumstances brought about by the failure of the 1848 Revolution and the emergence of the Second Empire in 1852 could not but cast new light on the events of the Revolution of 1789–94: Michelet's

Revolution down to the abolition of feudal rights on 4 August 1789. The two volumes of Michelet's history published before 1848 included his philosophico-historical introduction to the origins of the Revolution, and his narrative of events down to the flight to Varennes in June 1791.

[6] II:696. The historicity of the utterance is also reflected in the fact that, in the 1869 edition of his history, Michelet included a new preface, occasional supplementary footnotes, and a new section on Robespierre entitled 'Le Tyran', written largely in response to Blanc's history which had been completed in the intervening period. In certain instances, the readers' responses to the history in progress are already written into its later volumes. For example, the response of Lamartine's critics is literally inscribed in the first edition of the work (published in eight volumes between March and June 1847): in the final volume, he included an extra page which was to replace the account of Target's relationship to Louis XVI and his refusal to take on his legal defence (volume 5), which Lamartine had already rewritten in response to complaints from the lawyer's family (1847, VIII). Similarly, in a footnote to one of the last volumes of his work, Blanc answers the charges laid against him by the daughter of Merlin de Thionville who had found, on reading his earlier volumes, that her father had been misrepresented (II:743–4). Thiesse (1980) shows a comparable phenomenon in her study of the interaction between Eugène Sue and his readers in the course of the serial publication of *Les Mystères de Paris*.

invocation of the *Fête de la Fédération* (1790) as a symbol of hope for the present meant something different when it was originally written in November 1847, than it did when he finally finished his history in 1853.[7] Even when recent events are not explicitly invoked by the historian (as in Blanc's parallel between Prairial and June 1848), they must be seen as providing an interpretative frame in which the narrated events are located.

The connection between the discourse and the historical events it represents is not only that of historical succession, that is, of the fact that the discourse follows the events in time. By definition, there is also an *ontological* connection between them: both the discursive act and the events represented are posited as belonging to the same historical world. This means that there is no transgression of any diegetic boundary, no shattering of any fictional illusion, when the historians represent themselves as writing the history of the Revolution, describe the mechanics of their research or writing, or anticipate the reader's reception of their work.

Thus Michelet represents himself in Nantes in 1853; recounts his joy upon reading the naive, fervent testimonies left by the *fédérés* of 1790 (I:405–6) and his emotion upon reading in the *Armoire de fer*, on 30 September 1849, the last letter written by the fugitive Pétion to his wife in 1793 (II:168); offers to take the reader by the hand and lead him back in his imagination into the underworld of the Cordeliers (I:497); explains the location of Danton's house through giving the name of the street as it is known to his public ('what is called nowadays the *rue de l'École-de-Médecine*', I:1287). Thus Blanc exhorts his reader not to forget the mitigating circumstances of the people's hunger (I:313) and to keep continuously in mind the fact that the Revolution was originally 'infinitely indulgent' (I:576); adds a footnote in defence of his own 1848 project for the *ateliers nationaux* (I:359); quotes from the *Revue du Progrès* which he published between 1839 and 1843 (II:13) and from his *Histoire de dix ans* (II:32); describes his research activities in the British Museum and, by implication, his exile.[8]

Such references to the 'situation of the utterance' are all the more

[7] See I:609: 'May this sublime vision lift all of us, readers and author, above the moral miseries of our times, and pass us a heroic spark from the fire which burned in our fathers' breasts!'

[8] As he writes concerning the petition which occasioned the assembly of the crowd at the Champ de Mars on what was to be the day of the massacre there (17 July 1791): 'The original petition still exists; it has been conserved in the Seine archives. Exiled from my country, it was not in my power to consult this unique document. My illustrious colleague, M. Michelet, was more fortunate than I was: I take the liberty of borrowing from him the following curious and characteristic details...' (I:730).

noteworthy in the case of Louis Blanc, since (unlike his colleagues, as commentators have frequently pointed out) he makes abundant use of footnotes.[9] He uses them, however, not only to indicate his sources, but also to indicate how he got hold of those documents (for example, at the British Museum, I:495); to give additional information or proofs; to take his colleagues to task (below, pp.48f); to add extra commentary and draw parallels with current events (I:359); to state his personal opinions (for example, on the meaning of the word 'peuple' and what it should mean in a truly democratic society, I:670).

Reference to the situation of the utterance is more than simply a theoretical possibility, then, or an inevitable, though unacknowledged, feature of these historical works. Instead, as the examples given above illustrate, the works considered here are characterised by the frequency with which attention is drawn to the historiographical act. Thus, belying those critics who have asserted that realist writing in general (Hamon 1973:428–9), and historical discourse in particular (Barthes 1982:16), are characterised by a sustained attempt to suppress all signs of the discursive act, the evidence of the texts themselves suggests that there was not only no suppression attempted, but that the historiographical act (and, to a lesser extent, the act of reading) was itself represented as a part of the historical *fabula*, as part of history itself. The fact that this representation of the discursive act is selective – like all representations – does not take from its signifying function within the context of the narrative.

These representations of the historiographical act suggest that the role of the historian is a historical one: a form of historical action taking place through the production of discourse. Blanc's rehabilitation of Robespierre is represented as belonging to the same history (if not to the same historical context) as the vilification of Robespierre by the victors of Thermidor, who, as the historian shows, tried to disfigure their enemy's image for posterity by erasing all traces which might speak in his favour (II:733; III:83). Similarly, in the introduction to his work, Michelet sets himself the task of resurrecting the men and the events of the Revolution which had been unjustly disfigured or relegated to oblivion in the intervening period (I:1–8).

If Michelet can describe how he himself would have chosen to sit between Cambon and Carnot in the Convention, that is to say, with the Montagne, but not among the Jacobins (II:347); if Blanc can impute Girondin sympathies to his principal rivals Michelet and Lamartine (II:44; II:586), and if he can quote some of Robespierre's opinions with

[9] See, for example, Aulard 1893:37; Godechot 1974:75.

approval or criticise him for having ignored the problems of Labour (I:675), this is because the historians and the revolutionaries are actors in the same historical world. The act of representing the past, and of thereby transforming the historical tradition, is thus represented in the historical account as a part of history: it is both a *faire-savoir*, or making known of the past, and a form of historical action (even a remake of the Jacobins/Girondins struggles), which seeks to influence the present and future course of events. Thus, in an optimistic anticipation of the effect of his representation, Blanc entitles his account of the *Fédération* of July 1790 (published 1852), a 'Vision sublime de l'avenir':

> Sans doute il ne fut pas tenu, ce serment qui se liait à des espérances, hélas! trop tôt déçues; mais la France n'en avait pas moins écrit là, et de manière qu'il fût impossible de la déchirer désormais, la première page d'un livre destiné à être repris plus tard et continué. (I:575)
>
> [Doubtless it was not kept, this pledge that was linked to hopes which were thwarted, alas!, only too soon; but France had written there, and in such a way that it can never be torn up, the first page of a book destined to be taken up again and continued.]

The intertextual context

Sources

In his memoirs of Paris during the Revolution (first published in 1796), Louis-Sébastien Mercier gives a graphic account of the scenes he witnessed in the National Convention between 16 and 19 January 1793, as one by one the 721 deputies pronounced sentence on Louis XVI. It is impossible, he suggests, for someone who was not there himself to imagine what it was really like: the fatigue, the incongruities, the taking of bets, the drinking, the ladies eating icecream – 'Of all that I saw there, nothing can be resaid exactly the way in which it happened... history will not succeed in reaching it' (1862, II:408).

Having depicted the atmosphere in the Convention on that historical occasion, however, Mercier goes on to comment on his general limitations as an eyewitness. He had indeed had the privilege of being present on a number of such historical moments; but at the time, caught up as he was in the events themselves as well as restricted by his personal viewpoint, he often failed to be fully aware of the general, *historical* implications of what was going on around him. The significance of what he was seeing only became apparent to him after the fact – a point which seems to anticipate and corroborate what Arthur C. Danto has more recently argued: namely, that history can only be written from an 'anachronistic', retrospective position in the light of subsequent events (above, p.14).

Those who watched like Mercier as each of the 721 deputies cast his vote in January 1793 were still in a position to lay wagers on the outcome: for them, the outcome of the vote was still an open question. It was only later that 'Louis XVI' came to connote 'guillotined', that the episode of 'the verdict on Louis XVI' was to become a mere prelude to its fixed sequel, 'the execution of Louis XVI'.

By definition, historical writing (including Mercier's memoirs) always comes after the fact, at a later point in time. Unlike the writer of memoirs, however, a historian does not write of 'memorable events' on the basis of his personal experiences or in his personal capacity as a 'former eyewitness'. Rather, he claims to base his account on his decipherment and collation of a variety of different, fragmentary source-texts.

On the one hand, then, the historian is dependent on other texts for his 'second-hand' information about the past and does not enjoy the first-hand privileges of 'having-been-there' himself. On the other hand, however, his potential access to a variety of different accounts as well as his temporal distance from the event gives him a historical perspective which is not accessible to any of the individuals who were watching the scene in the Convention in January 1793.

Since a historian can only refer to the past via the implied or explicit mediation of another, primary text, one of the defining characteristics of historical discourse lies in the fact that it is, in De Certeau's words, a 'construction dédoublée' ('a dual construction'):

> Se pose comme historiographique le discours qui 'comprend' son autre – la chronique, l'archive, le mouvement –, c'est-à-dire celui qui... se donne... le pouvoir de dire ce que l'autre signifie sans le savoir. Par les 'citations', par les références, par les notes et par tout l'appareil de renvois permanents à un langage premier (que Michelet nommait la 'chronique'), il s'établit en *savoir de l'autre*. Il se construit selon une problématique de procès, ou de *citation*, à la fois capable de 'faire venir' un langage référentiel qui joue là comme réalité, et de le juger au titre d'un savoir. (1975:111)
>
> [Historiography presents itself as a discourse which 'understands' its other – the chronicles, the archives, the movement: it is the discourse which... authorises itself to say what the other signifies without knowing it. Through 'citations', through references, through notes, and through the whole apparatus of permanent referral to a primary language (what Michelet called 'the chronicle'), it sets itself up as *knowledge of the other*. It is constructed according to a problematic of judgement or *citation*, at once capable of 'summoning' a referential language to function as reality and empowered to judge that language on the strength of its own knowledge.]

The primary record concerning the Revolutionary events as they were taking place, or had taken place, was deposited in a capricious and inconsistent manner in the many traces, documents, records, narratives, memoirs, left by the Revolution. (As we have seen, it was only in 1842 that Alluaud made the account public of his meeting with Vergniaud.) The information provided by the *chronique*, the *ensemble* of primary texts, is linked to the discursive form in which that information is transmitted and to the function of that discourse within the historical context in which it was produced. This applies as much to non-narrative records as it does to discursive representations of events (such as newspapers). François Furet suggests, for example, that the *cahiers de doléances* submitted by the *Tiers état* in 1789 largely adopted the vocabulary and idiom of the *ancien régime* jurists (1978:71–2); while Victor Fournel shows how the *procès-verbal* drawn up by the Municipality of Varennes, giving an account of the king's detention there, had first been corrected by the departmental censor who found the original version too Royalist in sentiment (1890:309f). The production (as well as the censorship) of records and of representations of the Revolution can itself be seen as an integral part of the Revolution-as-event. Half a century later, as we have seen, Blanc was to lament the fact that there are many (by implication, redeeming) features of Robespierre which can never be known since it was in the interest of those who seized power on 9 Thermidor to wipe out any such positive traces. The discursive representations and analyses of events which were produced either contemporaneously with the Revolution, or at a later date by those who had participated in it, make up the main body of the sources used by the mid-nineteenth-century historians, providing at once information about what happened and a point of view on events.[10]

In the *Avertissement* to his *Histoire des Girondins*, Lamartine gives due recognition to the fact that one of the pre-conditions for its readability as a historical (versus fictional) work is that it be based on the evidence of

[10] Certain types of documents (e.g. provincial and municipal records, commercial records) which later historians were to consider pertinent evidence for the history of France in the Revolutionary period, were generally unavailable to the historians considered here, the archives not yet having been catalogued and made available to researchers. Michelet was the only one to use archival material, having himself been actively engaged in a professional capacity in the organisation of the national archives from 1831 to 1851. For the rest, as Godechot shows (1974:60–70), Lamartine, Blanc, Michelet worked from a common pool of already published materials (including earlier histories of the Revolution, Buchez and Roux's parliamentary history, the principal newspapers of the time, and various collections of memoirs, e.g. those written by Bouillé). These were complemented in each case by a set of particular sources to which the historian had access and which marked out his informational edge over his rivals: Michelet's use of the archives and oral testimonies; Lamartine's private collection of memoirs and his correspondence; Blanc's use of the Croker collection in the British Museum.

some other testimony. He only composed his history after scrupulous research, he insists, and there is nothing in his account which is not authorised by authentic memoirs; in short, he is not asking to be 'taken at his word':

> Nous avons écrit après une scrupuleuse investigation des faits et des caractères. Nous ne demandons pas foi sur parole. Bien que nous n'ayons pas embarrassé le récit de notes, de citations, et de pièces justificatives, il n'y a pas une de nos assertions qui ne soit autorisée soit par des mémoires authentiques, soit par des mémoires inédits... soit par des renseignements oraux et véridiques, receuillis de la bouche des derniers survivants de cette grande époque. (1847, I:i-ii)
>
> [I began writing only after a scrupulous investigation into facts and characters. I am not asking to be taken at my word. Even though I have not encumbered the narrative with notes, quotations, and supporting documents, there is not one of my assertions which is not authorised by authentic memoirs, by unpublished memoirs... or by reliable information taken directly from the mouths of the last survivors of that great age.]

In practice, of course, as our catching Lamartine *in flagrante* with respect to Vergniaud so clearly demonstrated, a text will not always actually be based on testimony even where it claims to be, and even where it names a particular source.[11] Nor will a source which has actually been used always be indicated or named in the text. Indeed, at the same time as Lamartine claims that his narrative is based on careful research, he also implies that the obligation to demonstrate bibliographically the source of his historical evidence goes counter to the aesthetics of 'vivid narration' to which he openly adheres. Michelet echoes this concern, announcing that he would not actually include his many bibliographical references on the grounds that, by distracting the attention of the reader, they would break up the coherence of the narrative, a coherence which is its own authority, which speaks for itself: 'what gives authority to a narrative is not a multitude of bibliographical curiosities, but its continuity and coherence'.[12]

[11] In theory, a historian should apply the methods of historical criticism to the analysis of his source documents: assess their authenticity and value, locate their bias, place them in their rhetorical context, collate different testimonies, and finally draw conclusions from the established evidence (see Halkin's 1973 *Initiation à la critique historique* for a succinct account of the different aspects of historical criticism). However central such issues may be for the historian, they lie outside the scope of my analysis to the extent that they are situated at the level of research and not at the level of the historian's textual transmission of his information about the past.

[12] I:14. While Blanc regularly identified his sources in more or less detailed bibliographical references at the foot of the page, he too invoked the argument of

While an intertextual structure is at all times presupposed in the historical representation, then, the manifestation of that intertextuality is optional for these historians. As long as an event is probable according to one or another cultural code, it is not necessary for a historian to indicate his sources; the coherence of the narrative, to use Michelet's phrase, takes over from the authentication or verification of particular elements. Or, as De Certeau has more recently put it, 'The *vraisemblance* of what is uttered constantly takes over from its verifiability' (1975:111). Thus, Michelet did not have to invoke the authority of another text in order to assert that the day was cold and the trees were bare as Madame Roland went to the guillotine in November 1793 (II:620): these climatic conditions are, in a sense, self-evident (for the same reason, they also contain little new, historical information).

If the event represented is improbable, controversial, or of a private nature, however, then presupposing a source for the representation is not enough to ensure its authority as history; an appeal to the historian's research and the authority of some other text is called for. Thus, one of the rare occasions on which Michelet identifies his source in the body of his text is when he describes the feelings which the queen entertained towards her husband; since this information is of a private nature, it is unlikely that Michelet had access to it – hence: 'She despised her husband too much ... His want of resolution at Varennes and on 10 August had led her to believe that he was completely lacking in courage (Campan, ch. XVIII et XXI)' (II:182–3).

A more or less precise bibliographical reference in the body of the text, or in a footnote, is only one way of indicating the mediating role of a source in the representation of events. Where a source is not simply presupposed by the narrative representation, it may either be directly quoted or simply cited and paraphrased (this is the case with Lamartine's use of Alluaud's testimony). In particular instances, each historian varies his general manner of incorporating sources into his text by deploying any one of the above options and applying it to particular source texts so as to achieve particular local effects within the representation. An especially improbable point or a controversial one may thus be reinforced by invoking the authority of the document which demonstrates it. A paraphrase or a direct quotation from a particular source may be used to

'narrative coherence' and readability in order to explain why he had not included his *critique historique* in the body of his text: 'I considered it my duty to clarify as much as possible, by historical analysis, the picture of events which I was to draw. But, in order not to interrupt the course of the narrative and to avoid distracting the reader, I took care to place at the end of the most important chapters the dissertation which belonged to them' (1847–62b, VII:ii).

represent a certain incident more vividly by appealing to the experience of an eye-witness (and, as will be seen later in my study of the Champ de Mars, by appealing to one eye-witness rather than another: below, p.132).

With quotation, Antoine Compagnon writes (1979:113), the question of the authenticity of the utterance (did x say y?) takes over from the truth of what is said (is y true?), the quoted text having a certain autonomy *vis-à-vis* the host text: 'Recourse to quotation replaces the test of truth by the test of authenticity, of verification.'[13] Thus, if quotation from primary texts is a way of increasing the authority of an assertion by evoking another independent document or discourse, or a way of increasing the authenticity of the representation by appealing to the first-hand testimony of an eye-witness, it may also be used, as we shall see, as a way of renouncing or delegating authorial responsibility; as a strategy to 'pass the buck', as it were, to the other text.

In describing the death of Madame Roland, for example, Blanc suggests that one source gave her last words as 'O Liberty, what crimes are committed in thy name!' whereas another one gave something different (II:583). In this case, the invocation of two different, contradictory sources serves to call into doubt the historical status of Madame Roland's famous last words, by suggesting 'O Liberty, etc.' is merely the version given by one witness, that these words are not universally recognised; and that, therefore, they may be merely legend and not history.

In his account of the death of Danton, Blanc introduces (if only to dismiss them as improbable) both Mercier's contention that Danton died drunk and Senar's contention that Danton's last words concerned his erotic adventures (II:722): in this case, the use of primary texts to which the historian does not give credence allows certain (improbable) occurrences to be suggested in the text – as possibilities, if not as facts. 'Le fait historique est lié linguistiquement à un privilège d'être,' writes Barthes, 'on raconte ce qui a été, non ce qui n'a pas été ou ce qui a été

[13] Compagnon 1979:88. Precisely because a text which is quoted directly in the historical text has an autonomy *vis-à-vis* the historian's discourse, it can have all the more authority as documentary evidence and, in certain instances, be all the more susceptible to distortion. Again, Lamartine's transgressions point to the convention at work – the 'Proclamation à tous les Français' which Louis XVI left for the Assembly when he secretly fled the capital and which Lamartine purports to quote directly, was in fact, as Court has shown, modified substantially by the historian: he leaves out those passages which might incriminate the king as a counter-revolutionary conspirator, and he adds a passage which expresses the king's intention not to leave France (Court 1985,II:81–2); in this way, Lamartine 'resolves' the controversy concerning Louis's travel plans and his alleged treason, by inscribing his interpretation into the original document he purports to be quoting.

douteux' ('The historical fact is linguistically linked to an ontological privilege: one narrates what was, not that which was not, or which was doubtful', 1982:18). Blanc's use of primary texts to introduce doubt and possibility into his representation implies that historical discourse may not in fact be as 'uniformly assertive' as Barthes pronounced it to be.

Under cover of the same citational immunity as in the above examples, and of the same renunciation of authorial responsibility, Blanc also exploits the political and the literary content of certain primary texts:[14] he quotes at length, for example, one of the satirical pamphlets written against the clergy (I:514) and regularly quotes directly from the satirical writings of Camille Desmoulins and the *Père Duchesne* (e.g. I:494, I:553, I:612) in a way which allows the caustically expressed opinions of these revolutionaries to become effective within his own account of the Revolution. Blanc's deployment of the discursive productions of the Revolutionaries points to the fact that historical works are dialogic constructs in which, as Georg Schmid puts it, 'past and present systems of semiosis are brought into relation with each other'.[15]

An important feature of the intertextual, 'dialogic' structure of these works is their incorporation of the polemic and programmatic speeches which were made by the Revolutionary leaders as they sought to direct the course of events in one way rather than another: speech acts and the production of discourses are part of the events-to-be-represented. But clearly, not every speech of every speaker can be reproduced and a selection is invariably made, the historian focussing on those discourses which he considers relevant to the reader's understanding of the Revolution. Lamartine, for example, quotes at length from, paraphrases, and comments on, Robespierre's polemical-programmatic speeches (e.g.

[14] In addition, it should be noted that Blanc's use of other texts is not restricted to primary sources (i.e. texts produced contemporaneously with the Revolution or subsequently produced by those who had participated in it). He introduces the *Grand Peur* of 1789 through a long quotation from George Sand's novel, *Mauprat*, in which she describes, in a fictional form, a peasant's reactions to a burnt-out château (I:465); the intertextual basis of his representation thus gives Blanc the freedom both to include fiction in his account ('this is only a quotation') and to profit from the literary work, the vivid or imaginative representations, and the purple prose of others. On occasion, Blanc even quotes some felicitous expression of his fellow historians; in a chapter on the 'Force attractive de la Révolution française', for example, he borrows Michelet's extravagant description of Kant ('I did not say it, he did'): 'In the depths of the Northern seas, there was a bizarre and powerful creature, a man? no, a system, a living scholasticism, spiked, hard, sculpted like a diamond out of the Baltic granite' (I:675).

[15] Schmid 1986:21. See also Ricoeur 1983–5: 'If…action can be narrated this is because it is already articulated through signs, rules, norms: from the outset, it is *symbolically mediated*' (I:91).

II:281; II:811f); in this way, Robespierre's ideas are not only given a new hearing, but his social programme for a christian democracy (as interpreted by Lamartine) is set up as a guiding principle in the narrative of events: will his ideals be realised or not? Blanc also gives extensive attention to Robespierre's speeches (and correspondingly less attention to those made by other parties); but his particular choice of passages for quotation and paraphrase, together with his interpretative commentary, succeeds in foregrounding Robespierre's programme for universal political equality rather than the religious and ethical dimension of his thought foregrounded by Lamartine.[16] In both cases, the manner of quoting from Robespierre's speeches leads to a somewhat different interpretation of his programme; but, in both cases, the quotation of his speeches allows the historian to introduce a polemical, programmatic discourse – the outline of what might be achieved – into his narrative account of what actually happened.

The above examples illustrate how primary texts are incorporated in a variety of ways into the host-text – to give expression to particular programmes of action; to express opinions concerning actual events; to distance, modify or intensify the effect of an event; to heighten the vividness of the representation or to focalise it in a particular way. Finally, as the following example makes clear, primary texts may even serve as an excuse for *not* representing certain incidents. In his narrative of the final days of Louis XVI, Michelet refers the reader to the moving account ('le douleureux récit') of the condemned monarch's farewell to his family written by the king's valet (II:185). Michelet recognises that the account is moving (as all the deaths of 1793 would be moving, he adds, although not all of the victims had the consolation of saying goodbye to their family); if his readers so wish, then, they can read all about that pathetic scene in Cléry's account; for his part, Michelet will pass over it since it has been described so well already. By opting to call upon the intertext on this particular occasion as a complement to his own account, Michelet exonerates himself from having to represent *in praesentia* the scene of the king's farewell to his family so favoured by the royalist historians; while pronouncing it moving, he obviates its potentially moving effect on the reader of his own text.

Since the historians' source documents are often themselves complex texts, the historian may accordingly use them in practice as more than simply throw-away source 'documents' whose sole function is to provide

[16] See, for instance, Blanc I:674. For examples of how Robespierre's speeches are mediated and interpreted through the manner in which they are quoted, see below, p.167.

information about 'what happened' or to act as guarantors of the account.[17] The selection of primary texts and the manner in which they are incorporated into the historical text give rise to specific effects at the level of the representation, effects which are clearly linked to the particular image of the Revolution which the historian wishes to convey. The fact that historical representation is, by definition, a 'dual construction' thus provides the historian with an important rhetorical instrument which is particularly his own, and the use of which goes far beyond simply a scholarly conscientiousness in showing the source of his information.

The historical tradition

The French Revolution: a 'received event'

Historians of the French Revolution do not set to work with a mass of primary source-texts from which they then, step by step, construct a particular series of events which they all happen to call 'the French Revolution'. Between 1789 and whenever the history of the Revolution is being written, not only have many memoirs become available, but other, more or less lengthy, narrative histories of 'the French Revolution' have already been produced.

'Le champ événementiel ne comprend pas des sites qu'on irait visiter et qui s'appelleraient événements: un événement n'est pas un être mais un croisement d'itinéraires possibles,' writes Paul Veyne ('The evenemential field is not composed of discrete sites to be visited and called events; an event is not an entity, but the intersection of possible routes', 1978:38–9). The fact that we can speak of 'the French Revolution', however, or that the different historians in the nineteenth century should collectively write histories of 'the French Revolution', presupposes a prior mapping out or organisation of the theoretically open evenemential field: certain events are already seen as together constituting coherent episodes in 'the French Revolution'. What happened in France between 1789 and 1794 may not have happened in the form of an 'untold story'; but in the meantime, it has clearly become part of the historical tradition or culture: it has become a story to be told, one which has already been told.

As scholars like Mona Ozouf (1970) have pointed out, the representation of the Revolution as a whole and of its constituent episodes already played an important role in the direction of the events even as they were taking place.[18] Indeed, as Furet argues, the notion that the

[17] For the pertinence of the distinction between 'documents' and complex 'texts' to the treatment of historiographical sources, see LaCapra 1985:19–51.

[18] See also Lynn Hunt's study of this aspect of the rhetoric of the Revolution (1984:19–51).

Revolution marks an absolute break with the past and initiates modern history is part of the legacy of the discourse of the Revolutionaries themselves (a legacy which, as we have already seen, was reflected in the metahistorical debates of the nineteenth century).

Through the different representations which have already been given from 1789 onwards, through the tradition or transmission of those representations, and the addition of others along the way, 'the French Revolution' has become what Veyne calls a 'received event' (1978:39). It is 'a site to be visited' or, if the nominal reference is to be expanded into a narrative account, it is a pre-arranged itinerary marking out the recommended scenic route (and the beaten track) from one major point of interest to the next – the Jeu de Paume (20 June 1789); the Taking of the Bastille (14 July 1789); the abolition of feudal privileges (4 August 1789); the women at Versailles (5–6 October 1789); the Flight to Varennes (20–22 June 1791); the crowd's invasion of the Tuileries (20 June 1792); the Storming of the Tuileries on 10 August 1792; the execution of Louis XVI (21 January 1793); and so on, through to the fall of the Girondins (2 June 1793), the *Terreur*, the trial and execution of Danton (13–16 Germinal *an* II, 2–5 April 1794), and the fall of Robespierre on 9 Thermidor *an* II (27 July 1794).

For all the differences between the three histories in length, in the degree of detail with which they treat particular episodes, and in the particular links they establish between them, each one is structured around these canonical events, these areas of common historical ground. Their common narrative skeleton is manifest in the titles of the different chapters and subsections of the individual histories. Thus Michelet's first book ends with a chapter called 'The taking of the Bastille (14 July 1789)', the second with 'The *peuple* bring the king back to Paris (6 October 1789)', the third with 'Concerning the new religion – nationwide Confederation (14 July 1790)', the fourth with 'The flight of the king to Varennes', and so on. The first volume of Blanc's narrative ends with the abolition of feudal privileges on 4 August 1789, the second with the crowd bringing the king to Paris from Versailles on 6 October 1789, the third with the reorganisation of the state, 1789–90, the fifth with the *Fête de la Fédération*, 14 July 1790, and so on. Lamartine departs from this narrative model somewhat in entitling his work the *Histoire des Girondins* and in beginning his history *in medias res* with the death of Mirabeau in 1791. Although it thus sets out to recount the story of the Girondins rather than of the Revolution as a whole, Lamartine's account remains nevertheless structured around the *journées mémorables*;[19] it falls back, as it were, into the tracks of the master-narrative. Particularly revealing in this respect is the fact that instead of closing with the death of the Girondins, the titular subjects of his history, Lamartine goes on to close, like Michelet, with the fall of Robespierre. Blanc entitles his account of Robespierre's death 'The denouement', thereby suggesting, like Michelet and Lamartine, that there was an identity between Robespierre's career and that of the Revolution; as a supplement or epilogue to this denouement, however, his narrative account goes on to relate the *Terreur* of the Thermidorean reaction and the events leading to Vendémiaire.

Although there is no exact agreement as to where the Revolution should end, nor – what is even more problematic – where it should begin, it is clear from the above narrative outlines that any divergence takes place within a conventional framework and through the reorganisation of a limited set of possibilities.[20]

The French Revolution is not only a 'received event' in the sense that it has already been given a basic narrative form, a *fabula* running *grosso modo* from the Estates General of 1789 to Thermidor (or Vendémiaire). Through the contemporary representations produced by the revolutionaries themselves, and through the various subsequent narrations of the events of 1789–94, the constitutive events of the Revolution and the Revolution as a whole have also been configured in particular ways and invested with particular, often divergent, meanings. (As Furet puts it:

[19] Unlike his colleagues, Lamartine simply gives a number to the different chapters and sections, without titling them. In response to complaints from the public regarding the absence of a table of contents and of topic indicators within the text itself, Lamartine inserted an 'Avis aux MM les souscripteurs' in vol. V of the first edition (1847), promising to include a table of contents 'free of charge' in the final volume.

[20] If historical events are inseparable from the events which preceded them, how can one ever 'begin' a history? The solutions adopted by the three writers reflect the narratological problems involved: Blanc and Michelet preface their narratives of the Revolution by lengthy historical and analytical essays which act as buffers filling the historical gap between it and the Reformation (Blanc) or the end of the Middle Ages (Michelet), anterior master events which function as the symbolic 'beginnings' of modern history; their narratives of the Revolution then commence with the court of Louis XVI (Blanc) and with the convocation of the Estates General (Michelet). Lamartine opts to begin his history with the death of Mirabeau in 1791 (Carlyle opts for a similar procedure in beginning with the death of Louis XV in 1774). Mirabeau's death symbolically marks the transition between the old and the new, and initiates the narrative movement by creating an absence or vacuum which leaves open the question: who or what will take the place of the deceased? Orr also considers the difficulties of such 'beginnings' in her study of Blanc and Michelet's introductions to the origins/causes of the Revolution (1989).

whatever a historian of the Revolution actually writes has 'a meaning which pre-exists his own work': any new history is read both as an account of the Revolution and as the disclosure of the historian's opinion – as a royalist, as a liberal, as a Jacobin – on that master event (1978:13).) The new historian's view on the nature and course of the Revolution will be expressed through, or reflected in, his particular treatment of certain specific topics and his representation of certain key events which have become the most controversial ones in the historical tradition: the trial of the king, popular violence, the role of Robespierre, the *Terreur*, and (most important of all perhaps in the context of the July monarchy) the relationship between 1789 and 1793. As we have seen earlier (above, p.8), the liberal critic Baudrillart complained of the positive attention paid by Lamartine, Blanc, and Michelet to the republican 1793 phase of the Revolution, a criticism which echoed that of the *légitimiste* Nettement who, in 1848, accused Lamartine and his colleagues of having 'rehabilitated' the 'exterminators' typical of the 93 democracy, thereby removing 'the hitherto insurmountable barrier of horror and indignation, which until now arrested the fall of opinion onto the fatal slope' (1848:587).

In his *A Theory of Semiotics*, Umberto Eco suggests that the statement 'Napoleon died on Saint Helena' was a factual judgement on 5 May 1821: that is to say, a judgement which 'predicates of a given content certain semantic markers that have never been attributed to it by a previous code' (1979a:159). From 1821 onwards, however, the same statement has constituted a semiotic judgement: that is to say, a judgement which 'predicates of a given content (one or more cultural units) the semantic markers already attributed to it'. Since the cultural code has fixed in the compositional tree of /Napoleon/ the definitional connotation 'died on Saint Helena', to restate the fact that 'Napoleon died on Saint Helena' is simply to re-affirm the workings of the code, rather than to give new information.[21] Confirming the workings of the historical code is, of course, the basis upon which new information will be communicated.

Using Eco's terms, then, we can say that in the passage of time between the French Revolution and the 1840s, 'The French Revolution' has become part of the cultural code, having fixed in its compositional tree –

[21] In contrast, we might add, the statement 'After the battle of Marengo, Napoleon drank a cup of coffee' remains a factual statement, and for it to be a historical statement, a source must be presupposed. Since it is *vraisemblable* according to the cultural code that the emperor might have taken some refreshment in the form of coffee after the exertions of the battle, the obligation to identify the source would be less heavy here than it would be in the case of a statement like 'Napoleon, before the battle of Austerlitz, won a pearl necklace in a game of forfeits'.

among other elements – the connotations 'Prise de la Bastille', 'Fuite à Varennes', 'Robespierre', 'Terreur', and so on.[22] In discussing the relations between Mirabeau and the court in the spring of 1790, for example, Michelet refers to the former's 'famous apostrophe' on Charles IX and the Saint-Barthélemy: 'I see from here the window etc.', leaving it to his readers to fill in the blanks according to what they already know of the famous speech; what is left unsaid here – the *etcetera* – is common knowledge; it is what has already been said (as Michelet puts it) 'in every memoir'.[23]

Moreover, as is illustrated by Blanc's invocation of 'that too famous day, 15 May 1848' (III:205) in his account of Prairial, and his invocation of the Bourbon restoration in his account of the surrender of Verdun in 1792, 'the French Revolution' figures within the historical code together with subsequent events in French history.[24] It also figures there alongside earlier events such as the Saint-Barthélemy, which Blanc recalls in the very title of his chapter on the September massacres, 'Souviens-toi de la Saint-Barthélemy', and which Mirabeau himself had already recalled in his 'I see from here the window from which a king...'[25]

In the course of Michelet's representation of the events leading up to the fall of Robespierre on 9 Thermidor *an* II (27 July 1794), the historian makes a brief reference to Brumaire *an* VIII (9 November 1799)': The Robespierristes were ready for their 18 Brumaire. Robespierre was not . . .' (II:948). Although he has not yet represented the later event (as it turns

[22] There is a certain difficulty involved for a twentieth-century reader – particularly a reader who is not French – in following these nineteenth-century histories of the French Revolution (or indeed more recent ones) since they depend so largely on the reader's foreknowledge of a particular cultural code to which the principal elements of the Revolution already belong.

[23] I:347. Famous *bons mots* or 'last words' have an important rhetorical function in these texts, which I discuss in greater detail elsewhere (1986:83f). As commonplaces, they function as points of recognition in the representation; but as commonplaces, they are also most susceptible to transformation, a point which is illustrated above by Blanc's undermining of the historical status of Madame Roland's 'O Liberty, what crimes...' Michelet himself gives two different versions of Mirabeau's apostrophe concerning the Saint-Barthélemy (I:347, 368).

[24] In describing the surrender of Verdun in 1792, Blanc comments: 'Already, compass in hand, the royalists were measuring out on the map the distance separating Verdun from Paris; already their wives were preparing to wave their white handkerchiefs – remember 1815! – as the desecrators of Paris passed by' (II:190).

[25] For a study of the function of the 'Saint-Barthélemy' as a commonplace in Revolutionary historiography (a sign of *ancien régime* violence to be set against the violence of the *Terreur*), see Delon 1981. It is a commonplace which also plays a very prominent role in Hugo's *Quatrevingt-treize* (1874), as do the 'famous sayings' of the Revolutionaries around which he builds his portrait of the Convention (1965:157f) – e.g. 'A king dead is not a man less' (Manuel); 'As it falls, the head of a king should not make more noise than the head of any other man' (Rouyer).

out, Brumaire lies outside the temporal framework of his Revolution), Michelet can presume that it already lies within the frame of reference of the addressee of his account: the name 'Brumaire' already makes sense, signifying Napoleon's *coup d'état*. Thus, the 'French Revolution' as a whole, including its later evolution into the *Terreur* of 1793–4, constitutes the 'horizon of expectation' for any reading of the events of 1789.

Precisely because it is historical, then, a narrative account of the Revolution is free to be anachronistic in structure: in a sort of temporal chiasmus, later events, already belonging to the historical code, can be used to illuminate the earlier ones which are the subject of the narrative. Conversely, the narration of earlier events may serve to illuminate the later ones and thereby change the reader's perception of them. Thus, Michelet takes care to note the presence of 'Marceau' among the *gardes-françaises* who helped to capturc the Bastille. As the historian himself admits, the famous Marceau did not distinguish himself particularly on this occasion; he 'contented himself' with playing a modest, unremarkable role:

> Dans ses soldats [i.e. les soldats d'Élie], il en avait un, admirable de vaillance, de jeunesse, de pureté, l'une des gloires de la France, Marceau, qui se contenta de combattre et ne réclama rien dans l'honneur de la victoire.[26]
>
> [Among his soldiers, there was Marceau, admirable for his courage, his youth, and his purity, one of the glories of France, who contented himself with fighting, without claiming any merit in the victory.]

Since Marceau is known to have become a great general in the revolutionary campaigns of 1794, his (unobtrusive) presence at the Bastille in his capacity as 'great-revolutionary-general-to-be' can be used to increase the symbolic value of that particular event: the presence of

[26] I:155. The name 'Marceau' is frequently used like this to point forward to the military glories of France's revolutionary army (among all the historians this is the glory which is the least disputed). Blanc, for example, invokes Marceau's name again in his account of the surrender of Verdun (1792): 'and when the king of Prussia asked the name of the young man who had been forced to deliver the capitulation of Verdun, the young man answered "Marceau", with an unforgettable look in his tearful eyes' (II:220). In Carlyle's history, we find a striking number of such anticipatory references to Napoleon: as Artillery Major in Marseilles, 1793 (1903, II:269); as that 'remarkable Artillery-Major' at Toulon, 1793 (II:280); as figuring prominently among the generals of the Republic in the post-Thermidorean *soirées* (II:366). The same technique is abundantly used by Alexandre Dumas in his *Les Blancs et les bleus* (1867–8): when Pichegru's officers read the account of the siege of Toulon in the *Moniteur* of the day, they 'happen to' pick out, among the various persons cited for bravery, the artillery officer 'Buonaparte', whose remarkable name and person they then proceed to discuss at length (n.d.:172–5).

'Marceau' at the Bastille allows 14 July to prefigure the future glories of the French Republic and to suggest that those glories, rather than the future violence of the *Terreur*, are the natural outcome of the founding event of the Revolutionary tradition.

In the lengthy preface to his history of the Revolution, Louis Blanc recounts how the Calixtins of Bohemia, having prized freedom over fraternity, ended up by betraying their Taborite brothers; and describes them as the 'Thermidoreans of those days' (I:11). The fact that 'Thermidor' can be presumed, from the outset of his account, to be part of the cultural inheritance of his addressee (as 'Brumaire' and 'Marceau' are presumed to be by Michelet), does not prevent Blanc from giving a lengthy representation, almost two thousand pages later, of Robespierre's downfall. But the 'Thermidor' which he represents will not simply be invested with the same semantic properties as the 'Thermidor' to which he nominally refers at the beginning of his history. Blanc's eventual account of Robespierre's downfall will elaborate on the blanket term of 'Thermidor' through the narrative representation of particular details; moreover, it will be situated in the context of his history as a whole, where, in the intervening two thousand pages, Robespierre has been given a prominent and value-laden role. In this way, Blanc's particular representation of Thermidor (and, by implication, his representation of 'the French Revolution' as a whole) can be said simultaneously to exploit the historical code and to seek to transform it.

'I define the Revolution...': 'the French Revolution' which Michelet defines in the opening lines of his history is at once 'the French Revolution' with which his reader is presumed familiar already and 'the Revolution' which is not yet known, but which will be revealed through his narration and re-configuration, episode by episode, of the famous events. As Michel de Certeau suggests, proper names as used in historical texts – be they 'Marceau', 'Thermidor', or 'the French Revolution' – are often the locus of a didactic shift:

> Le nom propre permet un double effet. D'une part, il signifie: 'Robespierre, vous savez, ce que c'est.' Il est *fiable*. D'autre part, il est l'objet d'un décalage didactique: 'Robespierre, c'est autre chose que ce que vous savez, et je vais vous l'apprendre.' (1975:112n)
>
> [A proper name allows for a double effect. On the one hand, it signifies: 'Robespierre, you know who that is.' It is *reliable*. On the other hand, it is the object of a didactic shift: 'Robespierre, he is different from the man you know, and I am going to tell you how.']

In practice, then, any representation of the French Revolution in the 1840s is what Harald Weinrich has called 'ein Umerzählen' (1973:519): a rewriting or 'narrating afresh' of a history which has already been written (and rewritten). The individual narrative acts in different ways as a didactic mediator between 'the French Revolution' which is already known and 'the French Revolution' which has never yet been represented. The specific features of any new representation of the Revolution will be measured out against the common, inherited schema of 'the French Revolution' as it is known already. It is in the correction of the basic schema (to use Gombrich's terms, 1969:116) through the re-presentation of the famous *événements reçus*, and through the introduction of episodes which are less famous (such as Vergniaud's meeting with his nephew), that the historian's selection of sources and his manner of incorporating them into his text comes into play.

The rewriting of events

That representing the Revolution fifty years later involves rewriting a story whose basic narrative outline has already been given is illustrated in a particularly clear, indeed literal, manner at the level of the verbal expression, the *elocutio*: in the metaphors used by the different historians to describe the Revolution and to chart out its course. That such metaphoric representation is common to the writers considered here (and plays a particularly important role in Michelet's work) is itself worthy of interest, since it points to the fact that the historians of the Revolution at this time did not aim for a transparent *écriture blanche* devoid of all figuration; that, on the contrary, a high level of metaphor was acceptable.[27] What is perhaps of even greater significance in the present context, however, is the fact that metaphorical description in the three histories is as much the locus of the commonplace – and of its transformation – as it is an occasion for individual experimentation and inventiveness.

As Ronald Paulson has shown, a reservoir of images with which to describe the new, unprecedented circumstances of the Revolution emerged almost simultaneously with the Revolution itself. These images were

[27] Curiously, although Lamartine's history was frequently described by contemporaries as the most poetic of histories, it is a work in which metaphoric description is comparatively rare, a fact which suggests that its 'poetic' qualities are to be sought less in its purely verbal texture than in its exploitation of a variety of literary commonplaces, eclectically culled from contemporary melodrama and from the popular novel à la Eugène Sue (see Reboul 1980), as well as from more classical sources. His extensive use of these literary topoi points to the fact that the intertextual tradition in which each new history was placed extended beyond the limits of the particular historiographical tradition of the Revolution to the literary tradition in general.

drawn both from the classical literary traditions and from a range of natural phenomena. Depending on the point of view adopted, the Revolution was regularly represented as a volcano, an earthquake, a torrent, an ocean, a natural regeneration, a sunburst (Paulson 1983: chap.1–3) – images which recur in a more or less elaborated form throughout the three mid-nineteenth-century histories considered here.[28]

When the king was brought to Paris from Versailles on 6 October 1789, for example, Mirabeau proposed in the National Assembly that a report be sent to the provinces to reassure them that the 'vessel of State was advancing more rapidly than ever towards port' (Blanc I:404). Three revolutionary years later, Camille Desmoulins described 'the vessel of the Republic' as trying to navigate a safe passage 'between the two reefs of moderantism and exaggeration' (Blanc II:680). A literary commonplace of long standing, the 'Ship of State' seems to have acquired a privileged status in the representation of the evolution of the new *régime* and its struggles to cross the ocean (representing the revolution, the counter-revolution, or revolutionary extremists, depending on the point of view). Certainly, this image has a privileged position in the subsequent histories of the French Revolution – again reflecting the way in which the discourse of those who participated in the events of 1789–94 is inherited by their historians.

The figure of the Revolutionary ship thus recurs in Michelet's description of Danton's speech to the Convention on the issue of liberty and property:

> C'était l'homme qu'on regardait comme l'orage même et le génie des tempêtes, qui venait, au moment où le vaisseau était relancé à la mer, jeter, fixer dans le granit les deux ancres invincibles auxquelles s'est tenue la France. (I:1181)
>
> [Thus, at the very moment the vessel was thrust back out to sea, the man regarded as the storm itself, as the very genius of the tempest, came and fixed in granite the two invincible anchors which held France steady.]

Later, Michelet describes the 'the rising tide of counter-revolutionary

[28] The general reservoir of classical commonplaces was also widely used by the three historians. Lamartine availed of it, for example, in the Roman analogy which he invokes in his account of how the Girondins threw money to the crowd as a sign of their indifference to life (see below, p.51); similarly, Blanc invokes a Roman analogy in his account of Madame Roland's death: she died in a manner worthy of the mother, or of a sister, of the Gracchi (II:583). In certain instances, the classical models had already been self-consciously adopted by the revolutionaries themselves: Michelet relates, for example, how Charlotte Corday spent the day preceding her assassination of Marat reading Plutarch's *Lives* (II:499). See also Paulson 1983:10f.

fanaticism' (II:220); relates how the Jacobins plotted to seize 'the helm of the Revolution'; how the Republic was like 'a superb vessel, reigning over the Ocean, but carrying in its hold a world of worms relentlessly working to devour it' (II:840).

Lamartine describes how, on 10 August 1792, 'France was heading for destruction. The Assembly would not take the helm' (I:655). Later on, he describes how Robespierre alone knew 'the secrets of the route, and marked out for the democracy the ever retreating port which they were hoping to reach across this sea of blood' (II:727).

Louis Blanc describes how, after the death of Mirabeau, people realised that they were launched onto the shipwrecking sea: 'with one such pilot less, who could affirm that the ship would not end up in pieces on the reefs, leaving the pale crowd struggling amidst the tempest in the immensity of space and waves?' (I:657). Having assessed the role of Mirabeau and the state of the Revolution, Blanc goes on to conclude his obituary with a reformulation of the same maritime figure, mixed with a classical analogy:

> [La Révolution] n'apparaissait-elle pas déjà flottant, dans un frêle esquif, sur une mer agitée? Sans doute, et qu'importe? Comme César, plus nécessairement que César, elle avait ses destinées à accomplir, et au nautonier, entre les flots de l'abîme soulevés et le ciel en feu, au nautonier saisi d'épouvante, elle avait certes le droit de dire: 'Va, ne crains rien: tu portes le peuple et sa fortune!' (I:660)
>
> [Did not the Revolution seem to be already afloat in a frail barque on an agitated sea? Doubtless, and what of it? Like Caesar, and even more necessarily than Caesar, the Revolution had its destiny to fulfil; and, between the burning sky and the waves rising from the abyss, it certainly had the right to say to the horror-struck captain: 'Go on, fear nothing: you are carrying the people and their fortune!']

Examples of the maritime commonplace of the ship (the state, the republic) trying to cross the sea of revolutionary events might be multiplied. Developed in more or less detail or simply invoked synecdochically under one or other of its aspects (the ship, the rudder, the reefs, the sea, the storm, the port which is sought), it recurs throughout the texts considered here, being used in each instance to represent different historical circumstances; more specifically, it is used as a metaphorical representation of the different relations between various actorial elements, the different configurations of power in the development of the Revolution.

Who stands at the helm in the different circumstances? (It is clear that, for Blanc, Robespierre takes over Mirabeau's role as pilot of the Revolution; for Lamartine, in contrast, Robespierre comes to the helm after the monarchy has been submerged by the popular flood ('le flot populaire', II:232.) Who should stand at the helm? (Blanc suggests that the pilot should be the servant of the Revolution.) Who is on board? (Blanc fills the ship with the *peuple*, whereas Lamartine puts the people outside, the *flot populaire* being the ship's antagonist.) What is the port towards which the ship is headed and what are the obstacles (the storms, reefs, tides) which stand in its way? (For Michelet, the ship is ultimately prevented from reaching port by the tide of counter-revolution and by the speculators who undermine the Republic from within.) What are the forces which help it towards its destination?

Like the topics of classical rhetoric, the commonplace of the revolutionary ship provides each writer with an empty frame or narrative grid, which can be filled in by different actors, depending on the particular configuration of the Revolution: the significant roles are already marked out, the historian only has to give them a figurative manifestation. Because the maritime image is a commonplace and not a particular invention of the historian, it allows the latter to mark out the changes taking place in the Revolution in its different phases and thereby make clear the specific features of his particular 'Revolution': as a cliché, it paradoxically provides the basis upon which differences can be measured and laid bare. At least in this instance, then, it can be said that metaphorical description functions as a sort of metacomment on the representation itself, 'a reader's guide' to its decoding, a way for readers to find their bearings.

Besides using a commonplace metaphoric representation of the Revolution and applying it in his text to particular figures and circumstances, the historian may also mark out and reinforce the significant features of his account through his transformation of the commonplace itself. When the Revolution was considered from the point of view of its violence, or when a negative image of it as a whole was to be put forward, it was commonly represented through the image of a raging torrent or a stormy sea; an anarchic, destructive force, it was to be feared, if not indeed abhorred. Writing in this intertextual context, Michelet takes the bull by the horns, and represents the Revolution in 1792 as the pacific Nile which, by the very fact that it bursts its banks, brings health and life with it, and which, as such, is something to be welcomed (Michelet reinforces this connotation by suggesting that everyone was in fact already blessing it): 'In two months, the Revolution had flooded its banks on all sides: it was rising, like the Nile, salutary and fertile, amidst the benedictions of men' (I:1133).

Michelet's fertilising Nile remains intimately linked to the commonplace image of the Revolution as a torrent by the very fact that it subverts it and seeks to take its place:[29] in Nettement's terms, to remove the barrier of horror surrounding the Revolution. The fact that he should use a subversive version of one of the commonplaces concerning the Revolution points both to the societal nature of his discourse and to its didactic function in converting its public: in this case, by first meeting his reader's expectations and preconceptions concerning the Revolution as a destructive or terrifying force, and then, through a 'didactic shift', by showing the real Revolution to have been quite the contrary – a wondrously productive, not terrifying, event.[30] It is also in this light that we can view the rewriting process in Lamartine's transformation of Vergniaud from a terrifying figure into a glorious one.

Intertextual antagonism

False histories and false historians

The historians of the Revolution write in the context of earlier, pre-existing representations of the events of 1789–94. As I have shown above, this historical tradition provides them with a preconfigured narrative schema and, to a certain extent, a vocabulary, through which they can represent the Revolution and mark off their particular *prise de position* with respect to that master event.

The intertextual context is also made up, however, of particular representations of the Revolution and particular traditions of interpreting the common elements. These particular representations may run counter to the individual historian's view on the matter or, simply by providing an alternative view, challenge his claim to be arbiter of the historical tradition, his claim to pass on historical truth and to speak with the authority of reality. Although a historian may actually write as a partisan – as a Liberal, Royalist or Jacobin – he does so in the name of the collective truth about events which has not yet been revealed: '*the* French Revolution' which has not yet been written. 'I have already said it several times,' writes Louis Blanc, 'and I could not become tired of repeating it: a special book could be written on the false histories of the French Revolution' (II:586).

[29] In Esquiros' *Histoire des Montagnards* (1847) we find a similar transformation of the commonplace: Danton 'fertilised the Revolution, like the Nile, by his outbursts and fits of anger' (II:347).

[30] It is presumably this type of strategy which the reviewer of *Le Charivari* had in mind when he proclaimed that the principal function of the histories of Michelet, Blanc, and Lamartine was to make the Revolution 'be loved': 'It is no longer a matter of judging the Revolution, but of making people love it. Lamartine, Michelet, Louis Blanc have dedicated themselves to carrying out this providential task' (12 April 1847).

'Unless at least two versions of the same set of events can be imagined,' writes Hayden White, 'there is no reason for the historian to take upon himself the authority of giving the true account of what really happened' (1987:20). Now, in the case of the historians of the Revolution, the existence of other, rival accounts of the same event is no mere theoretical possibility, but a historical fact. If it is to succeed in its claims to speak with the authority of historical reality, then, the historian's discourse must assert this authority over the claims of any possible alternative accounts of the same events.[31] In order to establish 'his Revolution' as a truthful representation of 'the Revolution', the historian will have to cut the ground from under the feet of his potential rivals and dislodge his predecessors – whether these are specific texts or specific traditions of interpretation which have generated their own commonplaces. He may have to overemphasise certain aspects of the events he is narrating or in other ways overstate his case, if he is to make his point and overcome the implied resistance or antagonism to his point of view, thereby swinging the historiographical scales back to a hypothetical zero.[32]

This is not to suggest that every historian attacks every other historian on any point where they happen to diverge. That would not only be an impossible task, but also a senseless one; for, as with all conflicts, there must be enough common ground between the two opponents for battle to be possible and the outcome of it to be significant. (An exhaustive account of all one's opponents' errors must be a task reserved for that hypothetical book on the 'false histories of the French Revolution'.)

The agonistic element in the historiography of the Revolution is particularly clear in the case of Louis Blanc. His text is the latest in the series considered here, and he avails himself of the new forum provided by the footnote to carry out a sustained critical evaluation of his opponents (who are presented as erroneous or pseudo-historians and not, of course, as rivals). His accounts of the principal canonical events – those areas of

[31] See also Paul Ricoeur's contention that a historian always writes in a 'situation de contestation et de procès'('in a situation of contestation and trial', 1983–5, I:261).

[32] In his study of the official iconography of the Republic between 1789 and 1880, Agulhon provides an illuminating example of how the context in which a sign is produced, and the implied resistance to the message which is perceived as part of that context, may lead to a particular form of hyperbole or intensification of the signifier. The official emblem of the July monarchy, he writes, was the Liberty Column surmounted by a tricolour (such a column had been symbolically erected in the Place de la Bastille). The only place where the king authorised the column to be surmounted by a Liberty goddess (the traditional emblem of the Jacobin Republic) was in Rennes, one of the seats of the *Vendéen* counter-revolution, where the column was strategically placed opposite the principal church (1979:67).

narrative ground shared by all historians of the Revolution – are followed up with a more or less lengthy *critique historique* in which he hauls his predecessors over the coals for their errors, omissions, and inventions. He thus represents his own text *historically* as having made progress *vis-à-vis* what came before it. His narrative of the September massacres, for example, is followed by six and a half, double columned, densely printed pages of criticism; his death of Danton by seven pages of such criticism, his death of Robespierre by two and a half pages, his massacre of the Champ de Mars by one and a half. In case his reader has not yet got his critical point, Blanc finishes up his blow-by-blow critique of previous accounts of the September massacres with the comment that: 'the preceding suffices to show whether it is indeed true, as so many people imagine, that the *History of the French Revolution* has already been written!' (II:215).

Although Blanc does on occasion refer to other historians such as Barante, Thiers, and Buchez and Roux, he focusses his critical efforts on Michelet and, to a lesser extent, Lamartine: the authors of the two histories closest in time to his own, and presenting, therefore, the most immediate challenge to his own work. Of these rivals, Lamartine is generally dismissed as a mere *fantaisiste*, by rights unworthy of consideration on the part of a serious historian like himself, but whose distortions of certain episodes must nevertheless be challenged because of the distorted view of the Revolution which they might disseminate.[33] Michelet, whose merits as a historian Blanc is willing to recognise (particularly on those occasions when he uses his text as an auxiliary to his own),[34] represents a much more serious opponent whom Blanc parries closely, and with increasing intensity, throughout his work.

Interestingly, Blanc's references to Carlyle tend, on the contrary, to take the form of a positive invocation: 'As one of the greatest writers in modern England put it...'[35] Because it is not written in the French context, Carlyle's work does not represent a challenge for Blanc, who is

[33] In the critique which follows his 20 June, Blanc prefaces his comments on Lamartine with the remark: 'Need it be said? M. de Lamartine was so badly informed, he was so completely unequipped with anything in the way of official documentation...that there is scarcely a fact in his narrative, a single important fact, which is not inexact' (II:135). See also his lengthy critique of the dangerous distortions contained in Lamartine's treatment of the September massacres (II:212f).

[34] In drawing on Michelet's description of Kant and his quotation of the Petition on the *autel de la patrie* (cf. above, notes 14 and 8), Blanc calls him 'an illustrious modern writer' and 'my illustrious colleague'; in citing Michelet's judgement of Mirabeau, he invokes his authority as 'a modern historian' (I:650).

[35] II:261. See also his invocation of Carlyle: I:366; I:479; II:286.

addressing a French public, and can be used instead to mark out Blanc's exclusive English position giving him access to English materials which are not available to his French colleagues.

The main argument which Blanc explicitly invokes against his opponents is that of their failure to respect historical fact, through omission, inaccuracy, invention, or distortion: faults which may be attributed either to the historians or to the sources which they have used. Michelet's particular failing, he suggests, is to distort facts by mere conjecture or interpretation (e.g. I:725), while Lamartine tends to base his account on facts which are simply inaccurate and even, at times, imaginary. In all cases, the implication is that he, Louis Blanc, has access to whatever facts are significant.

Moreover, exemplifying what De Certeau sees as the tendency of historians to establish their own authority by setting themselves up as different from fictional discourses, Blanc presents himself as a conscientious historian who seeks to oppose the historical distortions wrought by the 'artists', Lamartine and Michelet. According to Blanc (who presumably respects his 'austere duties' as a historian), both of these writers indulged, the former consistently and the latter occasionally, in an artistic and, by implication, misplaced sensibility.[36] It is this sensibility which explains their common partiality for the Girondins, the *artistes* of the Revolution, a sympathy which the (non-partisan) true historian Blanc clearly does not share: 'And, it is precisely because of their being artists, that [the Girondins] have found such favour with all the great artists who have spoken of them, like Messrs. Michelet, de Lamartine, and Sainte-Beuve' (II:44).

Blanc, however, is obviously selective about the points where he invokes these arguments in order to attack his opponents: his intertextual challenges are a function of the *prise de position* which he himself seeks to establish. He does not, for example, challenge Lamartine on his account of Vergniaud's last meeting with his nephew: even if he was in possession of information to the contrary, having himself been in contact with M. Alluaud, the incident is simply not pertinent to his argument and to his account of the death of the Girondins; whether Lamartine's version of the incident is veracious or not makes no difference since the reactions of a ten-year-old are, in this instance, beside Blanc's point. In contrast, whether or not on the day they were sentenced to death the Girondins

[36] In the *critique historique* which follows his account of the death of the Girondins, Blanc writes that Michelet, 'sacrificing his austere duties as a historian to his generous sympathies, has taken particular care to pass silently over *all* the circumstances unfavourable to the party which the tenderness of his soul had adopted from the outset' (II:586).

threw money to the crowd with the cry 'Friends, to our aid!', in an attempt to escape the scaffold, is very much to Blanc's point. He includes this particular incident in his account of the Girondins' execution (II:581) and refers to it again in considerable documentary detail in his critical assessment and rejection of Lamartine's account, where the Girondins had been represented as throwing away their money to the crowd, like the Romans, as a sign of their stoic indifference to life and not of their wish to escape death (II:528–9). In a similar way, it is pertinent to Blanc's argument to establish whether or not Mlle de Sombreuil was in fact made to drink human blood in order to save her father from instant death at the hands of the *septembriseurs* – as Lamartine and royalist hearsay had suggested. In his account of the notorious incident (II:204), Blanc explains, without any mention of Lamartine, how such a fiction might have arisen and the true circumstances in which the act of filial heroism took place; and in the process of contradicting the alternative, legendary account, he gives evidence of a redeeming modicum of compassion on the part of the alleged cannibals (what really happened, he suggests, is that they gave a glass of water to the unfortunate Mlle de Sombreuil). In the lengthy *critique* of Lamartine's work which follows, Blanc returns once again to the incident: 'We have told the true history of the glass of blood supposedly offered to Mademoiselle de Sombreuil; here is M. de Lamartine's version...' (II:213), thereby making clear the nature of the misconception his own account has sought to rectify. Indeed, the six-and-a-half-page *critique historique* which follows Blanc's account of the September massacres – the length of which is already a measure of the opposition the historian seeks to overcome – picks up, by way of a detailed analysis of the errors committed by both Michelet and Lamartine, the various points which have already been made in the narrative account. In this way, the critical analysis serves both to reinforce the points made in the representation and to bring into relief the significant features of the later historian's representation by showing its significant difference from the earlier one: 'this is what happened' and 'what happened has never before been truthfully represented'.

In a similar way, Blanc focusses his ongoing critique of Michelet on what he perceives as the latter's consistently unjust treatment of Robespierre, and on the consistent favoritism which he accords on the other hand to Danton: in this way, Blanc's critique of his principal rival brings out *a contrario* the pertinent or differential features of his own account (clearly it is a matter of considerable importance to him that the misrepresentation of Robespierre in particular be redeemed). Again, the seven-page *critique historique* which follows Blanc's account of the death of Danton, and which is explicitly directed against 'Dantonist' historians such as Michelet, is in many ways a repetition in a non-narrative form of the points which the historian has already made in his narrative representation of the event: that Robespierre did not have Fabre d'Eglantine arrested through fear of his satire, that Robespierre did not deliberately sacrifice Danton, that there are elements of truth in the official version of Danton's trial, that he was not simply a victim of the machinations against him, and so on.[37]

In this way, the *critique historique* functions, like the iconographical schema discussed earlier, as a form of gloss or metacommentary on the historical representation. It reinforces Blanc's *prise de position* by repeating or re-stating it in another, explicitly dialogic form and it draws his reader's attention to the significant, noteworthy features of the representation. Moreover, while bringing into relief the significant features of the preceding narrative account, it also makes clear the illegitimacy and partiality of any rival versions: 'this is what happened' and 'what happened is different from what has hitherto been represented in the "false histories"'. As the incident with Mlle de Sombreuil suggests, however, discrediting rival accounts serves not only to discredit the individual historian but, as importantly, the alternative image of the Revolution: Lamartine's hyperbole provides Blanc with a pretext from which to show up the 'fictional' versus historical status of a notorious incident which, if admitted as historical, would discredit the Revolution and reinforce its ill-repute.

Blanc's use of the paratextual *critique historique* illustrates in a particularly clear, even schematic, way the agonistic basis of historical writing and the intertextual basis of historical signification.[38] But intertextual antagonism is not simply restricted to such explicit statements of dissent. Blanc's rewriting of the death of Danton or of the Sombreuil incident points to the fact that the competition between rival versions is, in the first place, actually written into the narrative representation of

[37] Michelet responded vehemently to Blanc's criticisms in the preface which he wrote to the 1868 edition of his history (I:9–20), in which he attacks Blanc for his sacralisation of Robespierre; suggests that any history of the Revolution written in London rather than in Paris could only be an amateurish one; and argues that, in any case, Blanc could never have understood the true French spirit ('He was born in Madrid. He is a Corsican through his mother, French through his father (from Rodez)', I:17) – an argument which Michelet invokes throughout his work to identify those who are foreign to the spirit of the Revolution, if not downright opponents of it (see Rigney 1989).

[38] I use the word 'paratextual' in the sense of Genette 1987, to indicate those textual elements such as titles, notes, prefaces etc. which accompany a narrative without actually being a part of it, but which can play an important role in guiding the reader towards its interpretation. For the particular function of footnotes, see Genette 1987:293–315.

events; that formal dissent in a *critique historique* is merely a gloss on a procedure which lies at the very basis of the representation itself. In the following pages, I will examine how intertextual antagonism is written into the representation of events, by focussing on a single episode in the Revolution: the vote in the Convention on 16 and 17 January 1793 which sentenced the king to death.

The sentencing of Louis XVI

According to Albert Soboul (1966:212), there were some fears of popular unrest, and even some rumours of more massacres or 'Septembrisades' in the days preceding the judgement of Louis XVI. Lamartine, for his part, brings these rumours to the forefront of his account of the sentencing of the king: he sets the scene for the vote by giving a general survey of Paris, the dominant motif of which is violence and the threat of violence. Conflating a number of different revolutionary groups, Lamartine relates how 'the Avignon assassins, September cut-throats, veterans of the Tenth of August', and so on, have been mobilised by the Commune and the Jacobins to put pressure on the national deputies to vote for the king's death (II:105). From the city, the narrative account moves into the surroundings of the Convention where the same ominous threats of violence dominate: as the deputies enter, they are confronted by sinister individuals, whom Lamartine describes as 'les statues de l'assassinat placées aux portes du tribunal du peuple pour commander la mort' ('homicidal statues placed at the door of the people's tribunal to prescribe death', II:108). Moving inside the Convention, the narrative foregrounds the signs of coercion which were also evident there. Sitting right in the front row of the public gallery, in pride of place as it were, there was nothing less than a group of apprentice butchers: the sign *par excellence* of barbaric violence.

> Les premières banquettes de ces tribunes populaires étaient occupées par des garçons bouchers, leurs tabliers ensanglantés retroussés d'un côté à leur ceinture, et le manche des longs couteaux de leur profession sortant avec affectation des plis de la toile qui leur servait de fourreau. (II:108–9)
>
> [The front seats of the public galleries were taken up by apprentice butchers, with their bloody aprons hitched up on one side to their belt and the handles of the long knives of their profession ostentatiously sticking out from the folds of cloth which served them as a scabbard.]

The scene being now set, Lamartine proceeds to give a general account of the way the individual deputies went up to the podium to cast their vote ('some did this', 'others did that'); he then homes in on the vote cast by one deputy in particular out of the 721: the influential Vergniaud, one of the leaders of the Gironde. Against all expectations, and betraying the promise he had made to his mistress the previous day, the Girondin leader went up to the podium, voted for the death of the king, and thereby – according to Lamartine – determined the outcome of the debate (for most of the Girondins were to follow his example).

Set in this narrative context which moves from the general, threatening aspect of Paris to the threatening aspect of the Convention, and then converges on the particular figure of Vergniaud, his regicide vote (and by implication the Convention's decision as a whole) is seen as not having been freely taken; it is made intelligible not as an act of principle or justice, but as a 'cowardly' surrender to the violent will to immolate the king, emanating from the 'peuple' and the Jacobins, and manifested in the knife-brandishing butchers. Vergniaud is thus a second Pontius Pilate (II:113) *vis-à-vis* whom Louis must – following the particular intertextual model which Lamartine calls upon in giving coherence to these events – have the role of another Christ; and in his subsequent account of the king's passion and death, Lamartine will develop this role to its fullest.[39]

Whereas Lamartine's narrative moves from 'Paris' into the Convention, Louis Blanc's *mise en scène* of the event begins with a lengthy *tableau* of the interior of the Convention and its public as these had been so vividly painted by that articulate and reliable eye-witness, Mercier (Blanc's *tableau* includes many details which also figure in Lamartine's account, thereby attesting to their common use of this source). Having represented what Mercier actually saw (although without mentioning the latter's reservations as to the reliability of his eye-witness perspective, cf. above, p.26), Blanc goes on to describe what this trustworthy, authoritative eye-witness did *not* see. Clearly, this is a very particular way of exploiting a source to show what it signifies 'without knowing it', to recall De Certeau's words (above, p.29). As it happens, the ventriloquial description of what the primary source Mercier *did not see* is a literal, though unacknowledged, quotation from the rival historian, Lamartine; a quotation in a negative form:

> Mais Mercier, qui, de son banc, dessinait la salle, et qui jamais n'oublia un trait caractéristique, ne dit pas que les premières banquettes des tribunes populaires fussent occupées par des garçons bouchers; il ne parle ni de leurs tabliers ensanglantés, ni de leur

[39] The Vergniaud who is here presented as a coward and a Pontius Pilate is to be transformed, several hundred pages later, into the glorious prisoner of La Force prison – himself now a victim of the Revolution. These inconsistencies or changes in Lamartine's portrayal of the different figures is one of the most striking features of his work (see below, chap.4).

affectation barbare à faire sortir des plis de la toile le manche de leurs longs couteaux. Ces muettes menaces de cannibale sont une fable royaliste. (II:303)

[But Mercier, who was surveying the room from his seat and who never forgot a characteristic detail, does not say that the first rows of the public galleries were filled by apprentice butchers; he speaks neither of their bloody aprons, nor of their barbaric affectation in letting the handles of their long knives stick out from the folds of their aprons. These silent, cannibalistic threats are a royalist fable.]

What the faithful Mercier did not see in 1793, then, are the elements of the royalist fable, as this had been embodied most recently in Lamartine's 1847 tableau of the Convention.

Moving outward from the Convention, retracing the path of Lamartine's account as it were, Blanc goes on to fix his attention on the situation in the surrounding city: there were no threats to the assembly, there were no – and here, Blanc actually echoes Lamartine without naming him – 'statues vivantes de l'assassinat' to be seen in the environs of the legislature (Blanc II:303).

In this way, at the same time as it relates the judgement of the king, Blanc's account also represents an absence, a 'non-event', something which never took place – except in some other text. There were no apprentice butchers in the front rows, fondling their knives. Presumably there were no gorillas or chimpanzees there either. But the particular absence of cannibal apprentices (as opposed to members of the simian race) is significant, not arbitrary, because of its relation to the way in which the event has previously been falsely represented in some other text: the 'perceived' absence of butchers ('Mercier did not see ...') is a counter-representation, a contradiction of a previous assertion – an assertion which in fact post-dates Mercier's actual perception of the Convention in 1793.

As Blanc presents them, the butchers are a fabulous royalist invention, and they are not, therefore, historical. Yet, the fact that they have a certain legendary power, a certain ontological currency, is suggested by the very insistence with which Blanc asserts that they did not exist: the (fabulous) butchers exist in a particular historiographical tradition – one which sees the king as victim of unprincipled violence – even if they never existed in historical reality. Whereas Vergniaud and his nephew could be let pass without comment, these butchers and assassinating statues must be reckoned with, since they are part of the (mis)representations or misconceptions of what is commonly recognised to be one of the central, and most controversial, episodes in the Revolution.

By choosing to attack Lamartine's account in its most melodramatic and hyperbolic aspects, where it is historiographically most vulnerable (the heavily significant, clichéd, knife-brandishing butchers), Blanc provides himself with a foothold from which to attack the very foundation of Lamartine's interpretation: namely, that the regicide vote was brought about by intimidation and did not reflect the will of the Assembly. Lamartine's particular errors provide Blanc, moreover, with a pretext on which to dismiss all the general charges of intimidation and violent unrest. For within Blanc's account, the non-existence or absence of the butchers serves as an argument in a more general attack on, and disarming of, the intimidation theory of the condemnation of the king (just as their bloodthirsty presence in Lamartine's text was an argument in its favour).

Blanc does not stop there, however. Having denied the historical reality of the butchers (and by extension of the menacing atmosphere in the Convention) he goes on to describe how Paris was going through an exceptionally calm period at this time with work going on as normal, with preparations under way for a *fête* in honour of the patriot dead (a detail suggestive of civil order and communal harmony, II:304). Indeed, relates Blanc, the only violence marring this general calm were the disorders at the Théâtre français; as it happens – and with this, Blanc reverses Lamartine's account – these were instigated by royalist supporters (II:304), and were opposed by the forces of order representing the Commune. Finally, if there was fear among the deputies in the Convention on the 16 and 17 January (and Blanc thus acknowledges that there may have been), this was only the fear *simulated* by certain Royalist deputies who sought to give the false impression that the vote was not freely taken (II:304). Any conspirators at work that day were to be found, then, not among the Jacobins and the Commune, but in the ranks of their opponents. In this way, Blanc both acquits the population of Paris of the accusation of barbaric bloodlust and of the general will to immolate the king; at the same time, he characterises that population contrariwise by its orderliness, transferring the role of 'subversives' to the supporters of the king.

Where Lamartine had presented Vergniaud and those who followed him as yielding weakly to intimidation, Blanc not only removes the intimidating force, but he also points to the great sacrifices made by those who fought for the Revolution and voted for the execution of the king: he anticipates their untimely deaths (a reminder that Louis was not the only one to be guillotined), or he anticipates the anathema which was to befall them (the case of the Abbé Grégoire who was banished as a *régicide* in 1819 is invoked, for example, II:308). Above all, Blanc suggests that already in 1793 the regicides had had to sacrifice their natural compassion (indeed, their pity for 'the defeated and imprisoned Louis XVI, that weak man, that miserable being', II:304) to the call of duty and their conscience.

It is in the context of these present and future sacrifices (rather than in the company of the knife-brandishing butchers) that Blanc – like Lamartine – singles out Vergniaud's vote for particular attention. While Blanc basically repeats the account given by his rival (Vergniaud's promise to his mistress, his change of mind, and so on), here the same sequence of events signifies something different: the fact that Vergniaud should promise his mistress to vote against the death sentence was a sign of the Girondin's humanity and, consequently, of the great effort it must have cost him to vote, nevertheless, as his conscience and the general will dictated (II:305).

To a large extent, then, the significance of Blanc's 'Judgement of the king' is the significance of its difference from a pre-existing royalist version of that event, as exemplified most recently and successfully in Lamartine's *Histoire des Girondins*. This difference is not left to the public to establish: the other, 'fictional version' of events is inscribed and, at the same time, subverted in the very representation of the events of 1793.

Unlike Blanc and Lamartine, Michelet does not represent the general atmosphere in Paris or the scene outside and inside the Convention during the judgement of the king – the crowded public tribunes, the half-darkness as the days became night, the weariness, and so on – and so passes in silence over the whole question of the presence/absence of butchers in the front rows. Whereas Blanc admitted violence and intimidation into his account while attributing them to different parties, Michelet admits neither of them. As we shall see, however, this does not mean that he overlooks Lamartine's version of the regicide vote.

Where Blanc focussed on the (non-existent) butchers and the homicidal statues, and from there moved outward to counter the various points in Lamartine's intimidation thesis through a counter-representation of the situation in Paris and the Convention, Michelet focusses on one of the central arguments underlying Lamartine's account of the judgement of the king: the Girondins, led by Vergniaud, were cowards who gave in to the threat of violence emanating from the Jacobins, in a way which was inconsistent with their self-proclaimed ideals.

Before proceeding to give his relatively brief narrative account of the voting, Michelet opens his 'Le jugement de Louis XVI' with a ten-page discursive defence of the courage and principledness of those who voted for the king's death, a defence which culminates in the alleged episode of

Vergniaud's loss of nerve (II:163–73). Although he does not mention Lamartine by name (simply referring to the fact that the event has been disfigured and that the regicides have been calumniated, II:165), his defence of the regicides is structured according to the two aspects of his opponent's attack: the 'barbarity' of the Montagne and the cowardice of the Girondins.

In countering the implied allegations of unprincipled violence, he mobilises an amalgam of arguments *à décharge*, designed on the one hand to vindicate the civility of certain Montagnards (the non-Jacobin ones with whom he would have sat, see above, p.27) and, on the other hand, to invoke the institutional and cultural achievements of the Revolution. To this end, he invokes the names of Joseph Chénier; Carnot (who succeeded in the Herculean task of organising the revolutionary army); Ducos and Fonfrède (whose cultivation and candid purity touched even Marat); the chemist Guyton-Morveau; Lakanal (who organised the Museum, the Ecole normale, and the Institut).

In the second part of his defence, Michelet turns specifically to the 'shameful' royalist tradition which has insulted the national honour by suggesting that the Convention became regicide from fear. There was a logical consistency behind the Girondins' vote: if they hesitated before voting against the king, this was because they would have preferred the king's sentence to have been decided by a national referendum; when the *appel au peuple* motion was defeated, they took the only other course possible consistent with their principles and, within a year, most of them would themselves be victims of the guillotine or have died pitiful deaths as hunted outlaws.

This last argument is the one which Michelet develops most fully; with a brief anticipation of Louvet's fugitive existence in the caves of the Jura; with a lengthy account of his own emotion on reading the torn, stained testaments which had been found on the bodies of Pétion and Buzot when these were discovered, half eaten by dogs; with a brief reference to the way in which the remaining 21 Girondins sang the *Marseillaise* on their way to the scaffold. It is above all, then, the courage and pity of their deaths in October 1793 and June 1794 which vindicates them in Michelet's account against the charge of cowardice on 16–17 January 1793. (As in Blanc's account, the anachronistic anticipation of the later event functions as an argument relative to the earlier one: the Girondins are already the victims-to-be.)

Following a procedure of denial, inversion, and transference similar to that which we have already seen in Blanc, Michelet not only denies the charge of cowardice, but argues (1) that, on the contrary, the Girondins sacrificed themselves courageously for their principles, and (2) that the real cowards are the historians who accuse the Girondins of cowardice. In a remarkable passage which again points to the role of the historian and his rivals as actors in the historical world which they discursively represent, Michelet attacks those who have attacked the Girondins:

> Lâches, osez me dire maintenant que les hommes qui moururent ainsi, dans cette héroïque douceur, ont été des lâches, que la Convention a eu peur, que Roland mort comme Caton, que Vergniaud mort comme Sidney, bégayaient et tremblotaient, aux cris des tribunes... Qui croirai-je, en vérité, ou de vous, ennemis acharnés, qui affirmez sans prouver, dans un intérêt de parti, ou de ces hommes eux-mêmes qui, par leur vie courageuse, par leur mort sublime, nous défendent de ces basses pensées? Vous venez me dire qu'ils ont eu peur devant un danger incertain, douteux, possible. Et moi, je vous dis qu'ils n'ont pas eu peur devant la mort même...[40]
>
> [Cowards, dare to tell me now that the men who died with such heroic serenity were cowards; that the Convention was afraid; that Roland, who died like Cato, and Vergniaud, who died like Sidney, that these men trembled and faltered before the cries from the galleries... Who should I in truth believe? You, relentless enemies, who make affirmations without proof, out of party interest? or the men themselves who, by their courageous lives, by their sublime death, defend us from such base thoughts? You come to me and say that they were frightened by an uncertain, questionable, possible danger. And I, I say to you that they were not afraid in face of death itself...]

It is at this point that Michelet introduces the episode of Vergniaud's alleged cowardice: a non-event (as the butchers in Blanc were a non-event), it becomes here a sign of the accusers' cowardice (a melodramatic, forged anecdote designed to be memorable and to be repeated, if only for the 'effet littéraire', II:169). Although a non-event, it has taken Michelet five pages to pronounce it a literary and not historical episode, and the very insistence with which he piles up such diverse evidence against the alleged 'barbarity' of the Montagne and the cowardice of the Gironde is a measure both of his concern to set the record straight and of the resistance he has to overcome in doing so.

[40] II:169. Whereas Michelet consistently presents Vergniaud's accusers both in the plural and as factionaries – 'relentless enemies', 'writers of great renown' (II:163) – he represents himself as standing out alone and as speaking (by implication, courageously and heroically) for history, for the men of the Revolution: 'I am alone here, I know it... What matter! History is on my side' (II:165). Blanc's valorisation of conscience over sentiment in his account of the judgement of the king recalls his representation of the 'austere duties' of the historian, duties which he (like the Jacobins and Robespierre) respects, but which Michelet and Lamartine with their Girondin sympathies do not. In both cases, the historian's role is represented as analogous to the roles played by the revolutionaries themselves.

Besides its role in rectifying the record and straightening out the facts, however, Michelet's particular selection of evidence has another function within the larger context of his representation of the king's judgement and execution. His insistence on the courageous deaths of the Girondins in October 1793 and his account of his own feelings upon discovering the tattered testaments of Buzot and Pétion in 1849, also serve, within the context of his history, to counteract *antequam* the potentially moving effect of the death on 21 January 1793 of that 'false martyr', Louis XVI (II:190). Michelet's contradiction of Lamartine's version of the judgement of the king provides him with the occasion or pretext to introduce other historical events (for example, the founding of the Ecole normale, the death of Pétion and Buzot) into the context of the judgement of the king, events which serve to attenuate the potentially negative light which that particular episode might cast on the Revolution as a whole. In this way, the invocation of these other events plays a double role: in relation to the version which Michelet's text seeks to supplant and in relation to the narrative account of the king's death which is to follow.

Of the 721 votes cast on 16–17 January 1791 for or against passing the death sentence on the king, it is thus the vote cast by Vergniaud which, in the different representations of that event, has become *representative* of the 'Judgement of Louis XVI' and the touchstone against which the mid-nineteenth-century historians' interpretation of that event becomes manifest. This focus on the Girondin leader is to be explained less by the actual role which Vergniaud's vote played than by the intertextual antagonism between Blanc, Michelet, and their common opponent, Lamartine, in whose text Vergniaud is not only represented as exemplifying the circumstances in which the judgement took place, but as actually determining the outcome of the debate.[41]

Both Blanc and Michelet seek to supplant Lamartine's version of the judgement of the king by simultaneously denying its authority and replacing it with another (more authoritative, non-fictional) account. These historical narratives are concerned, then, not only with events which did take place, but also with those which never took place (except in some other text) – 'No, no: Vergniaud did not know fear'; 'Cowards, dare to tell me now that the men who died in this way... were cowards'. In both Blanc and Michelet, the representation of what really took place

[41] Soboul (1966:213) and Lefebvre (1951:279), for example, give much more prominence to the vote cast by Mailhe, whose example Vergniaud actually followed: having voted for the death sentence, Mailhe then proposed that the assembly should debate whether or not the sentence should be postponed until after the war – a proposal which he (like Vergniaud) made clear was independent of his vote itself.

in the Convention on 16 and 17 January 1793 is inseparable from the representation of what did not take place on that occasion: Vergniaud is represented as not being a coward, the sentencing of the king is represented as not being the work of barbarians, and so on. Indeed, it is in the very act of contradicting an alternative, fictional version that the 'original' event is revealed. In a similar way, it is through his contradiction of other fictional and falsifying versions that the historian accredits himself with the authority to speak for reality.

As the examples above illustrate, the representation of the 'real event' involves not only a re-configuring of an inherited schema, but also a re-configuring of a previously *disfiguring* version of that event. Through a complex re-working of narrative elements and through the procedures of negation, reversal and transference (the roles of 'coward', 'martyr', 'conspirator', for example, are carried over into the supplanting text while manifested in a different set of actors) the representation *en relief* of what happened remains intimately bound up with the alternative, fictional reading it replaces: the representation *en creux* or representation *quod non*.

'No event has been more cruelly disfigured by history than the trial of Louis XVI,' writes Michelet as the *incipit* of his own account of that event (II:163) – 'history' meaning here the historiographical tradition in the literal sense of the transmission or 'handing on' of the event to later generations. What has emerged from my brief study of the 'sentencing of Louis XVI' in the histories of Blanc and Michelet is that narrating 'what happened in the Convention on 16 and 17 January 1793' involves both re-presenting the past and transforming the historiographical tradition. In order to make known the real past and free it from the party bias which has hitherto distorted it, the historical account addresses itself to contemporary preconceptions and contemporary misconceptions about the past – contemporary ignorance – and seeks to transform it. Indeed, the events as represented can be said to bear already the marks of the later historians' re-reading and rewriting of them. Louis XVI was a 'false martyr', writes Michelet. The fear of the royalist deputies was simulated (not real), writes Blanc: they deliberately produced and fomented the false idea that the Convention was being subjected to violent threats – the very notion which Blanc, fifty years or so hence, is trying to combat.

Conclusion

'Vergniaud voted for the king's death despite the promise he had made to his mistress the previous evening not to do so': a sign of Vergniaud's cowardice for Lamartine, a sign both of his humanity and of his sense of duty for Blanc. The two interpretations are significantly different from each other. However, if this sequence of events signifies one thing rather than another, it is not merely because of the discursive interventions of the narrators who ascribe it this significance (although they clearly have a role to play); it is, in the first instance, a function of the position which Vergniaud's vote occupies within the economy of each particular narrative representation of 'the events themselves'. In Lamartine's account, for example, it is the juxtaposition of Vergniaud's vote with the apprentice butchers, and all the other signs of violence, which constitutes it as a sign of his cowardice. In Blanc's account, in contrast, Vergniaud's vote figures together with a number of motifs relating to the orderliness of the new *régime* and the conspiratorial designs of the royalist faction, and is followed up a few pages later by a focus on Robespierre's private regrets at having had to make such a painful decision (II:308); given this narrative context, combined with the discursive interventions of the narrator, Vergniaud's decision becomes intelligible as the triumph of a civic conscience over merely private motives.

Having outlined the discursive conditions in which Lamartine, Michelet, and Blanc wrote their histories of the Revolution, I shall now turn my attention more specifically to the way in which they narrate 'the events themselves': to the way in which they represent certain episodes by particular figures and incidents, to the way in which they present and conjoin those elements through the medium of their narrative discourse, so as to invest them with one meaning rather than another. In what follows, I shall concentrate on the different representations of 'Le 10 août' – that 'seconde Révolution française', as Lefebvre called it (1951:237), which marked the transition from the first, constitutional phase of the Revolution to its later, Republican phase.

2

The narrative configuration of historical events

Story and tissue, faint ineffectual Emblem of that grand Miraculous Tissue, and Living Tapestry named *French Revolution*, which did weave itself then in very fact...
Thomas Carlyle, *The French Revolution* (1837)

Narrative representation: 'Le 10 août'

Representation, as Paul Ricoeur puts it, is always a form of 'lieutenancy' (1983–5, III:149) to the extent that it involves making effectively present something which stands for, or in the place of, something which is absent. Historical events are by definition absent: they have already happened in the past and can never be repeated, reproduced or replicated in the present; they can only be represented by something else.

'Le 10 août', the insurrection which led directly to the deposition and incarceration of Louis XVI, is one of the canonical or 'cardinal' events which invariably figure in any history of the Revolution.[1] It has traditionally been defined by such incidents as the gathering of the various sections of the *garde nationale* in response to the ringing of the tocsin; the formation of a new, insurrectionary Commune at the Hôtel de Ville; the organisation of the defence of the Tuileries; the summoning of Pétion, the mayor of Paris, to the Tuileries and his escape from there; the summoning of Mandat, head of the defences at the palace, to the Hôtel de Ville where he was killed; the defection of the national guards posted at the palace; the royal family's taking refuge in the Assemblée nationale which was in session at the Salle du Manège at the bottom of the Tuileries gardens; the attack of the insurrectionary forces on the palace; the slaughter of the *avant-garde*; the subsequent success of the renewed attack undertaken by the main body of the insurrectionary forces; the king's order to the Swiss

[1] The term 'cardinal' is used here in the meaning of '*fonctions cardinales*', as defined by Barthes (1977:21): i.e. actions or events which play a role in directing the further course of events, as distinct from 'catalyst' actions ('*fonctions catalyses*') which simply serve to carry out or complete the decisive ones.

to cease firing; the escape of some Swiss and the slaughter of great numbers of them; the suspension and imprisonment of the king.[2]

The very length of this summary already indicates the complexity of what can be nominally referred to as 'The Tenth of August'. (And, of course, 'the nocturnal summons of Pétion', 'the king's leaving the Tuileries', 'the attack on the palace', and so on, are in their turn but shorthand, nominal references to what are themselves complex events, potentially describable in terms of an indefinite number of other events and incidents.) If everything known about 10 August 1792 or the Revolution were to be included in the representation – even within the limits of the extant primary sources – the account would become unreadable. In the first place, it would be simply much too long. (As it is, the sheer length of these mid-nineteenth-century histories makes reading them a daunting proposition.) Secondly, and more importantly, the sense of a developing situation would be lost amidst the circumstantial detail and the activities of so many particular actors. The *fabula* of 'The Tenth of August' involves a great number of actors, engaged in a great number of diverse incidents, taking place in a number of different locations and – this is the crucial point – taking place at the same time: it does not 'naturally' take the form of a unified, linear story.

In the first volume of his *Temps et récit*, Paul Ricoeur argues that all historical narratives have both an episodic and a configurational dimension: the configuration of events involves extracting 'a unified, temporal whole' from the diversity of small-scale events (1983–5, I:103). Ricoeur, however, does not discuss in any detail *how* the configuration of particular historical events actually takes place through the mediation of a narrative discourse. How is the narrative discourse used in order to represent the events of 10 August 1792 for a later public and, at the same time, configure them as 'an intelligible whole' signifying one thing, one 'Le 10 août', rather than another? In what follows, I shall examine the narrative representations of the insurrection of 10 August 1792 in the light of the semiotic possibilities afforded to the historians, and the constraints imposed on them, by their specific discursive medium: the finite, linear narrative discourse which both 'makes present' the past and directs the attention to be paid to its different aspects.

As Gérard Genette has shown (1980, 1983), narrative discourse (the *récit*) may organise or 'dispose' the same story-stuff or *fabula* in

[2] This summary of the events of 10 August 1792 is based on a collation of the various accounts given by Lamartine, Michelet, and Blanc, and on the detailed account given by Marcel Reinhard in his study, *La Chute de la royauté: 10 août 1792* (1969).

significantly different ways: the same event may be represented in a more or less extended form or related more than once within the same text; a set of events may be represented in an a-chronological order different from that in which the sequence of events purportedly took place; events may be focalised through a particular actor. Although I shall focus here on the narrative representation of events, it must not be forgotten that the discourse of the retrospective, historical narrator is not homogeneous. As we have seen in the preceding chapter, it is not exclusively concerned with narration, but also involves apostrophes of the latter-day reader, metacommentary on the narrative production itself and, even more importantly in the present context, interpretative commentary. Throughout, this plays an important supplementary role in actually articulating the diverse events and in making them yield an intelligible coherence which might not otherwise have been evident.[3]

Events in their narrative context

The order of representation

Since narrative is linear whereas action is 'solid' – as Carlyle put it (1895, II:258) – it is impossible to narrate simultaneously what was taking place simultaneously at the Hôtel de Ville and the Tuileries in the early hours of 10 August 1792, or in the Assembly and at the Tuileries later that morning. Yet, what was happening at the same time in these different locations or centres of activity is all part of 'Le 10 août' and must figure, therefore, in the narrative representation of that event.

The very act of narrating these historical events through the linear, sequential form of a narrative discourse must necessarily involve reordering those events and disposing them in a particular contextual relation to each other: by narrating the activities of one set of actors only at those moments at which they intersect with those of another set, as for instance, when actors or reports of actions arrive from somewhere else; or by narrating consecutively events which took place simultaneously, via an analeptic or 'flashback' account of what had been happening 'in the meantime' somewhere else.[4]

[3] The argumentative/interpretative functions of the narrator's discourse remains a relatively neglected topic in narrative studies. For brief discussions, see Bal (1985:126f) and Suleiman (1983:156f).

[4] The terms 'analepsis' and 'prolepsis' will be used here as defined by Genette 1980: an analeptic account involves evoking after the fact 'an event that took place earlier than the point in the story where we are at any given moment', while a proleptic account involves 'narrating or evoking in advance an event that will take place later' (p.40).

Lamartine's extensive account of the hours preceding the outbreak of the insurrection is situated for the most part within the Tuileries where it focusses on the anxieties of the inmates and their preparations for the defence of the palace: of the 37 pages covering the period from the evening of 9 August to the king's departure from the Tuileries at around 8 o'clock the following morning (I:568–605), less than 7 pages of the narrative deal with events taking place elsewhere in the city.

It is following one of his many accounts of the anxieties of the queen that Lamartine relates how Pétion, the mayor of Paris, 'still had not arrived' to give his report on the state of affairs in Paris; how he finally arrives, but only refuses to allot further arms to Mandat, head of the defences at the Tuileries; how upon receipt of a summons from the Assembly, he left and 'did not appear again at the palace' (I:587). His departure is followed by a brief, page-long cross-cut to the Hôtel de Ville and a brief account of the formation of the insurrectionary Commune (an event which had been generally recognised by historians as one of the defining, key features of 'Le 10 août', and which could not be ignored with impunity, therefore, even in Lamartine's court-centred account). After this brief excursion, the narrative then cuts back to the Tuileries to give an account of the different measures taken by Mandat to ensure the security of the palace; this account leads up to his receipt of the summons which *had been* sent by the new Commune ordering him to go to the Hôtel de Ville to justify the commands he had given for the defence of the palace. The narrative follows the anxious Mandat and his son to the Hôtel de Ville, where, after being interrogated and condemned for the orders he had given, the commander of the palace defences is murdered on the steps outside the building. With this, the narrative cuts back again to the Tuileries and relates the reaction among the royal family and their supporters to the news of Mandat's death, signifying as it did the loss of their military leader.

In this manner, Mandat's expedition to the Hôtel de Ville, like that of Pétion to the Tuileries, is only related in the context of the situation in the palace: Pétion arrives (we do not know what he did on the way to the palace or the circumstances in which he received the summons); Mandat receives a summons (we do not learn the circumstances in which it was sent). While Mandat's reception of the summons is represented in its chronological position, that is to say, preceding his response to it, the writing of the summons only figures as a 'pluperfect' event or antecedent.

Whenever the narrative does shift location (to recount the formation of the Commune or Mandat's fatal trip to the Hôtel de Ville), the displacement is only momentary, serving to fill in a vital piece of information concerning an event elsewhere, which has a bearing on the morale of those at the palace and on the situation of their defences: the brief account of the formation of the Commune prepares for Mandat's reception of their summons in the following sequence. In this way, the narrative 'montage', with its particular articulation of the different actorial spheres, serves to demarcate a dominant narrative development to which all other occurrences are subordinated in the representation: the erosion of the palace defences. The fact that the account of the formation of the Commune should immediately precede the death of Mandat at the seat of that newly formed body serves, moreover, to associate the Commune from its very beginnings with the shedding of innocent blood.

The representation of 'solid action' through the linear medium of a narrative discourse serves to link up different occurrences, to bring them into the context of each other in such a way as to build significant sequences at the micro- and the macro-levels of the narrative. The very constraint of discursive linearity and sequentiality provides, in this way, an important source for the production of meaning.

Whereas Lamartine's account is focussed on the anxieties of the court and marks out the different stages in the erosion or destruction of their defences, Michelet's narrative account of 'Le 10 août' begins with a description of the hopes and fears of those about to engage in combat and the difficulties confronting the newly elected Commune: the strategic positioning of the royalist troops and, especially, the placing of the cannon at the Pont-Neuf on the orders of Mandat; the slowness with which the different sections responded to the tocsin; the absence of Pétion the mayor, and the fact that as long as he was held hostage at the Tuileries, the sections could undertake no action. This reference to the absence of Pétion triggers an analeptic account of the mayor's activities since 4 August, leading up to his reception of the summons from the Tuileries, his going to the Tuileries, his interview with the king, his walk in the garden, and finally, his reception of a summons from the Assembly and his return to the Hôtel de Ville. With the mayor's return, the obstacle to the insurrection and to the action of the Commune is removed and the narrative analepsis is complete: 'Having ensured his safety, they were now free to act' (I:972). The primary story line then goes ahead with the removal of the cannon from the Pont-Neuf, which the narrator presents (proleptically) as the decisive moment of the battle, since it was to enable the conjunction of the insurrectionary forces from both sides of the river later that morning.

It is only at this point that Michelet cross-cuts for the first time to the interior of the palace in order to describe the disposition of its forces, leading up to the moment when the national guards stationed there defect. Using the subsequent isolation of the palace as a narrative hinge, the account moves on to describe the palace as an isolated island in the midst of insurrectionary Paris where the Revolution had 'already been realised' at the Hôtel de Ville ('The palace was already alone, like an island within Paris... The Revolution had just been completed [*venait de s'accomplir*] at the Hôtel-de-Ville', I:977).

This *venir de* introduces an analeptic account of the death of Mandat (who had been summoned to the Hôtel de Ville by the Commune) and how his death had provided the catalyst for the sounding of the general alarm and for precipitating the gathering of the national guard (which had been delayed until now). The narrative of Mandat's death thus leads into the account of how the insurgents came together in their thousands and how at 8.30 a.m. an impatient *avant-garde* set off for the Tuileries. At this point, the narrative cuts back to the palace which the royal family 'had just left' (I:979), and introduces an analeptic account of their departure followed by an account of the disposition of the forces which they left behind. This account leads up to the first successful, bloody encounter between those guarding the palace and the *avant-garde* of the Revolution; the palace guards' initial sense of victory is transformed in a sudden, dramatic *peripeteia* as the main body of the insurrection forces comes into sight coming from the Pont-Neuf:

> La jonction de Saint-Antoine et de Saint-Marceau s'était faite au Pont-Neuf. On pouvait, du pavillon de Flore, voir au Levant, déjà au quai du Louvre, l'armée vengeresse du peuple, la forêt de ses baïonnettes, flamboyante des feux du matin. (I:984)
>
> [The union of the districts of Saint-Antoine and Saint-Marceau had taken place at the Pont-Neuf. Looking eastwards from the *pavillon de Flore*, one could see the avenging army of the *peuple* already at the *quai du Louvre*, the forest of its bayonets flaming in the morning light.]

This vision of the army of the Revolution introduces an analeptic account of how the conjunction of the forces from the two sides of the river had actually taken place.

The above sketch of Michelet's use of 'chronological deviations' (Bal 1985:53) to link up one sphere of activity with another might be continued on throughout the insurrection and its aftermath. Enough has been shown, however, to indicate both the importance of such deviations in articulating the different centres of activity and the variety of shifters or hinges which Michelet uses to motivate the cuts from one sphere of action to another: a theme (the isolation of the palace); the fact that one party sees another (the Swiss guards see the insurrection approach); that one party approaches another (the *avant-garde* setting off for the Tuileries triggers a cut to the palace).

If each analepsis begins by going back in time, recentering the action on another actor, it ends up by bringing the story forward in time. The *enchaînement* of events is such that every step back in time (which usually coincides with a step across in space) is followed up by a number of steps forward. The end result of all this is that the precise chronological order of the different events becomes obscured and effectively replaced by the order or logic of the narrative; that is to say, by the particular relations established between the events in the unfolding context of the representation.

The semiotic importance of Michelet's montage of events, however, lies not only in the new links established between events, but in the very choice of cutting points. In Michelet's representation of the build-up to the insurrection, the very fact that certain incidents should be used as hinges, or that they should figure as the final or initial incidents in a particular sequence, in itself serves to foreground their significance as key episodes:[5] the need to remove the cannon from the Pont-Neuf (the Pétion story); the removal of the cannon (shift to the Tuileries); the defection of the national guard from the palace (shift to Paris); the coming together of the insurrection and its movement towards the Tuileries (shift to Tuileries); the arrival of the insurrection (shift to the insurrectionary forces and how the conjunction of forces was made). In this way, the different points of articulation between the various centres of activity in the narrative can be seen to mark out the progress of what is in fact a single, continuous sequence or action: namely, the removal (more specifically 'the falling away') of all obstacles confronting the insurrection and its emergence into being. Moreover, by postponing the account of the final conjunction of Saint-Marceau and Saint-Antoine until the entire revolutionary army is suddenly seen *en masse* by the Swiss guards, Michelet heightens both the *fact* of the insurrection – the popular army exists no longer as a potentiality, but as a reality – and the symbolic and strategic import of the coming together of the forces from each side of the river.

Whereas Lamartine's account of the prelude to the insurrection is centred in the Tuileries and recounts more or less chronologically the events which took place there, outside events being described only in terms of their import for the state of the royalist defences, Michelet's account of

[5] For a discussion of how the significance of certain incidents in the narrative can be enhanced by their position either in the initial or the final position in a sequence (the 'primacy effect' and the 'recency effect'), see Perry 1979:53, 57. See also the discussion of the foregrounding effect of 'strategic location' in Eco 1979b:26.

what is basically the same set of events is characterised by its chronological deviations, by its sophisticated braiding together of different narrative strands. Nevertheless, the strategic timing of Michelet's deviations ultimately serves a purpose similar to that of Lamartine's general practice of non-deviation: namely, to articulate diverse events together in the narrative in such a way that they make up a single plot or narrative progression – a structured, intelligible sequence. In both cases, moreover, the construction of a single, narrative progression or plot serves to place one sphere of activity at the centre of attention, as the subject of the narrative action: it is in relation to this actorial centre and its programme or wishes that all subsequent occurrences are not only seen, but evaluated – as an obstacle or benefit, as the case may be. In Michelet's account, Pétion's expedition to the Tuileries is set in the context of the hopes and fears of the emergent insurrection (to which his absence poses an obstacle); in Lamartine's account, in contrast, Pétion's delay in arriving and his refusal to grant more arms to the soldiers defending the palace is embedded in the context of the court's hopes and fears regarding the adequacy of their defences. In Michelet's account, the (accidental) death of Mandat is the final catalyst which sets the longed-for revolution in motion; in the context of Lamartine's narrative, in contrast, his death signifies an intensification of the defenselessness of the palace as it faces a powerful and violent conspiracy.[6]

Degrees of presence

Condensation and expansion

'An event may take five seconds or five months,' Louis O. Mink writes, 'but in either case whether it is one event or many depends not on a definition of "event" but on a particular narrative construction which generates the event's appropriate description' (1978:147). An event, be this 'the French Revolution', 'Le 10 août', 'Pétion's expedition to the

[6] Cross-cutting frequently between the fermentation in the city and the situation within the palace, Blanc's articulation of events establishes the insurrection as its subject, at the same time as it foregrounds the difficulties of organising it and the resistance which its project to realise the sovereignty of the *peuple* must meet. This resistance is both military and ideological, being signalled, on the one hand, by the strength of the professional, organised defences within the palace and, on the other hand, by the ardour with which the courtiers and the queen seek to defend their aristocratic privileges. It is the aristocrats' defence of their class privileges which ultimately leads to the erosion of the palace defences from within and the defection of the national guards: the national guards within the palace rush to the side of the insurrection on being told by the queen that they should model themselves on the *gentilshommes* and take orders from them (I:167).

Tuileries', 'the king's departure from the Tuileries' or 'the massacre of the Swiss guards', may be represented more or less extensively according to the function which it is to play in a particular narrative context. Indeed, it is thanks to the fact that the same event can be represented on a variable scale that a historian may at once *refer* to a particular event (such as Pétion's expedition to the Tuileries) and at the same time endow it with a more or a less prominent role within the narrative (thus Lamartine subordinates Pétion's expedition to his account of the court's concerns about their defences).

There is no fixed scale by which the extensiveness of any representation can be measured, the amount of text space accorded to any one event being measurable only in relation to that accorded to the other events which figure within the economy of the representation. The amount of text space set aside for each event can thus be seen as a way of patterning the attention to be paid to different events in the *fabula*: 'The attention paid to each element can only be analysed *in relation* to the attention paid to all the other elements' (Bal 1985:69).

The important point here, then, is perhaps less the fact that the 'same event' may be represented more or less extensively depending on its role within different accounts; but that, within the economy of any particular narrative, the different events of the *fabula* will be represented on a differential scale. It is this differential scale that determines the role which a particular event actually plays within the context of the representation and which lays the ground for what Menachem Brinker has called its 'signifying relief' ('relief significatif').[7] As the preceding analysis of 'Le 10 août' suggests, the amount of attention paid to a particular occurrence is a function of its implications for the aims of the actorial group which has been made the centre of interest, the subject of the particular narrative account.

At around 8 o'clock on the morning of 10 August, Louis XVI decided, on the advice of Roederer (who had taken over the command of the forces at the palace), to seek refuge for himself and his family in the Assemblée nationale. While the monarch's departure from the palace is one of the

[7] 1985:435. Seymour Chatman argues that 'differential scale' is perhaps the defining feature of narrative; although his remarks concern visual narrative in particular, they are pertinent also to the discussion of historical narrative: 'In a highly realistic painting, what is shown is determined by what was visible to the painter, and that is a function of his distance from the depicted scene. Scale, then, controls the number of details. But narratives are not restricted by spatial scale and undergo no such control: a visual narrative, a comic strip or movie, can move from close to long shot and return without effort. And there is a virtually infinite continuum of imaginable details between the incidents, which will not ordinarily be expressed, but which *could* be' (1978:29–30).

cardinal episodes which figures in all accounts of the insurrection (it had important implications for the military and the political outcome of the day), the precise amount of attention to be accorded to this cardinal event as a whole or to its different constitutive or 'catalyst' events is not fixed once and for all.

In Michelet's account, we are told how Louis and his family made their way to the exit of the palace, and how at the last moment the monarch had some passing qualms about the fate of the guards and supporters he was leaving behind him; these qualms being only passing ones, 'he let himself be led away, and left them to die' (I:776). While the narrative presupposes that the king then left the palace and sought refuge in the Assembly, neither his walk across the gardens of the Tuileries nor his reception by the Assembly figures *in praesentia* in the context of Michelet's representation of 10 August: these occurrences belong to the *fabula*, but they are not made effectively present as elements in the representation. To all intents and purposes the royal family walk off the stage of the action, while the narrative pursues the topic of 'those they left behind'. (Only in the following chapter, entitled 'Le 10 août dans l'Assemblée' – thus distinguished from 'Le 10 août' – does Michelet pick up the story of the king with an analeptic account of his walk across the garden and his reception by the Assembly.)

Lamartine, for his part, briefly recounts the reaction of those in the palace to Louis's decision to seek refuge in the Assembly, *before* he relates Louis's own qualms about leaving them (which he presents without Michelet's comment as to their fleeting nature). This is followed up by an extensive account (2 pages long) of the walk across the garden in which the various stages of the procession are described in considerable detail: the dauphin playing with the dead leaves; the meeting with the deputation from the Assembly; the verbal abuse on the part of the assembled crowd; various threatening incidents, and the particularly menacing behaviour of one Rocher; the king being upbraided in familiar tones by one of the guards outside the Assembly; the entrance of the *cortège* into 'the dark and narrow' corridor leading to the Assembly (I:608); Rocher taking hold of the dauphin – to the great distress of the queen – and finally putting him down on the desk of the president of the Assembly (the last incident is foregrounded by virtue of its strategic location, both at the end of the sequence and at the end of a chapter-subsection).

In Lamartine's expanded representation of the cardinal event, 'the king left the Tuileries', so much text space is devoted to the royal walk across the Tuileries that this aspect of the event effectively takes over from the reactions of his supporters, which are only briefly mentioned (and then forgotten) at the outset of the account. But Lamartine's representation of the walk across the Tuileries is not only more extensive than the others: it also includes a number of other 'catalyst' events and descriptive details which do not figure either directly or by implication in Michelet's account, and which together build up an original sequence of incidents within the framework of the pre-configured episode. 'Louis left the palace' is amplified, in the course of Lamartine's representation, into the royal family's encounter with violent threats and obstacles, leading up to their final entrance into the Assembly, through the dark and narrow passage, as refugees from violence ('The mother [Marie-Antoinette] was trembling for her son', I:608). Nothing has changed in the course of events as such; but the *role* played by the king in those events has been redefined or transformed in the course of Lamartine's expanded representation of them: 'a leader who deserts' in Michelet's account, he comes to assume here (together with his family) the role of 'victim of aggression'.

In each case, then, the particular narrative representation of this cardinal event in the *fabula* (which incidents are given a more expanded treatment and in what context?) serves to foreground certain aspects of that event and to foreground them in such a way as to define, in one way rather than another, the role of the particular actors involved.

Scenic representation

In their 1958 'Treatise on Argumentation', Perelman and Olbrechts-Tyteca argue that 'presence' is an essential, albeit long neglected, factor in argumentation. By the very fact of selecting certain elements and presenting them to the audience, a speaker implies that they are important and relevant for the discussion; at the same time, he endows these elements with a *presence* which leads to an inflation of their value:[8] 'Accordingly one of the preoccupations of a speaker is to make present by verbal magic alone, what is actually absent but what he considers important to his argument or, by making them more present, to enhance the value of some of the elements of which one has actually been made conscious' (1969:117).

We have seen above how the narration of the 'king's departure from the Tuileries' is characterised by the unequal treatment in the representation

[8] Perelman and Olbrechts-Tyteca 1969:116–17. They refer in this context to experiments by Piaget showing that 'when two things are set side by side, say a fixed standard and things of variable dimensions with which it is compared, the things on which the eye dwells, that which is best or most often seen, is, by that very circumstance overestimated'.

of the different events of the *fabula*; by the over-valuation or 'inflation' of certain, presumably more important, moments or incidents. Some events receive more attention than others; some incidents and – what is inseparable from this – some actors are made more present than others in the text. While the foregrounding of certain elements is a function of the amount of textual space accorded to them and of their 'strategic location' within the narrative or the chapter unit, it can also, as I shall show in the following pages, be a function of the manner of representation; literally of the 'making present' of the person or moment.

Let us return once again to Louis's departure from the Tuileries. Michelet's narrative comment on Louis's fleeting qualms concerning the fate of the guards and his account of the king's departure is preceded by a dramatic re-presentation of the conversation between Roederer and the king as the royal *cortège* reaches the foot of the stairs on its way out of the Tuileries – a conversation which the historian quotes directly from Roederer's memoirs, where it had been reproduced.[9] In this scene, the monarch expresses some concern about the possible fate of those he is in the act of leaving behind; but Roederer (apparently thinking only of the royalist volunteers and not of the 1,300 Swiss guards who made up the main body of the palace defences) assures him that since they were not in uniform, his supporters would be able to slip away unnoticed:

> 'Que vont devenir toutes les personnes qui sont restées là-haut? – Sire, elles sont en habit de ville. Elles quitteront leur épée et vous suivront par le jardin – C'est vrai, dit le roi...'
>
> Ce dernier regret, ce petit mot de sensibilité, cette hésitation, ce fut tout ce que Louis XVI donna à ses défenseurs. Il se laissa entraîner, et les abandonna à la mort. (I:980)

> ['What is going to happen to all those persons who have remained upstairs? – Sire, they are dressed in city clothes. They will leave behind their swords and follow you through the garden – True, said the king...'
>
> This final moment of regret, this tiny expression of feeling, this hesitation, that was all that Louis XVI gave to those who defended him. He let himself be led away, and left them to die.]

[9] The dramatic re-representation of dialogue is an example of what Genette calls 'scenic' representation (1980:94): the extensive representation of an event tending towards a temporal equivalence between the duration of that event and the time taken to narrate it. As Genette argues (1969:53–5), the only thing which language can imitate perfectly is language itself: dramatic representation, unmediated by a narrative discourse, is the only true *mimesis*. In the context of the present study, it should also be pointed out that the only elements of the past which can be reproduced or replicated at a later point in time are its discursive and textual productions – hence the authority which these can have as unmediated portions of the past.

The scenic representation of the conversation between the two men serves to foreground the issue of desertion (the conversation occupies considerable textual space) at the same time as it 'makes present' the moment: the event, Louis's weakness, literally speaks for itself in a dramatic form, without the intervention of the retrospective narrator. This dramatically re-presented conversation serves then to authorise the comment which follows in the narrative discourse, interpreting and underscoring the significance of 'the events themselves'. Thus, the events speak for themselves and are then *made to speak*, made to yield a particular meaning, by the narrative discourse.

Lamartine's expanded definition of the walk across the gardens of the Tuileries involves another form of scenic representation or 'making present', one which has particular importance in the texts considered here. In the course of narrating the passage of the royal family from the palace to the Assembly, the narrative discourse *pauses* to describe what the royal procession looked like as it made its way across the garden of the Tuileries in the still light of a morning in late summer.

> Les parterres, les fleurs, les statues, les gazons brillaient de l'éclat d'une matinée d'été. Un soleil brûlant se réverbérait sur le sable. Le ciel était pur, l'air sans mouvement... Rien n'en troublait le silence que le pas mesuré des colonnes et le chant des oiseaux dans les branches... Seulement les précoces chaleurs de cette année avaient jauni déjà les marroniers des Tuileries. (I:607)
>
> [The flowerbeds, the flowers, the statues, the lawns were glittering with the radiance of a summer morning. The heat of the sun was reflected in the sand. The sky was pure, the air still... Nothing troubled the silence except the measured marching of the troops and the song of the birds in the trees... But the precocious warm weather that year had made the chestnut trees in the Tuileries already turn yellow.]

The function of this description of the Tuileries gardens in the morning light is, in the first place, literally to increase the presence of the event, to make it present as a scene, as something which can be visualised or revivified in the imagination of the reader through the life-line of such familiar details as yellowing leaves, sunlight, trees, and the (perhaps less universally familiar) lay-out of the Tuileries gardens. On a purely formal level, moreover, the slowing down of the narrative ensures that attention is focussed on the particular moment being described.[10]

[10] Consider, in this context, the suggestions of Perelman and Olbrechts-Tyteca regarding the rhetorical function of setting (e.g. lighting, crowd effects, scenery, music, and various devices of stage management) in intensifying the force and influence of a particular scene (1969:23).

In verbal narrative, as opposed to cinematic narrative, setting is always optional (Chatman 1978:106); and the morning light on the lawns and the yellowing of the leaves are certainly incidental to the fact of Louis XVI's leaving the Tuileries. However, precisely since it is uncalled for, the fact of describing the décor in this context suggests that there is indeed some connection between the setting and the event, a connection which endows both these elements with significance. Because it is otherwise uncalled for, the description of the gardens implies that the event itself invests the setting with meaning. Seen in retrospect, of course, this moment could be interpreted as marking the fall of the monarchy since Louis was never to return to the Tuileries. Lamartine's amplified account can be seen as a retrospective attempt to mark that historical significance: paradoxically, by freezing the moment and isolating it from its historical antecedents and consequences.

Lamartine proceeds to follow up his description of the yellowing leaves, moreover, by the king's comment on the fact that the leaves were turning early that year; by an analeptic reference to the comment made by a journalist a few days earlier to the effect that the monarchy would not last beyond the fall of the leaves;[11] by a description of the dauphin playing with the fallen leaves, which is finally topped off with the discursive comment, 'Enfance qui jouait sur le chemin de la mort' ('Childhood playing on the path to death', I:607). Through these multiple references to the turning of the leaves, the specifically autumnal content of the décor is brought to the fore, serving to invest the scene with a heavily symbolic value (as the fall of the monarchy) and to mark it with an unmistakable elegiac quality. In this way, the décor, with its pre-coded symbolism ('autumn signifies decline'; 'autumn is elegiac') functions as a signifying supplement to the narrative account where, at the level of the *fabula*, the king simply walks across the garden on 10 August 1792.[12]

In this case, Lamartine's use of the décor as a signifying supplement illustrates not only the semiotic complexity of his narrative text, but also

[11] The fact that the king's comment and that of the journalist should also figure briefly in Blanc's representation of the king's walk across the Tuileries (II:168), as well as in the account which Michelet gives of this event in the following chapter (I:997–8), suggests these are commonplaces belonging to the pre-configured '10 août': although they are not 'cardinal' incidents affecting the outcome of the insurrection, they nevertheless tend to figure in any representation of that *journée révolutionnaire* since they are already part of the hearsay concerning it.

[12] Meteorological references or references to the season play an important role in all three histories considered here, providing a reservoir of pre-coded signifying elements ('sunshine is a positive sign', etc.) which can be used to colour or reinforce the significance of the scene presented. In certain instances, the weather

the fact that his representation of the past works with a specifically rhetorical aim: in accentuating the autumnal character of the garden and its elegiac quality, Lamartine can be said to inscribe in the historical scene – as an inherent or natural part of it – the attitude which his own reader is presumably to adopt towards the historical event being enacted.

We have seen how the 'vivid' re-presentation of the past was one of the principal goals of the early nineteenth-century historians. In practice, as I have shown, some events from the past are made more vividly present than others for the reader of the historical text – a 'presence' which is both a function of the extent of the representation and of the scenic manner of representation. Moreover, Lamartine's *mise en scène* of the walk across the Tuileries, like Michelet's dramatic representation of the conversation between the king and Roederer, suggests that 'signification' and 'vividness' work closely together; that those instances where unique historical moments are scenically represented – where 'the events themselves' appear to speak for themselves or where the reader is made an 'eyewitness' to events – may be paradoxically the locus of the heaviest symbolical and rhetorical investment on the part of the historian.

Scenic representation and the spectator function

The emergence of the army of the insurrection on 10 August is described by Michelet as a forest of bayonets emerging from the east, radiant in the light of the rising sun. 'Looking eastwards from the *pavillon de Flore*, one could see the avenging army of the *peuple* already at the *quai du Louvre*, the forest of its bayonets flaming in the morning light'. But this is not only a 'scene' in the sense that the descriptive details enable the reader to visualise the (highly symbolic) birth of the insurrection. It is also presented as a spectacle, a scene which was actually witnessed in this particular way by someone on 10 August 1792.

In what follows here, I shall briefly consider the function of such 'spectators': (1) as they direct attention towards the 'spectacle' and

may even be presented as a 'response' to the events being enacted. Michelet tells us, for example, that Madame Roland died on a 'cold November day' and that 'Nature, stripped and mournful, expressed the general mood' (II:620). Blanc insists that the sun was particularly bright on 6 October 1789 as the *cortège* of women brought the king back to Paris from Versailles (I:405), whereas Michelet stresses the autumnal, rainy aspect of the same scene, so different from the sun of 14 July (I:279). Although it rained for the greater part of the *Fête de la Fédération* (14 July 1790), the sun broke through the clouds, Michelet insists, just as the assembled crowd prepared to pledge their commitment to national unity: 'Le ciel écoute, le soleil perce tout exprès le nuage' ('Heaven hears, the sun deliberately breaks through the clouds', I:423).

thereby foreground its presence ('X sees Y' is only possible if X is in the immediate presence of Y); and (2) as they provide a reader's guide to the nature of its impressiveness (a phenomenon which we have already briefly encountered in the meeting between Vergniaud and his nephew, above, p.20).

Having followed the royal family to the Assembly, Lamartine goes on to relate how those present in the Assembly could not take their eyes off the royal family, who had been installed in the logographer's box:

> les regards, respectueux et attendris, se portaient involontairement sur le roi, sur la reine, sur Madame Elisabeth, sur la jeune princesse, déjà dans tout l'éclat de son adolescence, sur cet enfant que la reine tenait par la main et dont elle essuyait le front... Jamais le sort ne donna plus de douleurs secrètes en spectacle. (I:609)
>
> [The eyes of all those present, respectful and softened, were involuntarily drawn to the king, to the queen, to Madame Elisabeth, to the young princess (already in the full radiance of her adolescence), to the child whose hand the queen was holding as she wiped his brow... Never had fortune presented such a spectacle of private sufferings.]

Louis Blanc also presents a *tableau vivant* of the king in the Assembly and also places him at the centre of universal attention:

> A voir le roi... on l'eût dit complétement étranger à la situation. Esclave, comme presque tous ceux de sa race, du pouvoir des appétits physiques, il s'était fait apporter une pêche qu'il mangeait tranquillement – *tous les yeux étant fixés sur lui* – pendant qu'à ses côtés la reine, le visage en feu, prêtait une oreille avide au retentissement de la fusillade.[13]
>
> [To look at the king... one would have thought that he had nothing to do with what was happening. Like most of his stock, a slave to the dictates of his physical appetites, he had ordered a peach and was now placidly eating it – *all eyes fixed on him* – while beside him the queen, her face aglow, was listening avidly to the reverberating gunfire.]

By presenting the king and his entourage as objects of public attention and contemplation in 1792, the two historians direct the attention of their own readers towards the royal figures, inviting them to look at the spectacle. At the same time, the fact that the king was actually the centre of attention in 1792 ('all eyes fixed on him') justifies the attention paid to these scenes in the historical narrative, scenes which are quite incidental to the

[13] II:171 (my emphasis). For a discussion of the importance of the visual language of spectacle and the *tableau* in the melodramatic tradition of the nineteenth century, see Brooks 1985:24f.

unfolding course of events, but which, as we shall see, have a signifying and rhetorical function in the narrative representation. In Lamartine's case, especially, the fact that Louis XVI and his family were the object of universal attention (the *tableau* quoted above is but one of the many which punctuate his account of 'Le 10 août'), allows him to maintain the royal family as the subject or centre of interest of his narrative representation, and to justify the attention he pays to them and their sufferings, even after the king has long ceased to be a centre of activity or the subject of any action.

While both historians present the *tableau vivant* as the focus of general attention, in each case the implied public (which is left anonymous) saw something quite different. In Lamartine's narrative, they saw the king, to be sure, but in his capacity as a *père de famille*, and in the company of the queen, his sister, his young daughter, and his son; moreover, they saw the queen – and she is the centre-piece of the *tableau vivant* – as she held the hand of her young son, bending over him to wipe his brow. In Blanc's account, on the other hand, the *tableau* is centred on the figure of the king and portrays him in a typical pose as he slowly eats a peach while the battle for the Tuileries rages outside (typical, that is, according to one of the commonplace images of Louis XVI as a gourmand).

Lamartine's *tableau* gives an image of familial unity and, in concentrating on this harmonious familial whole, deflects attention away from the outer frame, that is to say, the situation which the king left behind him in retreating to the Assembly. In contrast, Blanc's *tableau* shows the king serenely concentrated on his peach and, on the other hand, the keenly attentive, tense queen (there is no mention of the children) who listens to the noise of the battle taking place outside, apparently still hoping that her party will come through as victors. Instead of portraying a unified scene, then, Blanc's *tableau* is composed of a number of juxtaposed or incongruous elements: the fact of being concerned with a peach in such circumstances, the manifest lack of a natural understanding or kinship between the king and the queen.

For all the differences in the way they compose their *tableaux vivants*, it is clear that each historian uses his portrait of the royal couple in order to direct the reader towards seeing the royal figureheads in one light rather than another.[14] In each text, then, the *tableau vivant* functions both as a signifying and as a rhetorical construct, designed to produce an effect of attraction and sympathy (as in Lamartine) or of repulsion and alienation (as in Blanc).

[14] In an unpublished article on the *Girondins* (in Guillemin 1946:130), Lamartine claimed that 'Des histoires de cet esprit sont des spectacles pour les peuples, mais

While the grotesque effect of Blanc's conjugal portrait is simply encoded in its composition, Lamartine makes explicit the 'pathetic', 'moving' impact of the *tableau vivant* by representing the effect which it had on the public present in the Assembly. In this way, the implied onlookers not only act as a guarantor of the historical status of the spectacle, but also as a guide to its reception:

> les regards, respectueux et attendris, se portaient involontairement sur le roi, la reine... La haine s'amortissait devant ce sentiment des vicissitudes soudaines qui venaient d'arracher ce roi, ce père, ces enfants, ces femmes à leur demeure, sans savoir s'ils y rentreraient jamais! Jamais le sort ne donna plus de douleurs secrètes en spectacle. (I:609)

> [The eyes of all those present, respectful and softened, were involuntarily drawn to the king, to the queen... Hate evaporated before the sense of the sudden vicissitudes which had uprooted from their home this king, this father, these children, these women, without their knowing whether they would ever return to it! Never had fortune presented such a spectacle of private sufferings.]

In recounting the reaction of the onlookers ('La haine s'amortissait' etc.), Lamartine presents the effectiveness and the particular effect of the pathetic scene as a *fait accompli*, a *historical* phenomenon. The fact that everyone who actually witnessed Lamartine's scene should have unanimously responded to it with compassion suggests that this response to 'the unfortunate family' is both the historical one (everyone actually reacted this way) and the natural one (one could not react in any other way). Lamartine's representation of the events in the Assembly on 10 August 1792 can be said, then, to anticipate or announce the unanimous response of his own public.

This rhetorical strategy is even more patently obvious in Lamartine's account of the way in which, on the previous evening, the queen had walked among the troops guarding the palace; the mere sight of her, her presence among the soldiers, provoked immediate cries of universal devotion:

> Son aspect attendrit, dans l'intérieur, les gardes nationaux les plus indécis et fit tirer du fourreau tous les sabres. Gardes suisses, gendarmerie, grenadiers, volontaires, gentilshommes, bourgeoisie, peuple; toutes les armes, tous les postes, toutes les salles, tous les

aussi des leçons' ('Histories written in this spirit are spectacles for the people, but also lessons'). The evidence of his text suggests that the relationship between 'lesson' and 'spectacle' was not only one of coexistence, but of close cooperation. Compare his presentation of the *Terreur* as a 'spectacle' put on for the pleasure of the masses, below, p.149n.

> escaliers s'émurent d'un même enthousiasme à son passage; tous les regards, tous les gestes, toutes les paroles lui promirent mille vies pour sa vie.[15]
>
> [Her appearance moved the most undecided of the national guards inside the palace, and caused all sabres to be drawn from their scabbards. Swiss guards, gendarmes, grenadiers, volunteers, gentlemen, bourgeois, *peuple*: all arms, all posts, all rooms, all staircases were moved by the same enthusiasm as she passed; all eyes, all gestures, all utterances promised a thousand lives for her life.]

In his representation of the event which effectively marked the downfall of the monarchy, Lamartine makes the figure of the queen the focus of his reader's attention, claiming that she was also the focus of universal attention and devotion in 1792. Since everyone ('gentlemen, bourgeois, *peuple*: all arms, all posts, all rooms...') who came into the charismatic presence of the queen was immediately converted to her cause, not everyone must have had the opportunity of seeing her, since the revolution of 10 August went ahead anyway... In thus bringing the figure of the queen to his public's attention and in projecting a unanimous conversion to her cause, Lamartine's narrative reveals itself to be not only a representation of what happened, but also an attempt to re-enact symbolically 'Le 10 août' in such a way that it can be seen to have had a potentially different outcome.

Repetitions and transformations

The singular and the recurrent

We have seen above how, in putting 'solid' events into the linear order of their narrative, the historians focus on particular actorial figures and link up the incidents in which they are involved so as to construct unique sequences. Linking up different incidents to form coherent sequences, however, is but one aspect of the historians' configuration of events. Different events may be linked together by similarity as well as by sequential contiguity. In what follows here, I shall consider how the repetition or reiteration of elements in the narrative serves to construct significant patterns or similarities among the diverse incidents which occurred on 10 August 1792.[16]

In the hours following the king's departure from the Tuileries, the forces guarding the palace – consisting principally of some thousand

[15] I:599. According to Antoine Court, one of the recurring sequences in Lamartine's text is 'encounter-seduction-conversion' (1985:chap.2, 85).

[16] As Susan Suleiman discusses at length in her *Authoritarian Fictions* (1983), 'redundancy' – the recurrence of a signifying element – is one of the basic

Swiss guards, 1600 gendarmes, and a couple of hundred *gentilshommes* who had rallied to the defence of their monarch – came into conflict with the insurrectionary forces – consisting of some 2,000 *fédérés* (national guards mainly from Brest and Marseilles), the different sections of the national guard from both sides of the river who had joined forces at the Pont-Neuf, and an indefinite number of 'passive' citizens or *sans-culottes*.

In the first encounter between the Swiss guards and the *avant-garde* of the insurrection, up to 400 of the insurgents were killed by a brief round of firing from the assembled Swiss in what seemed to many to have been a carefully planned ambush. With the arrival of the main body of the insurrectionary army, and with the commencement of their bombardment of the palace, the Swiss guards lost ground and began to retreat through the Tuileries gardens, while the *gentilshommes* escaped through the palace (the king finally did order a cease-fire, but whether this was before or after the Swiss guards had lost their advantage remains uncertain); in the course of trying to escape from the Tuileries, a large group of the Swiss guards was slaughtered in a number of separate incidents. Whatever the precise number of dead on both sides may have been, the legend of 'Le 10 août' was linked from the outset to the blood which was shed in the battle for the Tuileries and its aftermath (Reinhard 1969:409–10; 583f).

Lamartine exploits to a maximum degree the potential 'expandability' of the death of the hundreds of Swiss guards, in representing what happened to them after the forcing of the Tuileries by a series of different incidents, covering six chapter subsections and seven and a half pages of text. His account tends towards 'singulative' narration, to use Genette's terms, that is, towards the separate representation of each single event, rather than towards the sylleptic bringing together of separate incidents in a single representation.[17]

As a group of 500 defenders of the monarchy tried to get through the gate leading to the Pont Royal, seven were killed as they passed through, while 'all' the unspecified number of Swiss guards were brought down together with two of the volunteer *gentilshommes* (whom Lamartine

conditions of 'readability', allowing for the conservation of information in the communication process. Redundancy in the context of a narrative can be a function of the level of the representation (for example, the same actor repeats the same act, the same thing happens to many different actors, different actors share the same characteristics); of the level of the discourse (the same manner of narration is used repeatedly throughout the text); or of the relation between the discourse and the representation (the interpretative commentary of the narrator is redundant with the event). See Suleiman 1983:156f.

[17] In his discussion of 'frequency', Genette (1980:113–17) distinguishes between 'singulative' narration, where one event is represented once in the narrative (e.g. 'the king left the Tuileries at 8 a.m.'), 'repeated' narration, where the same event is

portrays as fighting side by side with the Swiss guards). As the remaining soldiers tried to retreat via the Pont Tournant, 60 Swiss guards were killed together with 15 *gentilshommes*. Of those who survived the attack, some ended up in the Assembly only to be imprisoned later (and in a proleptic reference to the bloody events of a month later, we are informed that they were massacred on 2 September), while the others got as far as the Champs Elysées only to be brought down there (a few did find refuge in the home of the Venetian ambassador; others were sheltered by some villagers in the forests of Meudon and Issy, while yet another group, having sought protection from former comrades-in-arms, were slaughtered). Again, another group (29 Swiss guards led by one of the queen's pages) ran into the courtyard of the Hôtel de la Marine and, having entrusted themselves to the crowd, were butchered. Another group of 60 reached the Place de la Grève only to be killed there to the last man...and so on and on through to the final bloody death of Clermont-Tonnerre, which closes with an account of his young widow's failure to recognise her husband's mutilated body. By giving such an extended, almost literally 'blow-by-blow' account of the massacre of the king's defenders, Lamartine increases the effect of systematic and prolonged violence, of what he calls 'a slow, excruciating massacre' (I:624). The effect of horror is further intensified by the constant itemisation of particular incidents and persons: one by one the 500 soldiers were to squeeze through the narrow railings (I:623); a group of ten was killed one by one as they fought their way from tree to tree across the Champs Elysées:

> Ils chargent à la baïonnette le poste de gendarmerie et de canonniers qui entoure la statue de Louis XV, au milieu de la place. Trois fois ils enfoncent ce poste. Trois fois des renforts y arrivent et cernent de plus près ces trente hommes. Ils tombent un à un, décimés lentement par le feu qui les enveloppe. Réduits au nombre de dix, ils parviennent à forcer le passage, se jettent dans les Champs-Elysées et combattent, d'arbre en arbre, jusqu'à la mort. (I:626)

presented a number of times in the narrative, and 'iterative' or sylleptic narration, where a repeated action is represented only once in the narrative (e.g. 'the Commune sent several messages to Mandat', or 'every hour, the Commune sent a message', as opposed to 'at 3 a.m. they sent a message, at 4 a.m. they sent a message', etc.). While 'a group of 400 men was killed fighting' would be an example of sylleptic narration (in that 'the narrative utterance takes upon itself several occurrences together of the same event', 1980:116), its syllepsis is a function both of the bringing together of different 'occurrences' and the grouping together of different actors. In the case of the collective events considered here, then, narrative syllepsis does not only involve the grouping together of different events or actions; it also (and as importantly) involves the grouping together of many different actors – a point which I shall discuss further in the next chapter.

> [They make a bayonet charge against the post of gendarmes and gunners surrounding the statue of Louis XV in the middle of the square. Three times they overrun this post. Three times reinforcements arrive and encircle ever more closely the thirty men. One by one they fall, decimated by the firing which envelops them. Reduced to ten, they manage to force their way through and, plunging into the Champs-Elysées, fight from tree to tree unto death.]

By referring to the numbers involved in each group (which is then subdivided into other groups) and by using such unspecific terms as 'some', 'the rest', 'all', Lamartine ultimately succeeds in confusing the exact numbers involved and thereby increases all the more the effect of multiple acts of a form of violence which, like the Hydra so often invoked as an image of the Revolution, endlessly subdivides and repeats itself. The almost pathological insistence with which Lamartine's account prolongs, and dwells upon, the violence perpetrated against the defenders of the king is at once an illustration of the imaginative power which horror could have as an argument against revolutionary movements, and an indication or measure of the particular ideological stakes involved in the event for this particular writer.[18]

In Lamartine's account, the blow-by-blow singulative narration of the death of the Swiss guards serves to create an effect of destructive repetition at the level of the events narrated: each separate event is linked to all the others, not so much as elements in an unfolding sequence of events, as different instances of the same unmotivated, relentless bloodshed directed against the king's supporters. Any non-violent episodes which are briefly mentioned are simply 'incidental' *vis-à-vis* the central action: momentary deviations which serve, by way of contrast, to highlight the atrocities and to underscore the constant pattern as it re-emerges with increased force.

Michelet's account of the fate of the Swiss guards is far less extensive than that of Lamartine, covering just over a page of text. Moreover, where Lamartine's representation takes the form of a nightmarish repetition of violence, Michelet shows that there are significant *differences* between the various incidents involving the Swiss guards. He begins his

[18] Going on the basis of Lamartine's portrayal of the royal family and the insurrection of 10 August, it seems extraordinary that he should have met with such criticism from the legitimist Nettement (above, p.22), or that he should have been praised by the reviewer of the democratic *Le Charivari* for seeking, together with Michelet and Blanc, to make the Revolution be loved (above, p.47n). However, the judgement of both camps seems to have been determined principally by his positive portrait of Robespierre (see below, chap.4). Within the broader context of his narrative, Lamartine's horror can be seen as directed, not against the ideals of the Revolution such as he interprets them, but against any attempt to institute change through popular insurrection.

account of the fate of the Swiss guards with a relatively detailed description of how they fought their way in an extremely disciplined fashion across the Tuileries gardens, and how their order broke down in an individualistic *sauve-qui-peut* only under the effect of the 'fearsome unanimity' of the estimated 40,000 national guards who opposed them (I:987). The rout of the Swiss, then, was the outcome of an intelligible sequence of events, with a beginning, middle, and end: the result of a fair fight.

In the brief 18 lines following, Michelet proceeds to narrate the subsequent rout of Louis's defenders, and lays out the fate of the various groups of soldiers: how 300 managed to escape, while another 'group' whose exact number is left unspecified, was captured and slaughtered in the Hôtel de la Marine; how 34 more Swiss guards were brought down by a single round of firing; how 30 more Swiss guards managed to defend themselves for a while at the foot of the statue of Louis XV.

Where Michelet actually recounts the fate of the different groups of Swiss guards, then, he does so in a sylleptic narration, in which multiple events (the deaths of 30 Swiss guards beside the statue of Louis XV) or multiple actions (the killing of 34 Swiss guards in a single round of firing) figure as single events in the narrative. No matter how many people were killed at the Hôtel de la Marine, within the context of Michelet's account, this was a single event which he does not represent at any length or in any detail. In Lamartine's account, in contrast, it is an unspecified number of insurgents who are brought down in a single round of firing, corresponding to a single event: 'The first volley of shots fired by the Swiss covers the tiles in the peristyle with dead and wounded' (I:617). The comparison between the two accounts shows up how the choice between 'sylleptic' or 'blow-by-blow' narration determines the significance of a particular act (or acts) in the representation.

In the paragraph following his account of the rout of the Swiss, Michelet presents a number of separate incidents, separate incidents which are nevertheless linked together by the fact that they commonly reflect the *repeated* influence of a generous and benign impulse behind the insurrectionary forces: some of the Swiss guards managed to reach safety in the Champs Elysées, where they were sheltered by 'de braves gens' ('honest folk'); the crowd who invaded the Tuileries behaved with courtesy to the women in the palace – going so far as to help them actually escape ('The victors escorted them so that they could escape, and helped them to disguise themselves ...' I:988); finally, the account of 'Le 10 août' closes with the dramatic reconciliation, in the presence of the National

Assembly, between one of the Swiss guards and one of the insurgents who offers him the hospitality of his home.

The pattern of events

Une scène extraordinaire, pathétique au plus haut degré, eut lieu dans l'Assemblée nationale. Qu'elle passe à la postérité, pour témoigner à jamais de la magnanimité du 10 août, du noble génie de la France, qu'elle conserva encore dans les fureurs de la victoire.

Un groupe de vainqueurs se jeta dans l'Assemblée, pêle-mêle avec des Suisses. L'un d'eux porta la parole: 'Couverts de sang et de poussière, le coeur navré de douleur, nous venons déposer dans votre sein notre indignation. Depuis longtemps une cour perfide a préparé la catastrophe. Nous n'avons pénétré dans ce palais qu'en marchant sur nos frères massacrés. Nous avons fait prisonniers ces malheureux instruments de la trahison; plusieurs ont mis bas les armes: nous n'emploierons contre eux que celles de la générosité. Nous les traiterons en frères.' (Il se jette dans les bras d'un Suisse, et dans l'excès de l'émotion, il s'évanouit; des députés lui portent secours. Alors reprenant la parole): 'Il me faut une vengeance. Je prie l'Assemblée de me laisser emmener ce malheureux: je veux le loger et le nourrir.' (I:989)

[An extraordinary scene, the acme of pathos, took place in the National Assembly. May it be handed on to posterity, as an eternal proof of the magnanimity of the Tenth of August and of the nobility of the French spirit, which was preserved even amidst the fury of victory.

A group of the victors, mixed up with some Swiss guards, burst into the Assembly. One of them acts as their spokesman: 'Covered in blood and dust, our hearts torn with pain, we have come here to register our indignation. For a long time, the perfidious court has been planning this catastrophe. We could make our way into the palace only by stepping on our massacred brothers. We have taken as prisoners these unfortunate instruments of the betrayal; several of them have laid down their arms: the only weapon which we shall use against them is that of generosity. We shall treat them as brothers.' (He throws himself into the arms of one of the Swiss and, from an excess of emotion, faints; some deputies come to his assistance. Then, continuing his speech): 'I must have revenge. I beg the Assembly to allow me to lead away this unfortunate man: I want to shelter and feed him.']

This scene, the final moment in Michelet's 'Le 10 août', is foregrounded in his representation through a variety of discursive and formal means. In the first place, it is explicitly introduced as worthy of particular attention: 'An extraordinary scene, the acme of pathos'. Secondly, it is represented dramatically and at length, the insurgent's speech being quoted directly and even accompanied by stage directions. Finally, it is strategically located at the close of the chapter on 'Le 10 août', a discursive position which suggests that the reconciliation between the Swiss and the insurgent represents the final outcome – the *terminus ad quem* – of the day's action.[19]

However, the unique historical moment represented and foregrounded in this scene is not an isolated event in Michelet's account: in bringing together as it does the notion of 'magnanimity' and the notion of 'patriotism', it is also the nodal point of a number of 'isotopies' in the narrative.[20] Indeed, the fact that the unique scene is foregrounded at all can be attributed to the role which it plays in picking up and reiterating elements which have already appeared in the representation.

Within the immediate context of the events around the Tuileries after the defeat of the Swiss guards on 10 August, the 'extraordinary' scene represents the final episode in the series of events in which the crowd's benign *élan* is repeatedly made manifest: the people's ultimate 'vengeance' takes the form of a determination to house and feed the guards, victims of the perfidious court. The final scene is explicitly introduced as a sign of the 'magnanimity' of 'Le 10 août' – an explicit decoding of the insurgent's gesture which is redundant *vis-à-vis* the event represented, to the extent that the gesture is by nature 'magnanimous' and it is situated in the context of the similarly magnanimous acts preceding it.

The same scene is also introduced, however, as a sign of 'the nobility of the French spirit'. Now, if the insurgent's gesture becomes a sign of the spirit of France, it is thanks to the discursive intervention of the narrator who, in a performative move, defines its significance – 'this is what the insurgent's gesture shall mean'. That the gesture indeed signifies this (and not, for example, the man's Christian ethos) is rendered plausible, however, by the predominance of a recurring patriotic motif in the preceding events.

In the first place: the particular catalyst of the transformation from a situation of violent conflict to one of benevolent reconciliation was the

[19] In contrast, Blanc's account of the same incident is followed up by another incident concerning the safeguarding of the queen's jewels, and by an account of the specifically political implications of the day's events and the reaction to them in the Assembly – material which Michelet relegates to the following chapter. Moreover, where Michelet gives a temporary closure to 'Le 10 août' (it succeeded fully), Blanc's narrative suggests that its aims are not yet fully realised and goes on to open a new question: namely, how is the sovereignty of the people as a whole to be realised in the organisation of the new regime (II:174)? See also below, pp.140f.

[20] The word 'isotopy' is used here in Greimas's sense, to designate the recurrence of semic elements in a text, which makes a uniform reading of that text possible (Greimas and Courtès 1979:197). See also Eco 1984:189–210.

spirit of patriotism and the Revolution; for it was by playing the 'hymne sacré' ('sacred anthem', II:618) of the *Marseillaise* that a certain M. Singier brought to order the angry crowd which had entered the Tuileries – 'And instantly, all these furious, bloody men forget their fury; they form a chorus, draw up around the harpsichord, and begin to dance in a circle, intoning the national anthem' (I:989).

Within the larger context of Michelet's 'Le 10 août', moreover, the reconciliation between the Swiss and the 'vainqueur des Tuileries' closes an account which begins with a direct quotation from one of the insurgents, describing his patriotic motives, hopes and fears in joining the insurrection (words which Michelet is later to recall in his discursive preface to the final scene, I:989):

> Quelle était la pensée forte et calme sur laquelle dormait le peuple, et qui servit d'oreiller à tant d'hommes dont cette nuit fut la dernière? Un des combattants du 10 août, qui vit encore, me l'a expliquée nettement: 'On voulait en finir avec les ennemis publics; on ne parlait ni de République ni de royauté; *on parlait de l'étranger*, du comité autrichien qui allait nous l'amener. Un riche boulanger du Marais, qui était mon voisin, me dit sous le feu le plus vif, dans la cour des Tuileries: "C'est grand péché pourtant de tuer ainsi des chrétiens; mais, enfin, c'est autant de moins pour ouvrir la porte à l'Autriche!"'
>
> Le 10 août, répétons-le, fut un grand acte de la France. Elle périssait, sans nul doute, si elle n'eût pris les Tuileries. (I:966–7)
>
> [What was the strong, calm thought with which the people were sleeping and which served as a pillow for so many men who would never have another night? One of the combatants of the Tenth of August, who is still alive, explained it clearly to me: 'We wanted to be finally rid of the public enemies; there was no talk of republics or of royalty; *we talked of the foreigners* and of the Austrian committee which was planning to let them in. A rich baker from the Marais, my neighbour, said to me in the courtyard of the Tuileries at the height of the firing: "It is surely a great sin to be killing Christians like this; but, after all, it means there will be fewer men ready to open the door to Austria!"'
>
> The Tenth of August, let me repeat, was a great act of France. There is no doubt but that France would have perished if she had not taken the Tuileries.]

The initial situation out of which the insurrection arises is thus presented in terms of the threat to the very existence of France, on the one hand, and of the individual's patriotic readiness to sacrifice himself in the interests of national security, on the other. As we have already seen above, Michelet's narrative of 'Le 10 août', for all its deviations, locates the centre of the action with the insurrection and marks out the different obstacles to its progress as, one by one, they fall away before it: in particular, the removal of the cannon at the Pont-Neuf which allows the sections from both sides of the river to come together as a united force – 'the avenging army of the *peuple*' – a conjunction of forces which is foregrounded by the order of the representation, by the fact that the united front of the insurrection is seen by those in the palace, and by the use of the physical setting as a symbolic supplement. In his subsequent account of the actual confrontation between the Swiss guards and the insurgents, as we have seen, Michelet attributes the military defeat of the Swiss guards to a very specific cause: namely, the disintegration of the extraordinary military discipline of the Swiss guards in face of the 'fearsome unanimity' of the people's army which had come together at the Pont-Neuf. (Lamartine explains the defeat of the Swiss guards only by the crowd's relentless thirst for bloody vengeance.)

The insurgent's magnanimity towards the Swiss, then, is not simply constituted as a sign of the 'genius of France' through the discursive intervention of the narrator. As a manifestation of the spirit of France, it is shown to arise naturally and consistently out of the preceding events where the spirit of patriotism plays such a dominant role. Within the particular context of Michelet's representation, the reconciliation scene between insurgent and Swiss becomes more than simply an instance of a humanitarian (versus violent) act: it signifies the victory or salvation of the *patrie* in face of the perfidy of the court and, as such, symbolically marks both the closure and the success of the insurrection.

Considered within the still broader context of Michelet's history, moreover, the final scene of 'Le 10 août' also perpetuates the main Revolutionary tradition, being in a way a re-run or repetition of the reconciliation between the 'besiegers' and the 'besieged' with which his account of the 'Prise de la Bastille' also ends (members of the revolutionary crowd offer to protect or adopt the soldiers of the *ancien régime*, I:162). In both cases, the final reconciliation not only makes manifest the patriotic or fraternal *élan* which was the motor behind events; the reconciliation itself – be this between 'besiegers' and 'besieged' or between the insurgents and their opponents – also functions as a sign of the new consensus brought into being by the recent event: the Revolution, as it were, can have no more enemies.

In the context of the isotopy of 'patriotism', which binds together both the different episodes of 'Le 10 août' and the principal *journées révolutionnaires* in Michelet's history, violent incidents are merely momentary deviations from the central action. As we have seen, the significance of the final, non-violent scene in the Assembly is over-determined in the representation, that is, a number of different strategies are applied simultaneously in order to foreground it, and what it signifies is in keeping with a number of other incidents in the narrative. In contrast, the massacre of the Swiss guards figures as an isolated, once-off incident which has no significant link – either sequential or thematic – with any other element within the economy of the representation. To be sure, there were indeed other victims of the insurrection and these are referred to in Michelet's account (in many instances, in the following chapter); but the representation has been organised in such a way that no attention is called to the possible similarities or connections between these different incidents. The death of the Swiss guards does figure in Michelet's account of 'Le 10 août', then, but it is represented as an accidental, rather than as a necessary or defining, feature of the insurrection.

Conversely, in Lamartine's account, it is the gestures of non-violence which represent deviations from the central action – an action which is defined, both within the micro-context of the death of the king's defenders and within the larger context of Lamartine's treatment of the insurrection as a whole, by the victimisation of the king and his associates. In Lamartine's account, moreover, the actions of the villagers of Meudon and of the Venetian ambassador in helping the Swiss guards are dissociated from the insurrection both by their humanitarian nature and by the fact that the actors themselves have no connection with the people of Paris. That courageous generosity, which is presented by Michelet as one of the Revolution's essential features, is situated in Lamartine's account on the side of those who are *not* associated with the insurrection.[21] These last examples suggest that there may be 'eccentric' actors as much as there are 'incidental' events – a problem to which I shall return in the next chapter.

Representation *en creux*

The narrative economy

The presence of knife-brandishing butchers in the front seats of the Assembly on 17 January 1791 could be denied: 'there were no butchers', wrote Blanc, contesting their historical existence (above, p.55). But the massacre of the Swiss on 10 August 1792 is not to be denied: as a recognised historical fact, it cannot be left out of any historical account – if only because its existence as a fact has been foregrounded, as an example of 'Revolutionary violence' or *terreur*, by a certain historiographical tradition. Least of all may the violence which marked 10 August 1792 be

[21] Parallel to Lamartine's reference to non-Parisians is Blanc's account of the murder of Mandat at the Hôtel de Ville at the hands of 'un inconnu' ('a stranger'), someone who, by definition, 'does not belong' (II:165).

ignored by those attempting, in Nettement's words, to 'rehabilitate' the Revolution and remove the barrier of horror surrounding it (the existence of such terms as 'rehabilitation' and 'barrier' is itself a measure of the resistance to be overcome, above, p.39).

So far, I have considered historical representation from the point of view of how certain events or aspects of events are 'blown up' and brought into significant relief. Inverting this *en relief* perspective in the following pages, I shall now reconsider historical representation *en creux*, 'inside out' as it were, and briefly examine some of the discursive procedures used by the historians to defuse, neutralise, or counter the potential significance of certain incidents whose status as historical facts they cannot deny and which must figure, therefore, in the representation; incidents which already are, or which might become, the source of an alternative version of the same event.

The narrative representation of historical events involves, as we have seen above, the unequal treatment of the events in the historical *fabula*: the production of meaning is a function of selectivity and inequality. The natural concomitant of the fact that certain aspects are blown up or brought into relief, of course, is that other aspects are not foregrounded, stressed, or brought into relief; to signify is to exclude: 'Every production of meaning implies exclusion, selection, difference, opposition; every mark is a demarcation...' (Hamon 1984:11).

If we read Michelet's account of 'Le 10 août' against the grain, then, and consider it from the point of view of what it does *not* stress, the representation can be seen as simultaneously directing the reader's attention towards the patriotic spirit manifest on that day and directing it away from the (deviant) violent acts which accompanied the day without defining it. Similarly, we can see how Lamartine's account, in playing up the role of the royal family as victims of the crowd's aggression, draws attention away from the king's lack of concern about the fate of the Swiss; how, in directing the attention of the reader towards the pathetic figures of the royal family as a group, represented in particular by the figure of the queen, it draws attention away from the less than inspiring person of the monarch himself (in Lamartine's account of 10 August 1792, Louis rarely figures in isolation from the charismatic queen, whose presence functions as a lightning rod in attracting the attention and devotion of all who see her).

The non-significance of the non-foregrounded aspects is not just by default, however. What is actually represented *en relief* can itself be a reflection *a contrario* of the aspects which the author chooses not to foreground. It just so happens, then, that Michelet's narrative shows the workings of the spirit of patriotism through its capacity to put an end to violence; it just so happens that Lamartine's expanded account of the king's walk across the garden ends up by portraying the monarch and his family as being victims, like the Swiss whom he abandons, of the crowd's aggression. In both cases, the non-foregrounded, 'incidental' element reappears in an inverted form in what is actually foregrounded: in case the reader might be led to think, or in case the reader might have started from the preconceived idea, that the king treated the Swiss badly or that the insurrection unleashed an outbreak of violence (even though these are not actually brought into significant relief in the narrative), the possible or alternative reading is being actively countered or displaced by those aspects of the event which are actually represented as significant.

Not only does Michelet represent the massacre of the Swiss in a relatively summarised form and in isolation from other similarly violent events; but the potentially negative effect of the massacre is further countered in the representation by the fact that it gives way in the narrative to a scene marked by its non-violence, the opposition to violence, and the active cultivation of a fraternal, nurturing spirit of reconciliation.[22] The non-violent actions which are thus privileged in the representation manifest both the insurgents' active opposition to violence and their determination to extend their protection to the victims of the perfidious court: a reminder that if there were any victims, they were not so much victims of the Revolution as of its opponents, that is, of those

[22] In the previous chapter, we have seen how in Michelet's account, the death sentence passed on the king is balanced out against the cultural, institutional, and educational achievements of the Revolution as a whole (above, p.58). Interweaving the violent and the beneficial aspects of the Revolution as a whole may also be reflected at the level of the narrative organisation in the articulation of different episodes or topics: Blanc, for example, follows up his account of the death of the queen by a discussion of the social reforms of the Revolution (II:567f), while Michelet follows his account of the death of the king by a chapter in which he relates the educational reforms brought in by the Revolution, and the violent death of Lepelletier Saint-Fargeau (the man responsible for them) at the hands of a royalist fanatic. The amalgam of the title itself indicates the number and diversity of the counter-arguments employed: 'The unity of the fatherland – Education – Funeral of Lepelletier (24 January 1793)'.
The strategy of transferring the negatively charged role to the other side and the strategy of balancing out the subject's negatively charged deeds by his positive ones are brought together in Michelet's description of the death of Marie-Antoinette in Paris; in his brief, attenuated account, this event is interwoven with two entirely different events which happened to take place at the same period (the dismemberment of Poland) and on the same day (the battle of Wattignies): 'Poland is killed with Marie-Antoinette' (II:602–3); 'At noon, on the sixteenth day of October 93 (at the very moment the head of the queen was falling onto the Place de la Révolution), Carnot, Jourdan were marching in silence with half of the army... towards the plateau of Wattignies' (II:607).

who had left the Swiss to their fate. In this way (following a rewriting procedure similar to those we have already encountered in chap. 1), the negatively charged deeds which accompanied the insurrection are transferred from the narrative subject to the antagonist. The insurrectionary forces may be the *apparent*, but the forces of the monarchy are the *real* cause of this bloodshed.

Elements to counter the historical import of the death of the Swiss can already be seen at work even within the brief, understated representation which Michelet gives of the diverse incidents making up this event. One group of Swiss guards, Michelet notes, managed to defend itself for a while at the foot of the statue of Louis XV, described in this context as 'that sad monument to the monarchy, so unworthy of their devotion and loyalty' (I:988). On the one hand, the spectacle of the dead Swiss before the statue of Louis XV recalls Louis XVI's betrayal of the Swiss and his ultimate responsibility for the fate which they met (an act to be recalled again in the final scene). On the other hand, the statue itself recalls the corruption of the *ancien régime* as represented by the notorious Louis XV. In this way, an element in the physical background, which already has a significance within the historical code, is used as a signifying supplement to the representation of the events of 10 August. By actualising this particular feature of the setting (and not the statue of Caesar, as Lamartine does, I:624), and by making explicit its significance, Michelet sets the death of the Swiss against the historical background of the *ancien régime*.

In a similar invocation of the historical code inscribed in the landscape, Blanc (II:163) refers to the church bells which rang out the call for the insurrection, gradually focussing in on the one which had also been used to announce the Saint-Barthélemy – the sign *par excellence* of the violence committed by the monarchy:

> Vers minuit trois quarts, le tocsin sonnant de divers côtés, et les fenêtres du château étant ouvertes, chacun s'y porta pour écouter. Et chacun de nommer la cloche qu'il croyait reconnaître: ici, celle de Saint-Roch, là celle de Saint-Jacques la Boucherie, et plus près, plus près, celle de Saint-Germain l'Auxerrois... la même, ô courtisans, qui sonna, il y a deux cent vingt ans, par ordre de Sa Majesté, le massacre de la Saint-Barthélemy![23]
>
> [At about a quarter to one in the morning, the tocsin having begun to ring on all sides, everyone went to listen at the open palace windows.

[23] II:163. The 'Saint-Barthélemy' is one of the most recurrent points of historical reference: see above, p.40n; also, Michelet I:36, 166. Generally, the historical context, whether it is invoked via an element in the represented context or simply

> And they took it in turns to name the bells which they recognised; here, the bell of Saint-Roch, there, the bell of Saint-Jacques la Boucherie, and closer by, closer by, that of Saint-Germain l'Auxerrois... the same bell, O courtiers, which announced two hundred years ago, on the orders of his majesty, the Saint-Barthélemy massacre.]

In a similar manner, in recounting how the king and his family were finally escorted to the prison of the *Temple* after 10 August, Michelet recalls the association between this building and another victim of the French monarchy, the templar Jacques Molay (Michelet I:1006).

In each case, the use of a feature in the setting as a symbolic hinge between 'Le 10 août' and its historical context serves both to justify the insurrection ('the French monarchy deserved its fate' or 'the Revolution was necessary to do away with injustice and corruption') and to reduce the *historical* significance of any violence which may be associated with 'Le 10 août' or with the Revolution as a whole: since the *ancien régime* was perennially marked by violence, violence as such cannot be the defining feature or *proprium* of the French Revolution as a unique historical occurrence.[24] If anything, the violence which marks the Revolution reflects the persistence of the old regime in the new.

The invocation of other historical contexts through pre-coded features in the landscape illustrates the semiotic complexity of the narrative representation and the set of checks, balances, transfers, established within the economy of each narrative. Such checks and balances are perhaps particular to historical narratives, where the narrator, by definition, is not free to orchestrate what happens, or rather what happened, next.

through a discursive intervention on the part of the historian, serves as an important reservoir of counter-arguments to remind the reader that violence was not invented by the Revolution and that the people suffered for centuries from oppression (the two arguments generally work in tandem). Michelet, for instance, places the relatively small numbers of guillotine victims in the context of the victims of the Inquisition (I:34–5), and at various points in his history invokes the persecution of the Albigensians, Waldensians, Protestants (I:369–71; I:809–11; I:818).

[24] Particularly in the later stages of the Revolution, cross-cutting between Paris and abroad, or between Paris and the Vendée, often serves to set the violence of the Revolution in the context of the barbarity perpetrated by the counter-revolution or in the context of the counter-revolution's attempts to destroy the Revolution: Blanc, for example, follows up his account of the execution of the king with a lengthy account of the counter-revolutionary intrigues initiated by Pitt (II:316f); having described the establishment of the infamous Revolutionary tribunal in Paris on 10 March 1793, Michelet ends his chapter with a brief account of the massacre perpetrated by the Vendéens at Machecoul, which began on the same day; the following chapter is then devoted to setting the massacre in the general context of the situation in the Vendée.

Checks and balances

Michelet's brief account of the violent death of the Swiss guards figures in isolation from all the other violent incidents occurring on the same day. The deaths of Suleau and the other prisoners on the morning of 10 August do not even figure in the context of 'Le 10 août' at all; instead, they are reserved for the following chapter, 'Le 10 août dans l'Assemblée', where they are attributed to the personal animosity of Théroigne de Méricourt and thereby dissociated from the insurrectionary crowd (I:991–5).

It is only in the following chapter, moreover, that we learn, via a brief analeptic reference, the precise number of Swiss (700) 'who had been killed that afternoon', information withheld in Michelet's narrative account of the events of 'that afternoon'. The complete narrative of the massacre of all the Swiss is, in this way, broken up and dispersed along thc narrative syntagm: while the actual death of the 700 remains an event in the *fabula*, it never figures directly in the representation.

Furthermore, no sooner has the high number of fatalities been mentioned than it is followed up, and more than balanced out, by the 1,100 insurgents who died on the same day, as we are now also told for the first time:

> Le soir du 10, on avait en hâte jeté au cimitière de la Madeleine les cadavres des sept cents Suisses qui avaient été tués. Mais le nombre des morts était bien plus grand du côté des insurgés. Les Suisses généralement avaient tiré derrière de bonnes murailles; les autres n'avaient eu que leurs poitrines pour parer les coups; onze cents insurgés avaient péri; beaucoup d'entre eux, gens mariés, pauvres pères de famille, que les extrêmes misères avaient poussés au combat, qui, entre une femme désespérée et des enfants affamés, avaient préféré la mort. Des tombereaux les ramassaient, les ramenaient dans leurs quartiers, et là, on les étalait pour les reconnaître. Chaque fois qu'une de ces lugubres voitures, couverte, mais reconnaissable à la longue traînée de sang qu'elle laissait derrière elle, chaque fois qu'elle entrait au faubourg, la foule l'entourait, muette, haletante, la foule des femmes qui attendaient dans une horrible anxiété. Et puis, à mesure, éclataient, avec une étrange variété d'incidents les plus pathétiques, les sanglots du désespoir.
>
> Nulle scène de ce genre n'avait lieu sans jeter dans l'âme des spectateurs un nouveau levain de vengeance... (I:1002)
>
> [On the evening of the tenth, the bodies of the seven hundred dead Swiss had been hastily disposed of at the Madeleine cemetery. But there was a far greater number of dead on the side of the insurgents. The Swiss guards had generally fired from behind stout defences; the others only had their chests to shield them; eleven hundred insurgents had perished; many of them were married men, fathers of poor

families, who had been driven into combat by extreme misery; faced by a despairing wife and starving children, they had preferred death. Their bodies were loaded onto carts and brought back to their *quartier*, where they were laid out to be identified. Every time one of these mournful carts – covered, but nevertheless recognisable by the long trail of blood it left in its wake – came into an area, the crowd of women surrounded it, silent, breathless, in terrible anxiety. And then, gradually, in a strange series of highly pathetic scenes, the sobs of despair burst forth.

No scene of this sort took place without sowing a new seed of vengeance in the hearts of the spectators.]

The potential pathos of the 700 dead Swiss is immediately defused by the numerical comparison with the dead insurgents, by the comparison between the way in which the two groups died, and simply by the sheer extent of the attention given to the dead insurgents. The effect of repetition is intensified through the insistence on 'each time' the funeral cart arrived, while the presence of the (repeated) scene is intensified by the deployment of multiple spectators: one after the other, the grieving widows and children of the dead *pères de famille*, see and recognise the corpse of their loved ones as time and again the funereal carriage approaches; and these scenes of familial grief are in turn witnessed by other onlookers who are moved.[25] In this way, then, the death of the Swiss is not only under-represented (we do not see their bodies and no one reacts to their death), but it is further eclipsed by the spectacular representation of the funeral of their victims, as focalised through the bereaved, and then witnessed by onlookers: 'No scene of this sort took place without sowing a new seed of vengeance in the hearts of the spectators.' At the same time that it reduces the importance of the death of the Swiss, of course, the description also serves to magnify the death of the insurgents.

What is of interest here is less the fact of this intense narrative attention to the death of the insurgents than its timing. For in his representation of

[25] This introduction of witnesses is paralleled in Lamartine's narrative by his account of how the young widows of Clermont-Tonnerre and Suleau recognise the mutilated bodies of their husbands (I:630, 614). If pathos is intensified through the introduction of a witness who is moved, the counter-strategy consists in noting the absence of witnesses or the presence of indifferent onlookers, each of which serves to reduce the 'spectacular' quality of the phenomenon. In his account of the execution of the king, for example, Blanc insists on the fact that it made no immediate impression on the people of Paris, so much so that there was dancing that evening on the *ci-devant* Pont Louis XVI (II:315); in a similar way, Michelet stresses the speed and the *lack* of effect of the queen's death: 'The queen was dispatched in two days, the 14th and 15th. She died on the 16th, the day of the battle, and her death had little impact in Paris' (II:602). As for the king's last journey towards the scaffold: 'There were few people on the streets. The shop doors were only half open. Nobody came to the door or windows' (II:186).

'Le 10 août', Michelet did not foreground the losses on the part of the insurgents or their role as victims (he refers to these only in his account of the first attack in the palace when 300–400 men were killed, I:982–4). Instead, as we have seen, he focusses on the heroic aspects of the day and the triumph of the forces of patriotism. In a sense, then, the human cost of the insurgents' achievement has also been *postponed* in the narrative representation of the events of the insurrection, and reserved until the following chapter, which goes on to conclude with a scenic representation of the general grief expressed on the occasion of the *fête funèbre* for the victims (27 August).

That Michelet, having marginalised the deaths of the insurgents in his account of 'Le 10 août', should then proceed to blow up this aspect of the event must be seen as an attempt to attenuate or combat *antequam* the horror of the September massacres (the next major canonical event with which his narrative must deal) by setting the events of 2–4 September in the context of the extraordinary grief of the crowd and the inevitable desire for vengeance which this grief could inspire in those who witnessed it. By foregrounding, in this particular context, the role of the insurgents as victims of the Swiss, Michelet's 'Le 10 août dans l'Assemblée' already prepares the way for the bloody events of September as an impassioned *reaction* to the blood shed by the Swiss on 10 August (rather than simply as a repetition or continuation of the same thirst for blood and destruction which, according to Lamartine, had already defined the people's action on 10 August).

The fact that Michelet's account of 'Le 10 août' should be divided in this way between the heroic aspects of the event (which figure together in 'Le 10 août') and its funereal mournful aspects (which figure in the chapter following, and prefigure the events of September) also suggests that his narrative is organised so as to mark out, within his representation of the events of 10 August 1792, the outlines of what the Revolution 'really' was in essence (as manifested, for example, in the scene of fraternal forgiveness in the Assembly), against the background of what it was, and was to become, in actuality.

Degrees of reality

We have seen how the configuration of 'Le 10 août' involves, on the one hand, foregrounding and conjoining certain events into intelligible narrative sequences and, on the other hand, narcotising or countering the potential significance of other events. As we shall see below in the case of Michelet, it may also literally involve reducing the ontological status of certain events or figures.

Whereas Lamartine gives a scenic representation of the royal family's walk across the garden in such a way as to underscore the symbolic significance of the moment itself, Michelet focusses on the person of Louis XVI, as he walks through the Tuileries, in an iconoclastic *mise en scène* which serves to reveal the 'real' identity of the king as a nonentity. He is entirely without force, being passively moved about like a mannequin, the passive object of a would-be sublime, but in reality, grotesque gesture:[26]

> Ce pauvre homme, lourd et mou, n'avait pu, même en cette nuit suprême de la Monarchie, veiller jusqu'au bout; il avait dormi une heure, et venait de se lever. On le voyait à sa coiffure, aplatie et défrisée d'un côté... Tel il était, et tel les maladroits le firent descendre, le montrèrent, le promenèrent. Pour comble de mauvais augure, il était en violet; cette couleur est le deuil des rois; ici, c'était le deuil de la royauté. Il y avait pourtant, même en ceci, quelque chose qui pouvait toucher. Mais on eut encore le tact de rendre une scène tragique parfaitement ridicule. Aux pieds de ce Roi défrisé, le vieux maréchal de Mailly se jette à genoux, tire l'épée, et, au nom des gentilshommes qui l'entourent, jure de vaincre ou mourir pour le petit-fils d'Henri IV. L'effet fut grotesque et dépassa tout ce que la caricature a représenté des voltigeurs de 1815. Le Roi, gras et pâle, promenant un regard morne qui ne regardait personne, apparut, au milieu de ces nobles, ce qu'il était réellement, l'ombre et le néant du passé.
>
> Par un mouvement naturel, tout ce qu'il y avait de gardes nationaux et d'hommes de toute sorte, se rejetant violemment de ce néant à la réalité vivante, crièrent: 'Vive la nation!' (I:975–6)

> [Even on this, the supreme night of the Monarchy, that unfortunate man, heavy and soft, had not been able to watch all night; he had slept for an hour and had just got up. One could see this from his wig, which was flattened and uncurled on one side... This is the state in which he was, and in this state his tactless supporters brought him down, showed him, paraded him. To top off the inauspicious effect, he was dressed in violet, which is the colour of mourning for kings; in this case, it meant mourning for royalty. Even then, there could have been something touching about him. But his supporters used their tact once more and transformed a tragic scene into a perfectly ridiculous one. The old Maréchal de Mailly throws himself to his knees before the dishevelled King, pulls out his sword, and, in the

[26] Where Lamartine relates the heroic gestures of devotion which the presence of the queen provoked, Michelet repeatedly describes them as amateur theatrics. Instead of a heroic or natural spectacle, pregnant with significance, the end result is mere theatre: 'The king's supporters were gathered for the most part in the billiard room, many of them standing on the seats in order to see what would happen next. M. d'Hervilly, his sword drawn, pronounced in a loud voice: "Usher, let the doors be opened for the Nobility of France." The effect of this *coup de théâtre* was very mediocre' (I:976–7).

> name of all the gentlemen present, swears to be victorious or to die for the grandson of Henri IV. The effect was grotesque, surpassing even what the caricatures made of the turncoats of 1815. Standing among these nobles, casting around a mournful eye which looked at nobody, the fat and pale King appeared as he really was: the shadow and the nothingness of the past.
>
> In a spontaneous reaction, all the national guards and everyone else who was present turned vehemently away from this nothingness towards living reality, and shouted: 'Long live the nation!']

Even as the figure of Louis XVI with his flattened wig and his mournful, vacant eyes is made present by Michelet as an object-to-be-contemplated, the 'presence' of the scene is a paradoxical one. The 'spectacular' representation of the king is escorted by a historically distant narrative voice which, in calling attention to 1815, reduces the immediacy of the king's presence and thereby deflects the potentially pathetic effect of the moment. Like Blanc's portrait of the king slowly eating his peach, Michelet's representation, indeed his caricature, of the fat, pale, passive Louis seeks to divest the person of the king of any of the symbolic aura he might possibly have retained: a symbolic stripping down. (In contrast, as we have seen, Lamartine's representation seeks to reinvest the person of the queen with a charismatic presence.) According to Michelet's explicit decoding of the spectacle, the person of Louis XVI *really* embodies only 'the shadow' and the 'nothingness of the past': he is present, but only negatively so.

This revelation of the king as a nonentity is a function of Michelet's portrait, of his commentary, and finally of his account of the reaction of the spectators to the sight of this monarch with his flattened wig and vacant eyes. As in Lamartine's representation of the queen considered earlier, Michelet's representation of the king anticipates the natural reaction and consensus of the public: everyone present spontaneously ('par un mouvement naturel') turns away from the negative epiphany of the royal 'nothingness' and turns towards the 'living reality' of the nation: 'Vive la nation!' In contrast to the spontaneous reaction of those present in crying out their devotion to the nation, de Mailly's gesture of devotion to the king is presented as a mere piece of literature or theatre belonging to a second-order reality. What is of particular interest here is the fact that the 'nation' to whom everyone unanimously and spontaneously turns is explicitly identified with 'living reality', while the monarchy is identified with 'the past' or 'non-existence': an opposition which recalls the terms of the historiographical debate which I outlined in my historical introduction.

In representing 'Le 10 août', as we have seen, Michelet gives more attention, more presence, to the forces of the insurrection than he does to those of the old order; here, he goes even further and actually portrays Louis XVI as a non-being (paradoxically, through creating what is in fact a vivid image of the king as a pale, fat man with empty eyes). His observation that 'living reality' was situated with the Revolution, while the monarchy was simply no longer a part of that reality, acts as a metahistorical gloss at the level of the discourse, through which the historian makes explicit and justifies his narrative configuration of the event as a whole.

Conclusion

In the preceding analysis, I have tried to bring out the complexity of these historical works as narrative constructs dealing with real events: how the historians exploit the tools of their narrative medium in order to give shape and meaning to the events they represent; how the description of persons, places, and scenes works together with the narration in investing events with a particular significance; how the discursive interventions of the retrospective narrator direct the reader in interpreting the significance of the representation; how the response or 'consent' of that reader is often already anticipated in the representation itself.

In each case, as we have seen, the narrative configuration of 'Le 10 août' serves to establish certain actors as centres of attention and sympathy in the narrative (in Michelet and Blanc, the insurgents; in Lamartine, the monarch and his supporters); it is their fears and desires which provide the horizon against which the unfolding of the historical events is seen and evaluated. Moreover, in the case of Michelet and Lamartine, the narrative subject is explicitly represented as the catalyst for a general consensus, indeed as the *de facto* object of a collective, natural allegiance: everyone present, as Michelet tells us, spontaneously turned away from the non-reality of the mannequin-king towards the 'living reality' of the nation; 'everyone', as Lamartine tells us, spontaneously turned towards the queen in devotion as soon as they came into contact with her.

However, the 'monarchy' which is the centre of Lamartine's narrative of 'Le 10 août' is not simply represented in the text through the figure of the monarch, Louis XVI: as we have seen, the fate of the monarchy is also represented through the figure of the queen, the royal family, and through their supporters and defenders, the Swiss and the *gentilshommes* – all of whom share the role of victims of the insurrection's anarchy. In Blanc and Michelet, in contrast, the Swiss are dissociated from these *gentilshommes* and are associated, rather, with the insurrectionary vanguard with whom they share the role of victims of the king and his supporters.[27] These differences indicate that the different actantial roles (for example, of subject and antagonist) are not simply distributed among a fixed set of actorial figures; that the representation and configuration of collective events are inseparable from the representation and configuration of the various individual and collective actors participating in them. It is this aspect of historical representation which will be the topic of the next chapter.

[27] See Blanc II:167, 170, 172.

3

The configuration of actors I

I believed, moreover, that if I concentrated more on narrating than on discoursing... I would be able to give a sort of historical life to the masses as well as to individuals, and that, in this way, the political destiny of nations would offer some of that human interest inevitably inspired in us by the unadorned details of the changing fortunes and adventures of a single man.
Augustin Thierry, *Histoire de la conquête de l'Angleterre par les Normands* (1825)

The representation of collective actors

It is one of the principles of our moral nature, wrote Lamartine in his *Cours familier de littérature* (1856–69), that 'interest never attaches itself to abstractions, but always to persons. The human mind wants to give a face to ideas, a name, a heart, a soul, a personality to things' (II:53). Now, novelists have traditionally organised their work around a limited number of individual figures, whose recurrence across the narrative syntagm provides the ground against which the continuities and the transformations in the represented world can be measured, and whose hopes and fears provide the basis upon which any such changes can be evaluated.[1] The historian-narrator of the French Revolution, however, does not immediately enjoy the facility of a unifying figurative focus, to the extent that he is dealing with collective events which involved the direct and indirect participation of a huge number of persons, acting alone or as members of a group: the crowd of women and the 20,000 or so national guards who went to Versailles on 5 October 1789; the crowd of petitioners calling for the suspension of the monarchy and the body of national guards who attacked them on 17 July 1791; the thousands who

[1] According to Hamon, '[characters] are the supports upon which the *conservation* and *transformation* of meaning is carried' (1977:161–2). My analysis is indebted to Hamon's study of the 'statut sémiologique du personnage' (1966) and to his more recent study, *Le Personnel du roman* (1983). As will become apparent in the following pages, however, the historical representation of collective events and collective actors raises specific problems which a model based solely on fictional narratives and individual subjects cannot fully account for.

participated in the battle for the Tuileries on 10 August 1792; the 'living mass' (Michelet I:1130) of the revolutionary army, commanded by Dumouriez, who won the decisive battle of Valmy against the Prussian army in September 1792; the 387 members of the National Assembly who voted for the execution of the king in January 1793 and the 334 who voted for a different sentence; Madame Roland, Vergniaud, Danton, Robespierre, and all the other individuals who, one after the other, went to the guillotine; all the victims of the Revolutionary wars, some of whose names are known or knowable, but many of whose names will never be: 'the unknown soldiers'.

The same individual and/or collective actors do not necessarily reappear from one episode to the next: some individual actors have only walk-on parts, as it were, in single episodes; some collective actors are simply *ad hoc* formations. Among those actors who do recur, there are few, if any, who do so throughout the length of the *fabula*: Vergniaud, for example, only came on the scene in October 1791 to fall from power on 31 May 1793 and, although Robespierre lasted from the Estates General in 1789 to Thermidor, he was not directly involved or instrumental in all the preconfigured events of the Revolution.[2]

What draws the different events of the historical *fabula* together is not the fate of any single individual as such, but the collective evolution of a social entity – the subject of 'History' – which is by definition impersonal or, rather, transpersonal. The development of this posited collective subject is manifested through the effective action and interaction of successive individuals and groups, groups which may be simply temporary *ad hoc* formations (for example, the particular crowd of petitioners at the Champ de Mars, the particular group of national guards who attacked them) or institutionalised entities/organisations which, although they

[2] To the extent that their subject-matter also involves collective events, historical novelists face problems similar to those of the historian. In Balzac's *Avant-Propos* (1842) to his *Comédie humaine*, where he set out his plan to be a social historian (above, p.5n), the novelist explicitly recognised the formal problems involved in his attempt to represent a social drama involving thousands of actors (1976–81, I:10). Using their freedom to invent fictional figures, however, historical novelists have tried to overcome the problem of actorial discontinuity and diversity in a variety of ways, especially through the use of a central fictional figure who moves between different episodes, observing them without necessarily playing a decisive role in the action itself: Scott's Waverley, who is a privileged witness to the intrigues of the supporters of the Young Pretender; Ange Pitou in Dumas's novel of the same name, who, while present at the taking of the Bastille, seconds the heroic deeds of his friend Billot, to whom the novelist attributes many of the heroic commonplaces of the day (1851, III:182); the young 'Citoyen Charles' in Dumas's *Les Blancs et les bleus* who happens to have personal meetings with both Saint-Just and Schneider within hours of his arrival in Strasbourg.

have a stable nominal identity, do not necessarily have a stable membership (for example, the Assembly, the Jacobins club, the *garde nationale*).

It was through the combined votes of 387 deputies, and not through the vote of any individual in particular, that the Assembly sentenced the king in January 1793. However, this is not to say that, in the narrative representation of that collective act, the reader's attention may not be drawn to the vote of certain individuals or of certain groups within the 721-strong Assembly: we have seen in chapter 1 how the particular figure of Vergniaud is regularly singled out as a key to the voting as a whole, for reasons that have to do both with the position of power which he actually occupied as leader of the Girondins, and with the intertextual tradition which has subsequently made of his figure the focus of the debate concerning the justice of that sentence.

Representing the Revolution, then, not only involves the representation and configuration of collective events; but also, and as importantly, the representation and configuration of the field of actors: the construction of 'actorial isotopies' (Greimas and Courtès 1979:197) from the masses of actors who participated together, both synchronically and diachronically, in the unfolding of events. To some extent, the personnel of the Revolution has already been pre-configured: there are certain key individuals (Robespierre, Danton, Vergniaud, and so on) who must inevitably figure in any history of the Revolution, together with certain groups such as the Montagne, the Jacobins, the *fédérés*, the *garde nationale*, the 'crowd'. Thus, re-configuring the personnel of the Revolution will involve, on the one hand, selecting the representative individual and collective figures acting within these pre-configured groups on any particular occasion, and on the other hand, establishing their synchronic associations, and their diachronic filiation, with the other actors figuring in the narrative.

Michelet, as we have seen, relates how those who witnessed the uninspiring figure of Louis XVI on 10 August 1792 spontaneously turned away from his 'non-vitality' to the 'living reality' of the nation: through what figures is this 'living reality' represented? The fact that the 'nation', rather than the 'King of France', should be the protagonist-subject of 'French History' can itself be considered, as I suggested in my Introduction, an outcome of the very Revolution which these histories set out to narrate. But if 'the nation' or 'France' is the implied collective subject of the historical narrative, in whose name the historian claims to speak, it is not itself an anthropomorphic figure whose fate can be traced out in the way that the story of the 'King of France' or 'Madame Bovary' can be. For this reason, the purely narratological problem of constructing a coherent story from the diverse figurative materials with which the historian deals inevitably goes together with the ideological issue of deciding which figures actually represent the collective historical subject at any particular conjuncture.[3]

In the light of these concerns and in the light of the narrative strategies I outlined in the previous chapter, I shall examine (a) the representation and configuration of group figures, and (b) the representation of the Revolutionary leaders and their symbolic function in the different narratives as representatives of, or spokesmen for, the nation.

The constitution of groups

The denomination of actors: proper names and common nouns

On the morning of 17 July 1791, two individuals who had hidden under the steps of the Autel de la Patrie, allegedly with the prurient intention of peeping under the skirts of the female patriots, were discovered, taken for conspirators, and killed by the crowd – a bizarre episode which was nevertheless to be instrumental in the declaration of martial law by the municipal authorities and result in the 'massacre' at the Champ de Mars later that afternoon.

Who were (or should it be, who 'was'?) this unhappy pair who so briefly played a part in the unfolding of events; who, almost as soon as they stepped onto the historical scene, effectively quit it – for evermore, as Carlyle writes, unless there is 'a day to be looked for when these two evidently mean individuals, who are human nevertheless, will become Historical Riddles; and...have their Dissertations' (1903, II:36).

Proper names, Hamon writes (1983:107), play a vital role in enabling a reader to identify an actor and to follow his progress throughout the narrative. While this may be obvious in the case of fictional narratives, it is only partially applicable in the case of their historical counterparts. In many cases, even where individual figures – such as our two would-be *voyeurs* – have emerged from the social mass into the historical light, they may remain anonymous: either because their names were never recorded in the first place or, what is related to this, because their 'personalised' name tags are not considered pertinent to the role which they are to play in the narrative.

Strictly speaking, proper names are semantically empty: they make sense only in their association with the unique, historical entity which they

[3] It is from this perspective that I understand Orr's view of nineteenth-century histories as attempts to work out 'the implications of democracy' (1984:246).

designate.[4] The name 'Danton', for example, refers to the unique individual called Danton and, like an identity card, it is in theory 'non-transferable'. In contrast, a common noun like 'a man' or 'a soldier' refers by definition to all 'men' or to all 'soldiers'.[5] As it happens, certain proper names designating certain historical figures have come to acquire meaning within the culture, and are already invested with a certain semantic value: if 'Napoleon', 'Danton', 'Robespierre' make sense, it is because we already know who Napoleon, Danton, and Robespierre were (to recall the words of De Certeau, 'Robespierre, you know who that is', above, p.42). Any statement concerning 'Robespierre' (for instance, that he was found under the patriotic altar on the morning of 17 July 1791) would be to reconfirm, add to, or contradict, the semantic values already associated with his name in the historical tradition ('Robespierre, he is different from the man you know...').[6] To relate that 'Hilaire Rigot' and 'Pierre Didesse' were found in suspicious circumstances under the altar might produce an *effet de réel*, to use Barthes' term.[7] But even if the statement were true, it would tell the reader no more than the tautological fact that the two men under the altar were called 'Rigot' and 'Didesse'. *Exeunt.*

Proper names enable us, John Searle writes, to refer publicly to a particular entity without being forced to raise issues and come to an agreement on which descriptive characteristics exactly constitute its identity (1958:172): again, 'Danton' was Danton. In the absence of a proper name, in order to assign an identity to a hitherto unknown proper name, or in order to re-define the identity of someone whose name we already know, the individual referred to may be described under a variety of different aspects. On the one hand, he may be identified by his actions,

4 In certain exceptional cases, proper names may function as signifiers independently of their designative function: such is the case with names which are clearly marked as 'foreign' (see below, n.8); such is also the case, for example, with a name like 'Clémence', whose *alter ego* as an abstract noun may on occasion be brought into play – as in Blanc's account of the scene in the Assembly on 10 August where one of the insurgents offered to shelter a Swiss soldier: 'The man who distinguished himself by this touching declaration was so moved in making it that he fainted. He bore a name which was in keeping with the beauty of his soul, he was called Clémence' (II:173).

5 According to Ducrot and Todorov (1972:321), while it is possible to refer to many different 'men' without the word 'man' becoming ambiguous, it is not possible to refer to 'Londons' without giving rise to confusion.

6 For a discussion of the semiotic functioning of historical names, see Eco 1979a:87f and above, p.39.

7 A 'reality effect', according to Barthes (1968), is produced by those descriptive details which, precisely because they have apparently no signifying function within a narrative, give the impression of being unmediated portions of reality itself.

according to what he has done or is doing. On the other hand, he may be identified according to what he 'is', that is, according to the different, more or less narrowly defined, classes or categories to which he belongs: by gender, profession, nationality, political affiliation, race, marital status, height, age, temperament, and so on. The narrator will select or foreground only that aspect or those aspects which are pertinent to the descriptive context, and to the role which the individual is to play in it. Thus, the man who dramatically embraced one of the Swiss guards before the Assembly on 10 August is identified by Michelet as one of the 'victors' (I:989), by Blanc as a 'citizen' called 'Clémence' (II:173), and by Carlyle as 'Clemence, the Wine-merchant' (1903, II:124). While proper names are unambiguous, clearly diversity sets in as soon as one attempts to identify an individual by any other means.

In each case, identifying the particular actor is inseparable from situating him, by association or difference, *vis-à-vis* all other individuals or groups who figure in the narrative. Indeed, 'Clémence' in Michelet's account is identified exclusively in his capacity as 'one of', as 'one among', the 'victors' of 10 August: there is nothing which marks him as different from any of the other combatants who are presumed here to constitute a single, homogeneous group; whether there were redheads among them, or differences in age or profession, is irrelevant to the description. We know no more about 'Clémence' in Michelet's account than that he was one of the *vainqueurs des Tuileries* and that he dramatically saved a Swiss: because he is left anonymous in this way, however, the entire class of 'victors' can be seen as a virtual agent in the generous deed.

Blanc's Clémence as a *citoyen* belongs to the class of *citoyens*. As it happens, other members of this class have already been represented in Blanc's account and all of them have figured on the side of the insurrectionary forces: as a *citoyen*, then, the humanitarian Clémence is associated with all those fellow-*citoyens* who helped take the Tuileries. In contrast, while 'Clemence, the Wine-merchant' is theoretically associated with all other members of his professional class, this is a class which is not otherwise represented in Carlyle's narrative of 10 August: the fact of being identified as belonging to this class, then, serves to reinforce his social isolation or eccentricity *vis-à-vis* the insurrectionary crowd, an eccentricity which is already expressed in the fact that, in Carlyle's representation, he goes against the collective current in undertaking a benevolent action. In this way, identity and deed act as mutual glosses: the marginality of the actor serves to marginalise the action and *vice versa*.[8]

Let us return now to the two men under the patriotic altar. Not one of the writers considered here identifies them by name. Not one of them identifies the hapless pair in the same way. While the fact that there were two men beneath the altar remains a constant, each writer produces a significantly different actorial configuration by reworking and re-organising a limited amount of information concerning the pair.

Carlyle identifies the two suspects as 'Two human individuals of mean aspect, one of them with a wooden leg' (1903, II:35): the two men make up a single homogeneous group, having in common both the fact of being found in suspicious circumstances and the fact of belonging to the category of individuals 'of mean aspect'; in this context, the wooden leg which distinguishes one member of the pair serves merely to reinforce the quality of 'meanness' which the two men have in common. Likewise, both Thiers (1865, I:143) and Lamartine (I:141) identify the men as constituting a single homogeneous group, presenting them as two undifferentiated members of the common class of invalid soldiers: 'deux invalides'. Blanc, for his part, identifies them as 'Two men, one of whom was an invalid soldier with a wooden leg' (I:728); and, a paragraph later, as 'the invalid soldier and his companion' (I:729): the pair is thus defined with reference to only one of its members, the *invalide* with the wooden leg, while the unmarked member is identified exclusively in his functional capacity as 'having been there' as the 'companion' of the other. Finally, Michelet foregrounds the member who is left unmarked in Blanc's account, identifying him as a 'hairdresser' (*perruquier*) who had chosen as *his* companion, 'an old invalid soldier' (I:698).

An individual who is identified as a member of a particular class is not only associated with all other members of the same class, but he is also presumed, until information is given to the contrary, to share all the attributes by which that class is defined. *Invalides* are by definition no longer able-bodied men (in doubling the number of *invalides*, then, and in confining the information about them to their class membership,

[8] In a similar way, Blanc identifies the only person to visit the queen on 10 August 1792 as 'Lady Sutherland, the wife of the English ambassador' (II:160), while, as we have seen, Lamartine identifies one of the rare persons to help the fleeing Swiss as Pisani, the Venetian ambassador (I:624). In each case, the 'foreignness' of the actor, which is doubly marked in both examples (by the morphology of the names and by the qualifying description), serves to underscore the deviant character of their actions. In certain instances, the eccentricity of a particular actor may be due to his personal idiosyncrasies rather than to his membership of a marginal group (Michelet, for example, suggests that Fournier, responsible for various acts of aggression on 17 July 1791, was a pathological case, I:701, 708).

Lamartine underscores the physical disabilities of the pair and, by extension, the senselessness of murdering them). And all hairdressers?

Before introducing the hairdresser at the Champ de Mars, Michelet gives a page-long discursive outline of the function of *perruquier* in the old and the new *régimes*: given a hairdresser's intimate acquaintance with aristocratic boudoirs, the members of this profession were notorious libertines; having lost their clientele through the emigration, they were also among the most ardent royalists. After thus specifying the particular attributes of the hairdressing profession in its historical context, Michelet then introduces our hairdresser as a typical member of the profession ('one of them...'), and hence as already marked by 'libertinage' and 'royalism'. His chosen companion is subsequently identified, not only as an 'old invalid soldier', but also as an individual who was 'no less' libertine and royalist than himself; in the context or company of the hairdresser, it is these attributes, more than the incidental fact of his being an *invalide*, which come to mark the second man.

For all that they belong to two different social groups, then, the two men are presented by Michelet as sharing a common denominator or, rather, denominators as libertines and as royalists. The fact that the two men, who belong to different professional classes, should figure in each other's company implies that the moral laxity and the royalism, which marks each of them individually, may be at the basis of their association. Moreover, given the semiotic function of recurrence considered in the previous chapter, the fact that the combination 'royalism'/'moral laxity' should be repeated in two different figures suggests that there may be a significant overlap in the general membership of these two classes. The men's prurient intent in hiding under the Autel de la Patrie is clearly a direct reflection of their morals; the significance of their common royalism remains ambiguous – a virtual rather than an actual force in this context.

When, later that day, hairdressers appear among the forces sent to impose martial law, and thus appear for the second time in Michelet's narrative, a significant link is effectively established between the two episodes in which hairdressers so unexpectedly and yet so prominently figure. Furthermore, the fact that the band of hairdressers should appear in the company of royalists serves to reinterpret retrospectively the earlier incident: instead of being simply the unhappy adventure of two (royalist) libertines, it becomes the sign of a more general intervention in events on the part of the forces of royalism. In Blanc's account, in contrast, the band of hairdressers later that afternoon appears out of the blue, as it were: anomalous, ridiculous, with no apparent connection to any other group or incident, and certainly not to the old *invalide* and his companion, who remain isolated figures in the narrative.

Thus, the different treatments of two anonymous individuals (out of the millions who participated in the Revolution) indicate some of the complexities involved in the representation of individual actors in their social, as opposed to their idiosyncratic, dimension. It points, on the one hand, to the fact that the very anonymity of historical actors can be a source for the production of meaning; on the other hand, to the fact that the identification of actors in the discourse is linked to the construction of an intricate set of associations and filiations between different actors in the narrative. Above all, the representations of the 'two mean individuals' (otherwise known as 'the *invalide* and his companion', the 'two *invalides*' or 'the hairdresser and his companion, the *invalide*') bring into relief the semiotic status which these historical individuals now have: the identity of the men and of the social group to which they belonged, while it is based on a limited number of possibilities, has clearly become a function of the role which these figures are to play as signifiers in each narrative text.

Figures in the crowd

'Danton', 'Robespierre' and 'un perruquier' designate individual actors – one man, one narrative figure, as it were. But there is not always such a direct one-to-one correlation between the number of significant figures in the narrative and the number of individual actors actually involved in the narrated events. Nowhere perhaps is the conventional character of language more apparent in these histories than in the many sylleptic references to *groups* as singular actorial figures. Such collective figures may designate a mass made up of an indefinite number of individuals and referred to simply by a collective noun ('the crowd' or 'the *peuple*'); an unspecified number of representatives of a particular class ('women', 'a band of hairdressers'); or a specific number of representatives of the same class (20,000 national guards). But, in every case, the identity of all the individual members of the group is, under that particular description, momentarily supposed. 'The *peuple* went to fetch the king': so Michelet entitles his account of 5 October, the word *peuple* here referring collectively to the thousands of women, the thousands of national guards, and the several hundred men from the Faubourg Saint-Antoine who went to Versailles.

Given the limits of the historical record, the limits of the discursive medium and, most importantly, the specifically collective nature of much of the action, an exhaustive listing or headcount of all the women and men involved in the different *journées révolutionnaires* is highly improbable. Nevertheless, the expanded narrative of 'Les journées d'octobre' or 'Le 10 août' does go together with an expanded, if not exhaustive, representation of the different crowds who participated in the various incidents constitutive of those events: thus, the singular *peuple* which figures in the title of Michelet's account of 5 October – 'The *peuple* went to fetch the king' – becomes expanded or de-composed in his opening paragraph to become the crowd of women, on the one hand, and the crowd of national guards on the other. The figurative representation of these complex, social events alternates between the de-composition of larger pre-configured actorial groups into their constituent elements, and the amalgamation or synthesis of smaller actorial units to construct larger wholes.

That a crowd of women was instrumental in the events of 5 October; that there was a crowd of petitioners attacked by the *garde nationale* on 17 July 1791; that an insurrectionary force successfully attacked the Tuileries on 10 August 1792: these are constants in all accounts of these events. What varies, however, is the number and the identity of the individual and collective figures which each historian-narrator cuts out or defines within these larger collective figures.

The composition of groups: 10 August 1792

In his account of 10 August, Blanc relates how the officers in charge of guarding the palace had led the Swiss guards to expect an attack by the rabble of Paris:

> Cette canaille parut: c'était le peuple.
>
> C'était le peuple, dans la plus large acception du mot. Car la première bande des assaillants... montrait, marchant côte à côte, des hommes de toutes les classes; la garde civique y était mêlée aux gens à piques; les bourgeois y fraternisaient avec les ouvriers; les départements, représentés par les fédérés, Marseillais, Brestois, n'y faisaient qu'un avec Paris.[9]
>
> [This rabble came into sight: it was the *peuple*.
>
> It was the *peuple*, in the broadest meaning of the term. For in the first group of attackers... one could see men from all different classes,

[9] II:169. As the opposition rabble/*peuple* illustrates, the term which is used to designate a particular collective actor may itself define its significance and its role *vis-à-vis* the implied collective subject or norm: e.g. 'a horde', as Lamartine refers to the crowd which attacked the Tuileries (I:627); 'some bandits', as Blanc refers to those responsible for the murder of the two men under the patriotic altar (I:729); 'les séditieux' ('the agitators'), as Lamartine refers to the petitioners at the Champ de Mars (I:145).

marching side by side: civic guards mingled with pikebearers; *bourgeois* were fraternising with workers; the provinces, represented by the *fédérés* from Marseilles and Brest, were united with Paris.]

Having first (re)defined the vanguard of the insurrection as being, or rather representing, the *peuple*, Blanc proceeds to give an expanded description or breakdown of its composition in terms of the different social classes to which its members belonged. In doing so, however, he gives no indication of the numbers of group members present in each instance: if there were a thousand workers for every bourgeois, or a hundred Parisians for every provincial, Blanc does not say. Nor does he make clear the degree of overlap in the membership of each group. The function of Blanc's definition, then, is less to give a precise breakdown of the composition of the actorial figure than to signal the virtual participation and cooperation of all these different groups in the insurrection through their representatives in the vanguard.[10]

In contrast to Blanc, Michelet defines the *avant-garde* of the insurrection as being specifically made up of 3,000 pikebearers or *hommes à piques* (I:979), accompanied by 'a few' *fédérés*, the national guards from the provinces (I:979). The fact that the vanguard should carry pikes and not another weapon signifies the bearers' social origin and, what is inseparable from this, their probable non-membership of the bourgeois militia or *garde nationale*, whose weapon was the bayonet. If there were any national guards in the vanguard besides the few *fédérés*, they were apparently not present in sufficient numbers to constitute a significant figure in the crowd; and even if they had been, the reader has no way of knowing it, for Michelet makes no mention of them.

Whereas Blanc's all-inclusive definition simply indicates the presence of members of different classes, Michelet makes clear that the members of one particular class outnumbered the other: while some *fédérés* went along and sought to direct the crowd, it is the crowd of 3,000 pikebearers which, because of its numerical predominance, defines the collective figure as a whole, whom he subsequently will refer to *en masse* as 'the crowd of attackers' (I:982).

The definition of the revolutionary vanguard on 10 August 1792 brings

[10] The fact that Blanc should insist on the bourgeois participation in the revolution of 10 August is all the more striking since, on most other occasions, he specifically defines the *peuple* as the deprived majority in its difference from the bourgeoisie (this class division is explicitly set out in the historical essay which precedes his actual narrative of the Revolution, see I:39f). Only in the first stages of the Revolution could the interests of the bourgeoisie be identified with those of the *peuple*: as he writes of the events of 27 June 1789, 'at least until that day, the bourgeoisie was the Revolution, the bourgeoisie was the *peuple*' (I:277).

into relief some of the options available to the historians in order to compose this collective figure differently, to identify and coordinate its constitutive elements in different ways (in the crowd, there were *fédérés*, workers, *bourgeois*, parisians, provincials; the crowd was made up of x number of pikebearers and y number of *fédérés*). As the example from Michelet also shows, however, defining a group involves not only coordinating different constitutive groups, but also subordinating one subgroup to another: one group may be preponderant numerically, constituting a majority with respect to 'the rest'. As we shall see in the following section, however, the preponderance of one figure over another may also be the product of the narrative discourse which foregrounds one subgroup or individual figure, so that they effectively come to represent the group as a whole in the narrative.

The representation of groups: 5 October 1789

Although 'the women' who went to Versailles on 5 October 1789 included several hundred men, it has generally been agreed that the crowd which led the expedition was predominantly female. Both in his discursive prolegomenon and in the narrative account which follows it, Michelet isolates a number of collective and individual female figures within this female mass: 'a 36-year-old woman, well dressed and honest, but strong and daring' (I:255); a 17-year-old flower girl called Louison Chabry; 'tradeswomen, *concierges*, prostitutes' (I:256) and a considerable number of market-women. It so happens that by virtue of their individual temperament or of the profession to which they belong (whose attributes Michelet re-defines), all these women have two features in common: namely, the fact of 'not being hungry' (that is, of not being destitute) and the fact of being 'compassionate and charitable' enough to go to look for bread for those too weak to do so themselves. It turns out, then, that when these women are seen together – having been randomly selected from the crowd, as it were – they make up a coherent, recognisable *ad hoc* group; indeed, the very fact that they should belong to different professional groups serves to underscore the common social and moral denominators which are the basis of their association. Michelet explicitly suggests, moreover, that as 'charitable and compassionate' women who engage in action for the sake of others, they also belong to the great heroic tradition of French womanhood, identified by such names as Jeanne d'Arc, Jeanne de Montfort, and Jeanne Hachette.

Michelet's women are given prominence and significance first of all by the very fact that they are thus brought into relief against the otherwise undifferentiated, unmarked female crowd.[11] At the same time, the fact that similar attributes should be repeated across a significant number of different figures suggests that the foregrounded group may be paradigmatic – a representative sample – of the crowd as a whole. This idea is reinforced, on the one hand, by the fact that no other information is given about the 'other women' which might contradict it and, on the other hand, by the fact that these 'charitable and compassionate' women are presented not only as akin to each other, but also as belonging to a certain historical tradition. The recurrence of similar attributes in the French women who acted in the past and those who are now acting on 5 October suggests that the same attributes might be further repeated on a significant number of instances among all those other women who, lost in the crowd, only figure *in absentia* in the representation.

Louis Blanc also draws the attention of the reader towards the presence of certain figures within the female crowd, above all through a *mise en spectacle* of the female procession:

> subitement grossi par des détachements accourus de tous les points de la ville, le cortége ne tarda pas à présenter le spectacle le plus extraordinaire. Armées de fusils ou de pistolets, de fourches ou de lances, et traînant deux pièces de canon, les femmes, au nombre de sept ou huit mille, formaient l'avant-garde, à la tête de laquelle se faisaient remarquer par leur beauté, leur jeunesse et leur ardeur, l'actrice Rose Lacombe, Pierrette Chabry, Reine Audu, surnommée la reine des halles, et, entre toutes, Théroigne de Méricourt, jolie Liégeoise que la révolution venait d'enlever au dernier de ses amants, et qui n'aima plus que la liberté le jour où elle l'aima. (I:389)

> [the procession soon presented the most extraordinary sight, its numbers having been suddenly swelled by groups arriving from all corners of the city. Armed with guns, pistols, pitchforks or lances, and dragging two pieces of cannon, seven or eight thousand women formed the vanguard; noticeable at their head were a number of figures striking for their beauty, their youth, and their ardour: the actress Rose Lacombe, Pierrette Chabry, Reine Audu, nicknamed queen of the market, and above all, Théroigne de Méricourt, the pretty Liégeoise whom the revolution had wooed away from her last lover and who, from the day she fell in love with liberty, loved no one else.]

[11] The narrator's delegation of a part to define or represent the actorial group as a whole is particularly well illustrated in Michelet's definition of the Swiss soldiers: 'A large number of these soldiers were from the canton of Fribourg; some of them no doubt were Vaudois, that is to say French, French by language, French by character' (I:982). Playing on the numerical indefiniteness of the 'many' and the 'some', and telescoping from one subgroup to the next, Michelet brings the 'Swiss' to signify 'Frenchmen'.

The women singled out from the crowd are not only foregrounded in the narrative discourse; Blanc simultaneously justifies the prominence he accords to them by suggesting that these figures were to be seen in the foreground of the crowd itself, at the head of the *cortège*: they 'stuck out' ('se faisaient remarquer') as remarkable figures.

While the four women thus foregrounded are identified as individuals by their proper names, they nevertheless form, like Michelet's ladies, a coherent group: they both figure together (they are literally seen side by side) and share the attributes of being remarkable, young, lovely, and enthusiastic. Since the rest of the female crowd remains otherwise undifferentiated, it is the four young and lovely lassies who represent and define the female crowd in Blanc's text.

However, if Blanc's women are to be construed as representative of the crowd as a whole, like Michelet's relatively prosperous and compassionate ones, it is clear that they are nevertheless exceptional, and not simply sample or typical figures: they represent the crowd at the same time that they are different from it, a paradoxical status which goes together with the fact that they apparently *lead* the crowd to Versailles (together with Stanislas Maillard, whom Blanc portrays as sharing the quality of 'youthfulness', I:389).

As it happens, Pierrette Chabry, one of the leaders of Blanc's crowd, has already figured in the narrative, having been singled out in the context of the women's earlier invasion of the Hôtel de Ville ('seat of the new *bourgeois* aristocracy, who treated the poor so harshly', I:388), an attack which Blanc represents by a series of incidents signalling the pacific, generous character of the female assaillants:

> Leur premier acte avait été de délivrer cinq prisonniers, retenus là pour de légers délits. Une jeune fille de dix-sept ans, ouvrière en sculpture, et nommée Pierrette Chabry, prit tout ce qu'elle avait dans sa poche, douze francs, et les donna, pour qu'on achetât à ces malheureux des souliers et des hardes. Les autres applaudirent, firent une quête en faveur des prisonniers et les renvoyèrent heureux. (I:388)
>
> [Their first act had been to set free five prisoners, imprisoned there for minor offences. A young seventeen-year-old girl called Pierrette Chabry, a worker in the sculpting business, took all the money she had in her pocket, twelve francs, and gave it away so that shoes and clothes could be bought for the unfortunate prisoners. The others applauded, started a collection for the prisoners, and sent them away happy.]

Pierrette Chabry's generosity here is more than a merely personal act; it is a personal act which conforms to the wishes of the entire crowd and provides a model for their future collective action: all 'the others' approve of her action and then proceed to emulate it. When the same Pierrette, recognisable as such by her proper name – and here we see its anaphoric function in linking up two narrative contexts[12] – reappears at the head of the *cortège*, her role as leader/representative seems to be motivated by the events themselves, by the common wish of the crowd. In thus narrating the reaction of the mass to one of its members whose actions they approve, whose actions presumably conform to their common aspirations, and whose lead they follow, Blanc can be said to represent the crowd in the process of defining itself (for his reader), in the process of (freely) designating its own representatives or leaders.[13] As we shall see in the course of the following chapters, representing the words or actions of particular figures as the focus of general approval or censure is frequently used in order to establish the role of a certain figure as a legitimate representative of the wishes of the general public and hence – what is no less important – to legitimise the representative role which the narrator himself is according to that figure in the narrative. This rhetorical strategy recalls the strategy, encountered in the previous chapter, of representing the '*de facto*' unanimous adherence of the public to the subject which the retrospective narrator has constituted as the subject of his history.

This brief description of the way in which Blanc and Michelet represent the crowd of women illustrates the complex interaction between, on the one hand, the role of the historian-narrator in appointing certain individuals to represent or 'stand for' the crowd as a whole and, on the other hand, the various appeals which are made to the events/actors themselves in order to motivate his selection: 'since a significant number of women were like this, then we may presume that the rest were the same'; 'the crowd recognised these women as expressing their aspirations and/or their values'.

At the same time, the different representations of the crowd indicate that the definition of a collective figure goes beyond the mere identification

[12] See Hamon 1983:107 regarding the 'anaphoric' function of proper names, i.e. their function in recalling earlier parts of the narrative text.

[13] Blanc's crowd of women will subsequently be shown unanimously rejecting the misbehaviour of certain fanatics ('forcenées') in that they silence those who threaten to kill the queen (I:390); in this way, the majority actively dissociates from itself certain actors who may figure in their company but who do not belong there, who are marginals. Later that day, Stanislas Maillard's patriotic speech in the Assembly (insisting that everyone should wear the national cockade) was greeted with universal applause, according to Blanc; with both trembling and applause, according to Michelet (I:262), who suggests thereby that Maillard is not truly a spokesman for, or representative of, the public at large.

of the participants in terms of the pre-configured social class or group to which they may belong (for example, *fédérés* or national guards): it also involves laying bare the basis of the association between different actors as they collectively engage in a particular action. Whereas Burke had presented the women as a motley crew with nothing more in common than their fury and the fact of being female ('all the unutterable abominations of the furies of hell, in the abused shape of the vilest of women', 1930:79), Michelet suggests that 'the women' who went to Versailles were compassionate and were not driven by material necessity; Blanc, that they were pacific, generous, young, orderly. As it happens, the common attributes in each case serve both to associate the members of the group with each other and to identify them collectively (and hence their projected actions) as the locus of particular symbolic, moral, and indeed aesthetic values: pacific and orderly, attractive, or filiated to Jeanne d'Arc, as the case may be. In this way, we can see that identifying the significant actorial groupings goes together with locating them with respect to certain implied norms.

After the initial composition of the *cortège*, the female ranks are kept generally closed for the rest of the expedition to Versailles, being referred to collectively as 'the women' or, what is apparently its synonym in this context for both Michelet and Blanc: 'the *peuple*'.[14] The initial definitions of the crowd, however, will subsequently function as a hermeneutic guide for the reader in recognising whether any newcomer figuring in the narrative is to be associated with, or dissociated from, the actions of the main body of women, the current representatives of 'the *peuple*'.

The association of individual figures

The preceding account of the representation of the female crowd on 5 October 1789 has shown some of the possible symbolic relations between individual figures and the group figure to which they belong. While these symbolic, representational relations are extremely important in the works of Michelet and Blanc, they are less so in the case of Lamartine. Indeed, Lamartine's work is perhaps above all characterised by the absence of mediating figures between the 'collective' crowd and the individual, his account tending to deal, on the one hand, with a largely undifferentiated, and negatively valorised crowd and, on the other hand, with individuals who are more often than not portrayed, by way of a digressive biographical sketch, in their private, idiosyncratic dimensions and in

[14] Michelet I:263, 265, 267; Blanc I:390, 392, 396.

circumstances which set them apart from the crowd; in fact, often in circumstances where they are its victims. The individual actors who are thus set over against the crowd do not only share the same role, however, but are also portrayed as sharing certain qualities – a fact which can be briefly illustrated by Lamartine's distribution of the qualities of 'familiality' among the actors involved in the events of 10 August.

Whereas Blanc refers to the queen on this occasion as 'the haughty daughter of Marie-Thérèse' (II:168), thereby marking her as an outsider and as a one-member class, Lamartine repeatedly presents her in her female and familial capacities as a devoted mother and spouse. Thus: 'queen and mother, trembling at once for her husband and for her children' (I:585); 'woman, mother, wife, queen' (I:586). As wife and mother, Marie-Antoinette is presumed akin to all other mothers and spouses or, what amounts to the same thing in Lamartine's account, to all those persons who value familial bonds. Presumably there are many women who are also wives or mothers; and presumably every individual fits in one way or another into some familial category, either as a daughter or son. It just so happens, however, that in Lamartine's representation all those who are marked in any way by 'conjugality' or 'familiality' belong to the royalist camp and/or to those who are victims of the insurgent crowd, where the only females are the negatively valorised 'mégères de la rue' ('harpies of the street', I:627). Thus, Mandat is accompanied to the Hôtel de Ville by his young son, who is then forced to witness the death of his father; thus, the wife of Clermont-Tonnerre must witness her husband's mutilation, and so on.[15] (In Michelet's account of the same event, in contrast, the women, children, and the *pères de famille* are located on the other side of the insurrectionary divide, I:1002; and as we shall see in Blanc's representation of 17 July 1791, the women, children and *pères de famille* are very clearly located on the side of those massacred by the government forces, below, p.130).

The recurrence of signs of 'familiality' among the different individuals who are victims of the insurrection serves, on the one hand, to reinforce an association which is already there at the level of the action and, on the

[15] In Lamartine's representation of 10 August, moreover, the antagonists and victims of the insurrection also have a monopoly on the quality of youthfulness: the young widow of Clermont-Tonnerre (I:630), 'the young Charles d'Autichamp' (I:626); 'several young royalists' (I:580); 'The old and intrepid Maréchal de Mailly, eighty years old, but young in his devotion to his unfortunate master' (I:581). In Blanc's account of 5 October, as we have seen, it is the crowd and its leaders who are marked as youthful. The property of 'youthfulness' serves not only to mark the figure as 'attractive' and 'energetic', but also to suggest that he or she has a *future* (unlike Louis XVI, in Michelet's narrative, who is explicitly defined as 'the shadow and nothingness of the past', above, pp.98f).

other hand, to mark as the locus of the implied collective norm, of 'normality', the minority group which Lamartine constitutes as the subject of his historical narrative, and which he portrays as victims of a numerically preponderant, but 'ab-normal' crowd.

Associations and dissociations

The whole and the part: 10 August 1792

Those actors who figure in the narrative do so, by definition, in the context of a particular action in which they are actively or passively involved. As I shall consider in greater detail below, the representation and valorisation of collective actorial figures takes place in conjunction with the distribution of various roles, and the allocation of certain responsibilities, among the different actorial figures defined in the text.

We have seen how, in his account of 10 August, Michelet attributes the first, vanguard attack to an actorial group in which both *fédérés* and pikebearers figure, but in which the latter group, made up of 3,000 men, predominates. We have seen earlier how Michelet also uses various narrative strategies in order to foreground the formation and emergence of the *second* group of insurgents from the combined forces of the Faubourgs Saint-Antoine and Saint-Marceau; how he accords the title 'the avenging army of the *peuple*' to this group in particular (where Blanc had given it to the vanguard); and how he specifically marks it by the predominance of bayonets – the emergence of the main body of the insurrection being signalled by the apparition of the forest of bayonets gleaming in the morning sun. What is the relation between pikes and bayonets, and what are their respective roles, in the insurrection of 10 August?

If Michelet's narrative is organised so as to highlight the emergence of the army of the *peuple*, it must now be seen as organised towards yet another end as well: namely, to indicate the difference in membership between the vanguard and the army of the *peuple* which formed the main body of the insurrection. In his discursive prologue to the episode, Michelet does suggest that there were up to 3,000 pikebearers dispersed amidst the main body of the insurrection (made up of 500 *fédérés* and 10,000 national guards); but these 3,000 pikes do not figure directly in his actual narrative account, having been assimilated to all intents and purposes by the majority group of bayonet-bearing national guards: at the level of the representation, the pikes have become lost in the crowd. In this way, then, Michelet attributes to the pikebearers the predominant role in the *avant-garde* phase of the insurrection, at the same time as he effectively eliminates them from the insurrection itself: their role is to have set the insurrection in motion and to have suffered, in the process, the deadly firing of the assembled Swiss. The result is, of course, that the serious fighting, as well as the victory, is reserved for the national guards who literally take over from the first group. By the time of the fighting in the Tuileries gardens, the national guards have become absolutely preponderant (there were up to 40,000 of them, Michelet suggests), while the pikebearers have effectively disappeared from the narrative – but not definitively, as we shall see.

In the brief account of the struggle in the environs of the palace, Michelet relates how a group of Swiss attempted to fight their way, sabre in hand, across the Place de la Révolution: unfortunately for the Swiss, however, the sabre was a useless weapon 'against the pikes of their relentless enemies' (I:988). Now, given the fact that there were allegedly 40,000 national guards involved in the battle for the Tuileries and apparently no pikebearers, or so few as not to have been worth mentioning, it is all the more surprising that pikes should momentarily reappear as the instruments of the Swiss guards' death, wielded by their 'relentless enemies'. Within the system of differences set up in Michelet's text, however, the reference to 'pikes' serves to dissociate the energetic pursuit of the Swiss from the main body of the 'people's' army, by implicitly associating it with those who had been part of the vanguard and who, having suffered the brunt of the Swiss guards' volleys, presumably had more cause for personal enmity towards them.

It is only in the discursive prolegomenon to his 'Le 10 août dans l'Assemblée' that Michelet defines the social composition of the group which he has hitherto simply identified metonymically by the weapons they carry: 'men with pikes'. Making explicit and (re)defining the class attributes of the pikebearers, he suggests that those who made up the main part of the vanguard were driven by desperate necessity, so poor that they no longer could even buy bread. Twelve pages later, in the narrative account of the funeral processions which we considered earlier (above, pp.95f), we are told that 'many' of the 1,100 dead men were 'married men, fathers of poor families, who had been driven into combat by extreme misery' (I:1002). Through the indefiniteness of the 'many', the group of victims is represented in the narrative, as was the vanguard, by impoverished *pères de famille*. Furthermore, there are those who, on beholding the grieving widows and orphans, swear to avenge the dead and seize hold of their weapons as a sign of their resolution – and these weapons are not bayonets:

> Nulle scène de ce genre n'avait lieu sans jeter dans l'âme des spectateurs un nouveau levain de vengeance; des jeunes gens reprenaient la pique, rentraient dans Paris pour tuer... (I:1002)
>
> [No scene of this sort took place without sowing a new seed of vengeance in the hearts of the spectators; young men took up their pikes again and went back into the streets of Paris to kill...]

The cycle of grief and vengeance, then, is an internal or domestic matter within the pikebearing, impoverished section of the community, who are both victims and avengers.

Recent narrative theory has shown how different actorial figures may play the same actantial role with respect to the realisation of a particular programme; it has also shown how the same actorial figure may play a number of such roles.[16] Michelet's configuration of the actors of 'Le 10 août' shows how, in the case of *composite* actorial figures, different roles may be delegated in a stratified or hierarchical way to their constituent elements. By bringing into relief the collective figure of 'the pikebearers' within the larger group of those who attacked the Tuileries, Michelet isolates or delimits a minority to whom he attributes the initial impetus for the attack and to whom he then indirectly attributes the negatively charged aspects of the insurrection and, *antequam*, of the September massacres. In the previous chapter, we have seen how the violent aspects of 10 August are presented, through a variety of representational and narrative strategies, as deviations from the central patriotic action; in this context, it becomes apparent that these deviant actions are also the work of a minority group. Moreover, the difference between the vanguard and the 'l'armée réelle de l'insurrection' ('the real army of the insurrection', I:967–8) also turns out, as we are retrospectively informed, to coincide with a difference of programme: whereas the aims of the latter group were ideological – they were motivated by a generous spirit of patriotism and the desire to save France – the former group sought material relief and was driven by necessity (I:1002). The bifurcation between 'necessary' and 'generous' acts is repeated in the battle's aftermath which involves, on the one hand, a quest for vengeance and, on the other hand, the desire to protect the Swiss; and again, the bifurcation at the level of the action coincides with the same stratification of the personnel.

The bayonet-bearing group, then, is predominant numerically; it replaces the vanguard; it is associated with 'higher', that is, selfless deeds not dictated by blind necessity; and it occupies what in Michelet's text is a particularly valorised position by virtue of its patriotic programme. It is

[16] See Greimas 1983:49–66 and Bal's summary, 1985:25f.

to this group that Michelet applies, first, the title 'army of the *peuple*' (I:984) and, secondly, the title 'vrais vainqueurs du 10 août' ('true victors of the Tenth of August', I:1005). It is this group which constitutes the 'real' army of the insurrection, which marks out the main tradition of the Revolution, and represents the 'noble spirit of France' (to recall the patriotic motif examined in the previous chapter). The other insurgents, who were motivated by material necessity and instinctive reactions, do not really belong to this class of *vainqueurs*: they played, rather, an auxiliary role in the primitive phase of the insurrection.

It is through the strategic recurrence of pikes and pikebearers in the course of his account of 'Le 10 août' and its immediate aftermath that Michelet creates an actorial isotopy running from the vanguard of the insurrection to the future vengeance of 2 September: a pike line, or rather lineage, which runs parallel, but subordinated, to that of the 'vrais vainqueurs des Tuileries'. As I shall show in the following section, however, the disjunction and discontinuity between actorial figures can play as important a role in the configuration of the action as the strategic recurrence of the same figure.

Insiders and outsiders: 5–6 October 1789

On the morning of 6 October, a crowd – which Burke had graphically depicted as a band of ruffians, assassins, ravishers – invaded the palace of Versailles: were the women from Paris among this crowd? If so, did the women make up a significant proportion of the invaders? Was a significant proportion of the female crowd involved or only a part of it? In the absence of proper names, a roll-call is obviously not possible.

Since almost all the figures which Carlyle identifies among the palace invaders are female, the signs are in his representation that basically the same actors are involved in the attack on Versailles as in the expedition which had set off from Paris in search of bread the previous day. If it is predominantly the same crowd, however, it is the same crowd at a different point of its historical existence; while the personnel may have remained substantially the same, what they collectively signify has changed: what began as 'hunger-stricken Maternity' (1903, I:202) has since become 'rabid insurrection':

> In few moments, the Grate of the inner and inmost Court, which they name Court of Marble, this too is forced, or surprised, and bursts open: the Court of Marble too is overflowed... Women snatch their cutlasses, or any weapon, and storm-in Menadic: – other women lift the corpse of shot Jérôme...

> Woe now to all Bodyguards, mercy is none for them!... Barricading serves not: fly fast, ye Bodyguards; rabid Insurrection, like the Hellhound Chase, uproaring at your heels! (1903, I:223–4)

If there was indeed a continuity between the predominantly female crowd which came from Paris and the crowd which broke into the palace of Versailles the following day, it is by no means so apparent in the narratives of Michelet and Blanc. In the first place, not only do they refrain from making any anaphoric reference to particular actors who had figured in the crowd the day before, but they do not even mark the palace invaders in any way by the presence of females. If the well-dressed 36-year-old woman or Reine Audu (the 'queen of the market') were there, they are travelling *incognito*, for neither they nor the figures of their companions reappear. This absence of anaphoric signs recalling the female crowd is coupled, moreover, with a discontinuity at the level of the nomenclature. While the female crowd was referred to collectively either as 'the women' or as 'the *peuple*', Michelet uses neither of these terms with reference to the palace invaders whom he designates as 'the crowd': 'la foule'. Now, this term has none of the positive connotations of 'the *peuple*' and its very neutrality (as not-*peuple*) can, in certain contexts, border on the pejorative. In contrast to Michelet, Blanc does refer to the invading crowd as 'the *peuple*' – or at least, he does so initially.

The immediate cause of the crowd's aggression, relates Blanc, was the death of 'a worker' (whom Carlyle identifies by the name Jérôme), killed by the palace guards: at the sight of the young man bathed in his own blood, 'furious, the *peuple* cried out with one voice for vengeance' (I:400). If it is the *peuple* who react to the young worker's death, it is, however, 'the crowd' which, six lines later, comes to the fore to avenge him and dispatch his killers: 'the furious crowd arrives, the guard is killed. At the same time, one of his comrades is seized and... dragged to the corpse of the young worker... (I:400).[17] This abrupt transformation in the anonymous crowd, whose name changes from *peuple* to *foule* depending on the type of action involved, illustrates clearly how 'reference' is inseparable from 'signification'. The fact that '*peuple*' should be replaced by '*foule*' in this manner suggests that, for Blanc and Michelet, the history of the collective subject is a selective one: that only certain deeds carried out by

[17] While the term '*foule*' is in many instances used simply to designate a mass of people, it also frequently occurs (as in the above passage from Blanc) in opposition to '*peuple*', as its negative mob-like pole. Michelet, for example, ends his account of the Tenth of August by relating how the statues of Liberty and the Law, the 'figures adored by the *peuple*', having been vandalised by royalists, the 'furious crowd' rushed in frenzy to the Assembly and demanded vengeance for the insult (I:1015).

the crowd belong to the trans-personal collective history. The collective figure of the *peuple* – the subject of their respective narratives – is thus defined in a circular way: its identity lies less in what it 'is', than in its involvement in certain deeds. 'The *peuple* went to Versailles' also means that 'the real *peuple* are those who went to Versailles to fetch the king'.

Neither Blanc nor Michelet contents himself, however, with simply designating the aggressive crowd or mob *en bloc*. Michelet distinguishes a number of different figures in the *foule* which had been lurking about the palace since the small hours: an infamous hunchback; a number of people from Versailles (the Versaillais, he suggests, are known to be more excitable than Parisians); several locksmiths and blacksmiths (members of these professions, he suggests, are naturally disposed towards aggression both by the nature of their work and by their drinking habits); an artist's model, with a long beard, dressed up in thc costume of a Roman slave. Thus, the only figures cut out from the aggressors are marked by qualities which are different from, and at times opposed to, those which marked the female crowd: male, non-Parisian, deformed and disguised (versus 'well-dressed and honest'). This motley collection of characters not only has the feature of alterity or 'ab-normality' with respect to the *peuple* in common: by profession or idiosyncrasy, each one of them is also explicitly marked as a marginal or eccentric. They may act in each other's company, then, but only *as* individuals. Moreover, in the case of the painter's model, who was responsible for the mutilation of the two bodyguards killed in the attack, Michelet stresses that his barbarity, far from being applauded or endorsed by the rest of the crowd, in fact horrified everyone present.

The figures which Blanc singles out among the palace-invaders of 6 October are also marked in their difference from the female crowd of the day before; a difference which is expressed primarily through the physiognomical contrast between the representatives of the two groups. Whereas the female crowd was headed by attractive, generous, young women, the *foule* is remarkable for the presence of a number of bizarre and unattractive figures to whom Blanc directly ascribes responsibility for the attack on the palace: the hunchback; men disguised as women; men with fine linen disguised as plebeians; a tall man with black hair and hollow eyes in the uniform of the *garde nationale* who was busy distributing money; a sinister-faced woman with red hair…

These misfits do not simply share the quality of being sinister, alien, 'different'; many of them are also disguised and secretive: 'other' than what they appear to be. Paradoxically, however, their sinister, conspiratorial significance is made patently clear through the over-coded, *clichéd* description which Blanc gives of their outward appearance, blowing their cover at the same time as he portrays it: could red-haired women, dark men with hollow eyes, and plebeians with fine linen, be anything but suspect?[18] Through this physical encoding of their role together with a number of references to the distribution of money and the exchange of pregnant comments, Blanc makes clear that this theatrical crew are working together as the paid agents of some faction. The precise identity of this cabal (Blanc suggests, among others, Monsieur working via Mirabeau) is perhaps less important than the existence of the plot as such: the presence of the plotters serves as a lightning rod in drawing the opprobrium of all violent deeds or violent intentions away from the crowd as a whole (of whom we are otherwise told nothing) and attributing them to a particular faction which, in fact, is secretly working against the *peuple*. The dissociation is multiple, then, in an all-hands-on-deck approach typical of these texts: the actors are defined by negatively valorised qualities, they look like aliens, they act for a particular faction, and they act as antagonists of the *peuple*.[19]

Thus, while Blanc and Michelet never explicitly deny the continuity between the female crowd of 5 October and the crowd of palace invaders, they not only refrain from making explicit any such connection, but they also represent the *foule* by figures whose membership of a particular faction is made clear, or by figures which are marked in their appearance and in their actions as untypical of the *peuple* as hitherto presented. If there were indeed women in the crowd, they are not made an effective element in the representation.

Nevertheless, after having suspended the *peuple*'s participation in the action, both writers go on to reintroduce the *peuple* into their narratives and identify it in each case with those who were active in opposing or

[18] In her study of different forms of redundancies in the *roman à thèse*, Suleiman describes how frequently cultural values are amalgamated with specifically ideological ones: e.g. a traitor (Jew, Communist) is 'ugly' (1983:188f). A similar 'technique of the amalgam' is used by Blanc in his representation of the conspirators on 6 October: it is by the fact that they are ugly, theatrical, unattractive, that the plotters can be recognised; and to a certain extent there is a sense that they are ugly and unattractive *because* they are conspirators.

[19] In the importance which is thus accorded to the existence of an undefined, and therefore ubiquitous, counter-revolutionary plot (and in this respect, the episode is typical of his history as a whole), Blanc's configuration of 5–6 October reflects a key element in the ideology of the Revolutionaries themselves. According to François Furet, the notion of 'conspiracy' played a central role throughout the Revolution in the conception, organisation, and interpretation of action: 'The idea was able to seduce both a religiously oriented moral conscience, accustomed to considering evil as the product of hidden forces, and a new democratic consciousness according to which the general, or national, will does not tolerate any public opposition from private interests...' (1978:91).

putting an end to the attacks on the palace: a pacific action *consistent* with the way in which the female crowd was defined in the first place.

Blanc and Michelet differ, however, in the figure they select to represent the *peuple* on this occasion. As Michelet describes the *peripeteia*, the dramatic turning point:

> La foule frappait, frappait, pour entrer dans l'Oeil-de-Boeuf. Les gardes s'y barricadaient; ils avaient entassé des bancs, des tabourets, d'autres meubles; le panneau d'en bas éclate... Ils n'attendent plus que la mort... Mais tout à coup le bruit cesse; une voix douce et forte dit: 'Ouvrez!' Comme ils n'ouvraient pas, la même voix répéta: 'Ouvrez donc, messieurs les gardes du corps, nous n'avons pas oublié que les vôtres nous sauvèrent à Fontenoy, nous autres gardes françaises.'
>
> C'étaient eux, gardes françaises et maintenant gardes nationaux, c'était le brave et généreux Hoche, alors simple sergent major. C'était le peuple qui venait sauver la noblesse. Ils ouvrirent, se jetèrent dans les bras les uns des autres en pleurant. (I:274)

> [The crowd was pounding, pounding on the doors to the *Oeil-de-Boeuf*. The guards had barricaded themselves in there; they had piled up seats, stools, and other pieces of furniture; the lower panel gives way... They prepare to face death... But suddenly, the noise stops; a gentle, strong voice says: 'Open up!' Since they did not respond, the same voice said again: 'Open up then, bodyguards, we have not forgotten that your men saved us, the *gardes françaises*, at Fontenoy.'
>
> It was they, the *gardes françaises*, now national guards. There was the brave and generous Hoche, as yet but a simple sergeant-major. There was the *peuple* come to save the nobility. They opened the doors and, weeping, threw themselves into each others' arms.]

The group of national guards (*ci-devant gardes françaises*) who rescue the king's bodyguards from the crowd are represented here by the figure of Hoche. Like the 'anachronistic' role of Marceau at the Bastille (above, pp.41f), Hoche's role here has obviously less to do with what he actually did as a 'simple sergeant-major' on 6 October 1789 than with the pre-coded significance of his famous name which functions as a proleptic sign or prefigurement of the future Republic, of the future of the Revolution under its glorious, military aspect. It is the great Revolutionary general-to-be in his present capacity as national guard whom Michelet *expressis verbis*, through his reiteration of the copula 'c'était', identifies as 'the *peuple*'. The presence of Hoche on this occasion and in these circumstances is thus constituted as a sign both of the virtual participation of the *peuple* as a whole and of the persistence of the heroic national tradition, which runs from the three Jeannes to the crowd of women and onwards to the future Republican armies.

For Blanc too, the incident is to be read as signifying the re-emergence of the *peuple* in the events of 6 October. The degree of overlap between the two accounts suggests their use of a common source, at the same time as it brings into relief the significant differences in the actual deployment of that source in their dramatic representation of the event. Whereas Michelet identifies the group of rescuers as national guards, Blanc leaves that bourgeois militia unmentioned in this context and instead simply identifies the men as grenadiers of the *gardes françaises*, referring to their leader (whom he leaves nameless), as a 'plebeian soldier':

> La porte retentit de coups redoublés, le panneau d'en bas est déjà brisé, c'en est fait... Mais voilà que soudain un profond silence succède au tumulte. On frappe doucement à la porte: 'Ouvrez, messieurs!' Les gardes hésitaient: 'Ouvrez donc! ou vous êtes morts!' Et Toulongeon rapporte que les mêmes voix ajoutèrent: 'Nous sommes les gardes françaises, et nous n'avons pas oublié que vous nous sauvâtes à Fontenoy.' Robert de Chevannes ouvrit: les assaillants avaient disparu, et les grenadiers remplissaient l'appartement. L'officier qui les commandait tendit la main à Robert de Chevannes, en lui disant: 'Soyons frères!' Le soldat plébéien échangea son bonnet militaire contre le chapeau du gentilhomme, on s'embrassa, des larmes coulèrent de tous les yeux: les gardes étaient sauvés. (I:402).
>
> [The door is shaking under the increasing intensity of the blows, the lower panel is already broken, their number is up... But suddenly the tumult gives way to a deep silence. Someone knocks gently on the door: 'Open up, sirs!' The guards hesitated: 'Open up, then! or you are dead men!' And Toulongeon reports how the same voices added: 'We are the *gardes françaises* and we have not forgotten that you saved us at Fontenoy'. Robert de Chevannes opened the door: the attackers had disappeared and grenadiers were filling up the room. Their commanding officer offered Robert de Chevannes his hand, saying: 'Let us be brothers!' The plebeian soldier exchanged his military bonnet for the gentleman's hat and, with tears flowing from every eye, they embraced: the guards were saved.]

Not only does Blanc suppress the particular identity of the rescuers as members of the national guard, he also marks the group by two signifying elements which together make up an isotopy of 'fraternity', the motto of the *sans-culotte* or post-1792 phase of the Revolution: 'let us be brothers', says the plebeian soldier, and exchanges his 'bonnet' for the hat of the gentleman soldier, to the universal joy of all the bystanders.[20] Like Hoche,

[20] It is interesting to note that the liberal Thiers, who also incorporates this scene into his narrative, specifically identifies the *gardes françaises* as 'belonging to Lafayette' (1865, I:80).

then, the 'plebeian soldier' both represents the *peuple* at this point in its history and prefigures its – specifically fraternal – future. The conjunction of these representative and prefigurative roles in both texts suggests that the re-emergence of the virtual agency of the *peuple* goes together with the re-emergence of the dominant, mainstream historical tradition (after a temporary deviation in the hands of marginals) as it is handed on from the past and heads towards the future.

Michelet and Blanc thus engage in a complex distribution of the different phases of the action of 5–6 October 1789 among the various actorial groups which they define in their texts: the 'negative' deeds involved in the attack on the palace are dissociated from the *peuple* (momentarily absent from the text) and attributed to marginals or factionaries, while the positively charged deeds are credited to the account of the narrative subject or *peuple* through a variety of discursive and symbolic relays. Whether it be in the alienation of negative actions or in the attribution of positive ones, the representation serves to conceal as well as to reveal: if Blanc attributes to the *peuple* the sublime fraternal gesture with which the combat was resolved, it is by letting the bourgeois national guard operate incognito in the narrative discourse, hidden under the general guise, as it were, of a bonnet-wearing 'plebeian soldier'. Indeterminacies and disjunctions, then, paradoxically provide the groundwork on which the conjunction of different actorial groups and the construction of a continuous, prevailing or predominant tradition is carried out.[21]

Inside out, or the part for the whole: the Champ de Mars, 17 July 1791

On the afternoon of Sunday, 17 July 1791, martial law was declared by the municipal authorities at the Hôtel de Ville in response, among other things, to the crowd's murder of the two men found in such suspicious circumstances under the Autel de la Patrie. The *garde nationale* led by Lafayette and Bailly, the mayor of Paris, converged upon the Champ de Mars and opened fire on the crowd of some 5,000 persons who, in the

[21] Through the use of the passive ('certain actions were done') or the indefinite *on*, certain negatively charged actions figure in the narrative in the absence of any particular actors: unclaimed symbolic baggage, as it were. Michelet, for example, describes the scene which took place at the Hôtel de Ville after the taking of the Bastille as follows: 'The pursuit of three *invalides*, believed to have been in charge of the cannon at the Bastille, was particularly relentless. One of them *had been* wounded; the commander de la Salle... managed to save him; as he was taking him outside, the others *were dragged way and hanged* from a street lamp' (my emphasis, I:160–1).

meantime, had gathered at the Autel de la Patrie in order to sign a petition calling for the suspension of the monarchy. While the number of casualties remains uncertain (anything between 13 and 50, according to Reinhard 1969:152), the event has traditionally become known as the 'Massacre du Champ de Mars'.

How was Michelet, whom we have seen extol the unanimity of the *peuple* in his 10 August, to portray this episode in the Revolution where the national guard massacres the crowd (*peuple*) which elsewhere it represents? Yet, how could Michelet avoid portraying this episode, given its canonical status as one of the core events in the pre-configured 'French Revolution'?

Michelet indeed follows the traditional outline of the massacre, at least to the extent that he describes how the crowd is (unjustly) attacked by forces sent from the Hôtel de Ville. But his representation of this event, as we shall see, goes together with a complex redefinition and reconfiguration of the significant actorial groups involved in the bloody affair and with a redistribution of the principal roles.

Blanc identifies women, children, and husbands among the crowd of petitioners gathered at the Champ de Mars, and refers to the group as a whole as 'a gathering of several thousand families' (I:729), who had respected all the legal requirements in organising their peaceful petition (I:728). Given the commonplace values generally associated with 'families', which we have already seen in Lamartine's account of 10 August, this is clearly Blanc's way of qualifying the crowd as non-aggressive, his way of identifying it as the locus of 'normality' and of positive values.[22]

Michelet too marks the crowd by its 'familiality'. But, unlike Blanc, he specifically notes the presence among the petitioners of members of the national guard: 'There was no one in this crowd who was armed, except for some national guards dressed in uniform and carrying their sabres; but most of them were accompanying their wives and had nothing threatening or suspect about them' (I:706). Again, in describing the actual petition, Michelet notes the frequency with which the title 'national guard' appeared after the signatures ('Many added to their name: *national guard* or *citizen soldier in the service of the fatherland*', I:703). In this way, the familial crowd in Michelet's narrative is doubly marked by national

[22] Peter Brooks has shown how the interrupted *fête* is one of the central structural devices in melodrama (1985:29). Blanc uses this device in his representation of 17 July, by insisting on the particularly festive nature of the gathering (I:729, 730), all the more to highlight the fact that the imposition of martial law against such innocent proceedings was both totally unexpected and totally unjustified.

guards, who were not only present among the crowd, but were also active in signing the petition which was the *raison-d'être* of the gathering.[23] The important point is not just that the peaceable crowd of citizens should be marked by the presence of national guards, but that the national guards themselves are also specifically marked by their conjugality or familiality (they literally figure together with their wives).

In Blanc's account, the (illegitimate) 'forces of order', who bear down on the peaceful, law-abiding crowd are represented by different companies of the national guard accompanied by a band of *perruquiers*. In Lamartine's account, the (legitimate) forces of order are represented by the national guard to whom he gives the title of 'national army' (I:145). This army is accompanied, moreover, by 'un peuple immense' (figuring in no other account), which functions as a sign of general, mass support for the campaign against the sedition of 'l'autre peuple' at the Champ de Mars (I:145); following a strategy which we have already encountered in Blanc's representation of the female crowd on 5 October, the '*de facto*' support given by this 'immense crowd' to the forces of law and order also serves to legitimise Lamartine's own representation of the crowd of petitioners as a lawless, seditious minority – 'the agitators' (I:145).

Michelet, for his part, distinguishes a number of different collective figures within the military force sent from the Hôtel de Ville, differences which are based initially on their spatial distribution at the Champ de Mars: the troops who entered by the Gros-Caillou, those who came by the bridge, and those who were posted next to the Ecole militaire. The first two groups, which made up the main body of the municipal forces, are defined, with the help of a variety of different arguments and a complex *découpage* or 'cutting out' of the personnel, as members of particular factions; but, above all, as royalists. 'Some' were ardent supporters of Lafayette; 'others' were fanatical royalists; there were 'more' officers than ordinary soldiers and 'almost all' the officers were 'chevaliers de Saint-Louis', that is to say, aristocrats; there were significant numbers of dragoons mixed in with the national guards ('and dragoons are well known for their royalism', he adds); finally, there was a band of hairdressers (and, as Michelet's reader already knows, *perruquiers* too signify royalism). To reinforce the predominance of royalists among the

[23] As he himself makes clear, Blanc relied on Michelet's text for information concerning the actual document of the petition (being in exile, he did not have access to the original, I:730). It is all the more significant, then, that in his representation of Michelet's account, Blanc should have eliminated the bourgeois national guards from participation in the crowd. (According to Reinhard, about one-third of the petitioners identified themselves as members of the national guard, 1969:152.)

troops even further, Michelet also manages, through a number of purely discursive relays starting from the *chevaliers de Saint-Louis*, to invoke the names (if not the presence) of both 'Lescure' and 'Henri de La Rochejaquelein', signs of the counter-revolution in the Vendée:

> Un journal assure qu'à cette époque ces chevaliers sont douze mille à Paris. Ces militaires se faisaient nommer sans difficulté officiers de la garde nationale: citons entre autres un Vendéen, ex-gouverneur de M. de Lescure; Henri de La Rochejaquelein le fut bientôt de même dans la garde constitutionnelle du Roi. (I:707–8)
>
> [A journal reports that there were twelve thousand of these *chevaliers* in Paris at that time. As military men, they had no problem in becoming officers in the national guard: among them, for example, was a Vendéen who had formerly been one of M. de Lescure's officers; Henri de La Rochejaquelein, likewise, was not long in getting a commission in the King's constitutional guard.]

For all the differences between them (dragoons, hairdressers, officers), every figure foregrounded among the national guards who approached from the Gros-Caillou and the bridge is marked as a counter-revolutionary royalist. Each segmentation of the group ('more', 'some', 'most') is carried out in such a way as to obscure the precise numerical proportion between these figures and the actorial group as a whole. As a result of all this, the 'national guard' is defined in the representation by its royalist, counter-revolutionary, aristocratic allegiances – which are not the attributes by which the national guard has hitherto been defined in Michelet's text. The men may have appeared in the uniform of the national guard, then, or under its auspices; but in fact, as Michelet's representation of them suggests, they were really, secretly something else. Of any typical or 'genuine' national guards who may have been among these crypto-royalists, we are told nothing.

The third, minority group of national guards posted at the Ecole militaire is dissociated in a number of ways from the main military body of 'national guards': first, by its peripheral physical position (it is out on a limb, as it were); secondly, by its composition (it is marked specifically by the presence of national guards from the famous *faubourg* of Saint-Antoine, whose conjunction with Saint-Marceau was to play such a strategic role in the revolution of 10 August, and whose name, therefore, signals the Revolutionary tradition rather than the 'counter-revolution' represented by the pseudo-national guards occupying the centre of the field); thirdly, and most importantly, by its non-participation in the actual massacre – indeed, by its active attempts to protect the innocent crowd (which in Michelet's account included some of their fellow national guards) and to defend this crowd against their enemies, the troops in the centre.

Blanc, too, mentions the humanitarian efforts of the national guards posted at the Ecole militaire in the course of narrating the actual outbreak of bloodshed; but in doing so, he presents this group as a minority within the national guard, whose action is simply eccentric or marginal *vis-à-vis* the main body of troops. In contrast, Michelet not only defines the troops on the periphery as representing the national guard and the Revolution, but he also manages to position this peripheral group at the very centre of his narrative representation of the event.

For, at this point, Michelet temporarily suspends his own role as retrospective narrator and relinquishes the privileged historical perspective which accompanies it. Taking advantage of the intertextual basis of his discourse, he hands over the actual narration of the bloody episode to an eye-witness. As it happens, however, this eye-witness/narrator is one of the national guards at the Ecole militaire who realises that he and his comrades have been misled into coming to the Champ de Mars by false reports of riot, and who watches with horror as the peaceful scene is suddenly and brutally transformed – by the others:

> 'Nous ne vîmes ni officiers municipaux ni drapeau rouge, et nous n'avions pas la moindre idée qu'il fût possible de proclamer la Loi martiale contre cette multitude inoffensive et désarmée, lorsque des clameurs se firent entendre et furent suivies aussitôt d'un grand feu prolongé. Des cris perçants, que ne purent étouffer ces détonations, nous apprirent que nous assistions non pas à une bataille, mais à un massacre... Des groupes d'hommes, de femmes, d'enfants, échappant à ce carnage, s'élancèrent vers nous, poursuivis par des cavaliers qui les chargeaient le sabre à la main. Nous ouvrîmes nos rangs pour protéger leur fuite, et leurs ennemis acharnés furent forcés de s'arrêter devant nos baïonnettes...' (I:710)

> ['We had seen neither municipal officers nor the red flag, and it seemed inconceivable that martial law could be proclaimed against this inoffensive, unarmed crowd, when suddenly we heard shouts, followed by intense, prolonged gunfire. From the heartrending cries which rose even above the gunfire, we realised that we were present, not at a battle, but at a massacre... Escaping from the carnage, groups of men, women, and children ran towards us, pursued by horsemen charging them with sabres in hand. We opened our ranks to protect them as they fled, and their relentless enemies were forced to halt before our bayonets...']

By handing over the narration of the event to one of the national guards at the Ecole militaire, who speaks in the name of his comrades ('we heard', 'we realised', etc.), Michelet's narration inflates the presence of this otherwise marginal group: the national guards are constituted both as the subject of the narrative action and as the subject of the narrative utterance. As testimonial source, as narrators, and as the subjects through which the events are focalised, the national guards at the Ecole militaire are endowed with a symbolic predominance with respect to all other groups which far exceeds either their numerical importance or their actual role in determining the outcome of events.

Moreover, in focalising the actual outburst of violence through a group which does not have any foreknowledge of what is to take place (unlike the historian and his public for whom 17 July at the Champ de Mars already means 'Massacre'), Michelet further underscores the dissociation between the royalist 'national guards' and the real national guards: in this case, the division runs between 'those who are in the know' and 'those who are not'. Like Blanc's narrative of 6 October, Michelet's narrative reveals and dramatises the operation of counter-revolutionary conspirators who have set up the situation for their own secret, factionary ends. (Seen now from this retrospective vantage point, the strange incident involving the *perruquier* and his companion ties in with the counter-revolutionary conspiratorial chain.) Whereas the event is unintelligible for the national guards at the Ecole militaire, through whom it is focalised and narrated, it was quite intelligible for the royalists who, as the historical narrator tells us, had inside information (I:707).[24]

Focalising the massacre through the national guards at the École militaire serves to counter or pre-empt any sense of a rift between the national guard and the familial crowd, by reaffirming the solidarity and continuity between those two groups. Not only are the national guards at the École militaire the horrified spectators of a massacre in which they do not participate, but it is even towards them that the people flee – or rather, as it is in the narration, 'towards us': 'we' protect them with 'our'

[24] The deliberate transfer of the role of narrator from historian to uninitiated eye-witness is all the more apparent since Michelet precedes it by a representation of himself and his reader *as* privileged witnesses, placed like the royalists, in a position dominating the whole:

> In order to understand what was going on, it was necessary to have a view of the whole scene. A number of royalists, apparently in the know, managed to get such a view...
>
> The American Morris, one of the palace intimates, climbed up to the heights of Chaillot. And it is from there that we also shall observe the scene; from this height, our view sweeps down and nothing can escape us; the Champ-de-Mars is at our feet.
>
> The curtain of troops there, right in the background, in front the *Ecole militaire*, that is the national guard from the districts of Saint-Antoine and the Marais. It is clear that Lafayette has little trust in them. (I:707)

bayonets and 'our' ranks are literally opened in a symbolic absorption of the children, women, and men (including presumably some fellow national guards), fleeing from the sabres of the other troops. In this way, the crowd and the (real) national guards are united in the narrative by their common opposition to the third party of the counter-revolutionaries, the faction from whose plots they themselves have collectively been excluded, and of whose plots they are both victims: the crowd having been literally massacred, the national guards having been deceived.

Michelet thus re-configures the 'Massacre du Champ de Mars' in such a way as to attribute responsibility for the bloody affair to the counter-revolutionary faction and, through his projection of an image of solidarity between the crowd and the bourgeois national guards, in such a way as to heal or symbolically compensate for any apparent rupture within the nation or the national tradition. This solidarity was perhaps all the more difficult for his readers in 1849 to imagine, and hence all the more important for Michelet to reconstruct symbolically, given the bloody events of the more recent past of June 1848.

Conclusion

Michel de Certeau suggests that traditionally one of the principal functions of historiography has been to carry out 'a symbolic social conjunction', by positing a common history shared by all members of society and linking them to previous generations: 'our history' (1982:24, 37). In the Introduction to this study, I outlined the importance for the post-Revolutionary historians of writing the history of 'men like ourselves'; whereas previous 'historians' had been merely concerned with the adventures of a few royal individuals, they themselves claimed to take 'the general life' or 'society' as their subject and to speak in its name.

The preceding analysis has shown how representing the events of the Revolution goes together with giving a figurative representation of the subject of 'our' history. In configuring the events of 1789–94 through the discursive means at their disposal, the historians establish certain collective and individual actors as the subjects of their narrative, and hence as representatives of the posited historical subject. These actors are constituted as the locus of the collective history at that particular moment and the vehicle for its 'tradition' to later generations (including presumably those generations situated after the final episode in the narrative and the public to whom the narrative is addressed).

In comparing the different works, I have brought out the complex narrative, discursive and representational strategies used by the historians in order to define the different actorial figures acting in the Revolution, and to connect up actors appearing at different points in the narrative syntagm. In doing so, I have shown the inevitably constructed, imaginary nature of the 'general life' which the historian claims to re-present across time; that the 'shared historical reality' does not so much pre-exist representation, as it is a product of the particular 'symbolic social conjunction' which the narrative configuration effects.[25]

But if my analysis has shown how the historians symbolically construct the social/historical subject they claim to re-present, it has also indicated some of the strategies which they use in order to invest their work with authority as a representation of the collective history. We have seen, for example, the importance of images of general consensus, where a group of actors is shown unanimously endorsing the leadership of a particular figure, embracing a common cause or course of action, or – as at the close of 10 August (Michelet), 6 October (Blanc, Michelet), and 17 July (Michelet) – embracing each other in a sign of concord, reconciliation, community. We have also seen the way in which the historian marks the foregrounded subjects of his narrative – even if these are minority figures (as in Lamartine) – with certain values presumed to be generally shared by his own public. These values serve to identify the narrative subject and his programme as the locus of the norm and, hence, as the representative in the past of the collective history with which the reader is to identify, and which he is presumed to have in common with his own contemporaries at large. In this way, we can see that the historical discourse does not only effect a symbolic conjunction between actors in the past, and between actors in the past and the contemporary reader; through its configuration of past events, it also gives an implicit representation of the contemporary 'general life' to which the reader is presumed to belong.

As the representations of 5–6 October and the Champ de Mars have illustrated, however, the symbolic conjunction of actors, past and present, goes together with the alienation or 'dissociation' of certain other actors, who are represented as marginals, minorities, eccentrics, factions (be these counter-revolutionaries, as in Michelet; counter-revolutionaries/bourgeois, as in Blanc; or the seditious, anarchic crowd, as in Lamartine). The activities of these actors do not accord with, and in many cases work against, the aims of the collective subject; their experiences and projects, therefore, do not belong to the mainstream of history, to 'our' history, although they may have actually had the power to direct the course of events.

[25] As representations/constructions of a shared social reality, these historical narratives are a particular form of what Claude Duchet, in his discussion of nineteenth-century realism, has called an 'écriture de la socialité' (1973).

4

The configuration of actors II

...it is only possible to play a great role in history if one is, what I have no hesitation in calling, a *representative man*... When nowadays opinion appears to be divided on the matter of proper names, what really divides it is the ideas, the aspirations, the tendencies, which those names represent.
Louis Blanc, *Le Temps*, 22 February 1866

Proper names and their symbolic function

Michelet may have proclaimed in the 1847 preface to his French Revolution that 'The principal actor was the *peuple*' (I:7), and described his own work as the first truly republican history, all previous histories having been essentially monarchic ones with either Louis XVI or Robespierre as king (II:991). But, like every other historian of the Revolution, he was dealing with a pre-configured *fabula* which included certain outstanding individuals: 'the great men'. These individuals occupied positions of political power and played a significant, if intermittent, role in the course of events – a role which becomes more and more prominent in the later episodes of the *fabula* as an ever-diminishing personnel engages in the power struggle leading to the final play-off of Thermidor.

'There was nothing about his features striking enough to arrest the gaze of someone scanning a large gathering; there was nothing written in physical letters about his completely interior power,' writes Lamartine of Robespierre as he appeared at Versailles in the early days of the National Assembly in 1789 (I:56). If Lamartine remarks at such length upon the inconspicuousness of the figure of Robespierre among the crowd of deputies in the National Assembly (no-one else noticed him at the time), it is in the anachronistic, historical light of the role which he is known to have played in the events of 1793 to 1794: as Lamartine adds, 'he was the last word of the Revolution, but nobody could decipher him' ('il était le dernier mot de la Révolution, mais personne ne pouvait le lire', I:56).

'The last word of the Revolution': Robespierre's name had become inextricably linked in the historical tradition to the events of 1793–4 or, more specifically, the *Terreur* (Furet 1978:96f). For Lamartine's readers, though not for the other deputies at Versailles in 1789, 'Robespierre' (like 'Mirabeau', 'Danton') is already a cultural unit, a 'word' which can be read, a 'name' in the sense of a 'reputation'. The unspectacular, unremarkable presence of Robespierre in the National Assembly in 1789 is historically, that is to say, anachronistically, of significance for the reader of Lamartine's text, for whom it already prefigures the final stages of the Revolution.

That Lamartine should foreground the figure of Robespierre in a context where his role is anything but prominent – indeed, where his insignificance is explicitly recognised – suggests that 'Robespierre's' profile in the representation is not always directly bound to the role he played in the particular action at hand. Even more importantly, it suggests that the earlier episodes of the Revolution are being re-represented, following the rewriting procedure which I discussed in my first chapter, in the light of the outcome which the name of Robespierre already invokes for the reader.

That Lamartine should explicitly describe the figure of 'Robespierre' as a sign-to-be-deciphered points to the paradoxical status of this name as both a proper name designating a particular, flesh-and-blood individual born in Arras in 1758, and a sign of a collective event – indeed perhaps the sign *par excellence* of that event in the historical culture. As we have already seen in the portraits of Louis XVI, individual figures allow for detailed figurative representation in a way that the anonymous masses do not. Yet, as the case of 'Robespierre' suggests, individual figures may also be the locus of a complex semiotic play as signs of a collective situation as a whole – or to use some of the terms encountered in the histories themselves: as summaries, concentrates, symbols, or personifications of a general situation.[1] If the flesh-and-blood Robespierre has now become a 'text' providing the key to the Revolution as a whole, it follows that any change in the composition of that text – in the definition of his reputation or the representation of his person – may also change the message which it relays to later generations concerning that event.

[1] Lamartine, for example, having praised the Convention for its ideals and criticised it for the way it attempted to bring these into practice, comments that 'Robespierre, more than any of his colleagues, personified these tendencies' (II:287). Blanc refers to Mirabeau's name as a summary of the situation in Provence: 'In Provence, one name sums up the disturbances...' (I:225). The lengthy historical survey of the origins of the Revolution which precedes his account of the Revolution as such, begins with an account of the Reformation, structured around the names of Huss (representing the unsuccessful spirit of fraternity) and Luther and Calvin (representing the successful spirit of individualism); in such cases, the individual name not only symbolises a collective event, but also the historical and ideological forces which underlay it.

Having considered in the previous chapter the various procedures used in the representation, definition, and diachronic conjunction of generally anonymous, *ad hoc* collective actors, I shall now adopt the opposite starting point and consider the symbolic function of those stable, or recurring points in the text, the 'big names' designating a fixed referent; in particular, those of 'Danton' and 'Robespierre'.

My decision to focus on these particular figures is based on their traditional symbolic importance: Robespierre, as a sign of the final phase and outcome of the Revolution; Danton as his opposite number (he not only played an important role as a leader, particularly in 1792; he was also one of the leaders who remained longest in the field, his death preceding Robespierre's by only four months). The three texts considered here differ in the amount and type of attention which they pay to individual figures (Lamartine's narrative is interspersed with multiple biographical sketches, with a particular focus, in the later sections, on the figure of Robespierre; Blanc's narrative tends to give Robespierre a foregrounded position throughout, while in Michelet's there is a greater tendency to foreground the role of collective actors). The three narratives also differ in the particular associations which they establish between various individual figures and between those figures and the *peuple*. Nevertheless, they have in common the fact of never forming any sustained alliance between Robespierre and Danton: although the two men may have worked together at certain stages in promoting the Revolution, the historians consistently define them in their difference from each other, even as incompatible, contrary terms, antonyms. As Michelet put it, the figures of 'Danton' and 'Robespierre' constituted the two poles of the Revolution: 'They were the two electrical poles, positive and negative, of the Revolution; together they created its balance' (II:480).

Personal records: Danton and Robespierre

The signing of events

Although neither Danton nor Robespierre took up a bayonet or a pike, nor actually participated directly in the insurrection of 10 August as members of the popular force, their names are inscribed in a number of different ways in the narrative representations of that event.

In the days preceding the insurrection, Michelet tells us, Sergent, Fréron, and Panis arranged for the Marseillais to be given quarters at the Cordeliers club, from where they could more easily approach the Tuileries in the event of the insurrection (I:759). 'Sergent', 'Fréron', and 'Panis'? The narrator simultaneously introduces and glosses these names, identifying the first two members of the trio as working 'under the influence' of their leader, Danton, and the third man as 'one of Robespierre's men'. Although there is only one Robespierre and only one Danton, then, there may be many 'Robespierristes' and many 'Dantonistes' in whose actions the name and influence, if not the person, of their leader are implicated.[2]

In Michelet's account, the general call to arms which rang out from all the church-towers in Paris on the eve of the insurrection was first rung at the Cordeliers in the very presence of Danton himself: 'From midnight onwards, the tocsin rang out from the Cordeliers, where Danton and the Marseillais were; subsequently it rang all over Paris' (I:962). Ten pages later, Danton again figures briefly *in propria persona* at an extremely strategic point in the narrative, immediately following the decisive moment when, the cannon having been removed from the Pont-Neuf, the conjunction of the two *faubourgs* was made possible: Danton, 'who until then had been at the Hôtel-de-Ville, calmly returned home ... The die was cast' (I:972).

The strategic recurrence of the name of 'Danton', as he figures in the narrative both directly *in propria persona* and indirectly *per procurationem*, serves to link his name firmly with the orchestration, if not the execution, of 'Le 10 août'. It was the 'avenging army of the *peuple*' which both conceived and executed the insurrection (and we have seen how Michelet insists on the popular impetus behind it); yet, if there was any name in particular to be associated with that popular movement – in a maieutic capacity, as it were – that name must be 'Danton'. At any rate, it was certainly *not* 'Robespierre', for he figures only once in the narrative and then he is shown to be opportunistically quiescent in the privacy of his own home, trying to manipulate events for his own dictatorial designs through his acolyte and agent, Panis (I:958–9).

In Blanc's account of the run-up to the insurrection, in contrast, it is the figure of Robespierre who plays the more prominent role. But this role is less a function of what he actually did in advancing the insurrection (even if he is shown to be active through his supporters or intermediaries) than of the degree of attention which is paid to him in the narrative discourse. By cross-cutting on a number of occasions to Robespierre as he privately ponders or publicly expresses his central concern (namely, the problem of

[2] One of the recurrent strategies used by Michelet to reduce the diversity of his personnel is simply to define an unknown or secondary figure in terms of the 'big name', under whose influence he is acting: e.g. 'The *département*, where Lhuillier (that is to say, Robespierre) had the greatest influence, passed a regulation ...' (II:357); 'three votes gained for Couthon and Saint-Just, that is to say, for Robespierre' (II:422).

how to ensure the full participation of *all* citizens in the future regime), Blanc simultaneously gives maximum presence to the man himself in the representation, accords him a consultative role as an ideologist or commentator on the political implications of the imminent change of regime and, through direct quotation, brings into relief his political agenda, which then serves as a touchstone against which the outcome of the insurrection will be measured. (Blanc himself goes on to close his account of 10 August with a question which echoes the concerns of Robespierre: 'But by whom was insurgent Paris to be represented in government?' (II:174)). Whereas the figure of Robespierre is, in this way, given a high narrative profile despite his relative inaction as regards the event as such, 'Danton' figures only once in Blanc's account of the run-up to the insurrection (where his energy and his ambition are brought to the fore) and once again, at the very end of the chapter on the insurrection where, in a new version of *Le roi est mort! Vive le roi*, we are told that 'Danton was minister, Louis XVI was suspended' (II:174).

Although Robespierre and Danton are by no means central figures in the actual events represented in each text, narrating 'Le 10 août' is nevertheless inseparable from marking out the nature of their involvement and/or their ideological position *vis-à-vis* what happened. In each account, the brief appearances of 'Robespierre' and 'Danton', whether at the level of the discourse or at the level of the events represented, make up a thin but persistent narrative thread or subtext which runs concurrently with the larger collective movement (Blanc's Danton was ambitious and became a minister; Michelet's Danton was present at the ringing of the tocsin and only left when victory was assured).

In each of these subtexts, one of the 'big names' is privileged over the other through the amount of attention paid to him in the discourse and through the role which he plays in the represented action, by deed and – what in many instances is as important – by word. For the foregrounded figure is associated in both cases with the will or programme of the collective subject, which is also the programme that is explicitly or implicitly endorsed by the narrator. Thus, Michelet's recurrent, strategic references to Danton suggest that the latter's concerns were identical with those of the *peuple* who initiated and executed the insurrection: given the huge symbolic value of 'Le 10 août' as the birth of the nation in Michelet's account, Danton's maieutic role is clearly a positive one. Blanc's Robespierre occupies a similarly valorised position in being defined by his overriding concern with bringing into being a new popular *régime*, though his role is less as an activist than as a watchdog for the people's interest: the fact that the (opportunist) Danton should come to power through the insurrection is clearly not something to which the people's watchdog (or Louis Blanc) could subscribe. 'The people's midwife' versus 'the opportunist Robespierre'; 'the people's watchdog' versus 'the opportunist Danton': the value of the position occupied by the principal figure as a representative of the *peuple* is thus brought into relief by the negatively valorised role played by the other, antagonist figure who is motivated by personal ambition. While Michelet's Danton works together with the people and his Robespierre seeks to profit personally from the situation, in Blanc's account the roles are reversed: Danton's personal ambitions not only highlight Robespierre's devotion to the people's cause, but to the extent that they seem to threaten the political achievements of the people, they also justify his vigilance.

The assignment of roles

August-September 1792

Whereas the *ad hoc* collection of women who went to Versailles on 5 October 1789 never appear directly again in the narrative, Danton and Robespierre figure on many, many occasions and, for this reason, can play an important anaphoric role in linking up the different stages of the Revolution and in marking out its trajectory. Through the way in which their names are inscribed in the different episodes of the *fabula*, 'Danton' and 'Robespierre' accumulate a record or reputation which provides the background against which their role in any new episode will be situated. Since 'Robespierre' and 'Danton' are already cultural units, however, the inscribing of their names in the different episodes is to a certain extent predetermined: any definition of 'Danton' and 'Robespierre' is a re-definition, meeting the resistance either of their legend or of their ill-repute.

The period between 10 August and the battle of Valmy, 22 September 1792, was marked by two events whose value – negative in one case, positive in the other – no historian disputes: the 'September' prison massacres (with which the names of Marat and the Commune are unanimously associated) and the great mobilisation of the national war effort in face of the foreign invasion (a patriotic movement epitomised in Danton's famous 'Il nous faut de l'audace' ('we need to be daring') speech of 2 September). How do Blanc and Michelet locate 'Robespierre' and 'Danton' *vis-à-vis* these two events?

Blanc portrays Danton as having condoned and promoted the massacres by permitting Marat to go ahead with his preparations (he even gives a dramatic presentation of a private conversation in which Danton explicitly argues for their political necessity, II:192). Michelet's Danton, in contrast, figures in isolation from the Commune and Marat, and he is presented as actually resisting their attempts to foment popular anger and direct it against the prisoners taken on 10 August and its aftermath: Danton expresses the need (both *in propria persona* (I:1005, 1011) and through the mediation of his acolyte Lacroix (I:1007, 1013)) for organising tribunals which, while respecting the people's grievances and appeasing the demands of the Commune for action against the prisoners, would nevertheless ensure that justice and not vengeance was administered. Whereas Blanc's Danton actively supported the massacres for his own ends, then, Michelet's Danton not only abstained from promoting the massacres, but actively opposed them.

Yet, Michelet is not content simply to clear Danton's name of all complicity with Marat; he also goes elaborately out of his way to discredit Robespierre, by foregrounding the latter's membership of the notorious Commune of 10 August. According to Michelet, this body was composed of a number of different groups, but was dominated above all by second-rate, narrow-minded 'scribes':

> Du 11 août au 2 septembre, elle appela dans son sein le scribe des scribes, le fol des fols, Marat, Robespierre. Tous deux sortirent de leurs trous et siégèrent à la Commune. (I:1003)
>
> [From 11 August to 2 September, it took into its fold the scribe of scribes, the madman of the mad: Marat, Robespierre. The two of them emerged from their dens and took their seats in the Commune.]

That Robespierre's association with the Commune is more than that of an ordinary member-at-large is suggested by the fact that he joins the Commune in the company of Marat (having emerged, like Marat, from some lair or hideout), and by the fact that (again like Marat) he exemplifies in a superlative manner the qualities by which the Commune as a whole is dominated and defined. In this way, through the mediation of the narrative discourse in which his name is woven together with that of Marat and with the other 'scribes', Robespierre's membership of the Commune and his association with Marat are not only foregrounded, but overdetermined. Although Robespierre may not be directly involved in instigating the massacres which began on 2 September, his name remains firmly allied in the representation with that of *l'ami du peuple* and, through him, to the prison massacres. (The basis of this hybrid alliance, Michelet suggests, was Robespierre's readiness to profit from the actions of the 'exterminator' Marat for his persistent dictatorial designs, I:1050.)

Blanc does not deny the fact that Robespierre was a member of the Commune at this time. But he does go out of his way to break down

Robespierre's apparent association with Marat and the massacres by presenting the Commune itself as a heterogeneous body, 'subject to two opposing influences, alternately inspired by Robespierre and inflamed by Marat' (II:179; recalled II:191). Far from being Marat's accomplice, then, Robespierre opposes him from within the Commune (II:191), attempts to regularise the administration of justice by instituting popular courts, and deplores the massacres, although only – and here Blanc criticises him – in private (II:205).

The result of all these complicated re-drawings of the actorial alliances is that Blanc firmly links up 'Danton' with 'Marat' while explicitly disconnecting 'Robespierre' from this pair and setting him up as their antagonist. Following a parallel procedure, Michelet firmly links up 'Robespierre' with 'Marat', while explicitly disconnecting 'Danton' from this pair and setting him up as their antagonist. Throughout these re-configurations, 'Marat', of course, remains a constant value: sign of revolutionary fanaticism. In each account, then, one figure in particular is foregrounded as the advocate of organised, popular justice, who unsuccessfully attempts to maintain the direction of a revolutionary situation which is being precipitated towards violence, anarchy, and a dictatorship by an amalgam of the 'others' (Marat and Robespierre in Michelet, Marat and Danton in Blanc).

I turn now to that other, 'positive' event which marked the early days of September 1792: the mobilisation of the war effort. The honour of having inspired this great patriotic effort is reserved in Michelet's representation for the figure of Danton, whom he portrays in an extensive *mise en spectacle* in the act of exhorting the women in the street, his colossal figure becoming transfigured as he ends up weeping patriotic tears together with his public: the very image of his solidarity with them (I:1024–5).

To have denied Danton a prominent role in the mobilisation of the *patrie* would have been to violate the historical tradition which has associated his name with that undisputably heroic moment. And so Blanc does not deny Danton's role (his famous 'audace' speech is duly quoted, II:193); but he does present Danton's action as neither unique nor decisive, as having been simply part, rather, of a far larger movement in which the Assembly (II:184) *and* the Commune (II:193) also played decisive roles. Now, if the Commune was subject to two opposing influences, and if it was the influence of Marat which gave rise to the 'furious' initiatives taken by the Commune (II:183), it follows from the logic of Blanc's representation that it must have been the beneficial influence of Robespierre which inspired the forceful, efficient measures taken by the Commune in response to the foreign invasion.

In both texts, then, the figure who opposes the violence is also more or less directly associated with the undisputed patriotic achievements of the same period: by virtue of being brought together in one single figurehead, the role of 'patriot' becomes amalgamated with that of 'antagonist of violence' and 'antagonist of dictators'. Concentrating these positively valorised roles in a single figure is inseparable from attempting to clear his name of those negatively charged deeds which would not stand to his credit or which would cast a shadow on his achievements. This schematising distribution of positive and negative deeds can be seen as an indication of the historian's attempt to reduce the 'ambivalence' of the Revolution by disengaging its positive features from the negative elements which accompanied it; its achievements from its accompanying shadow. Thus, although Danton may have appeared to be working with the Commune, he was in fact seeking to oppose Marat (Michelet); although Robespierre was part of the Commune, he was not in fact working with Marat (Blanc). As it happens, moreover, Michelet's cleansing Danton of the blood of September goes together with his transferring some of the taint to the name of Robespierre: 'if you are going to blame anyone in particular besides Marat and the extremists in the Commune, then blame Robespierre rather than Danton'. In this way, following a counter-representational procedure similar to those I examined in chapter 2, what is potentially the 'ill-repute' of Danton is taken into account by the representation, only to be displaced onto the scapegoat figure of Robespierre.[3]

The negatively and positively valorised positions occupied by the two figures in each account of September form a direct continuation of the positions which they also occupied in the run-up to the insurrection of 10

[3] Michelet suggests, moreover, that if Danton failed in his attempts to direct the situation, it was because of the Assembly's mistrust and misconception of him as 'a man of the Commune' (I:1049) – a misconception which Michelet's text *a posteriori* is clearly trying to rectify. In his *mise en spectacle* of Danton's exhortation to the women in September 1792, he invokes the commonplace image of the Revolution as 'volcanic eruption', while transposing it to the particular figure of Danton: 'And on this strange face, ravaged by smallpox and resembling the scorias of Vesuvius or Etna, great drops of water began to appear, and these were tears...' (I:1025). A volcano which brings forth tears rather than lava: in this way, Michelet's representation of the event acknowledges and, at the same time, transforms the false image of Danton as a man of violence and accomplice of the Commune. By extension, the same transformation is performed on the commonplace, but false, image of the Revolution as a destructive eruption of violence.

August: Blanc's Robespierre and Michelet's Danton, who are portrayed in September as attempting to steer the Revolution forward into its next phase, were also shown playing this role in August (the concern of Blanc's Robespierre in August was how to ensure a genuinely popular form of government in the new regime, one of his principal concerns in September is how to organise popular courts for the administration of justice).[4]

The continuity between the two episodes not only illustrates the anaphoric function of proper names in linking up different episodes; but it also shows how the *repeated* valorisation of a particular actor can serve to establish his position as an authority or reference point in the text and (what is linked to this) to create a certain predictability as to his role in subsequent episodes. The particular roles repeatedly ascribed to Danton and Robespierre in the two accounts also suggest that the 'tradition' of the Revolution can be read through, can be seen as represented by, the personal career of 'Robespierre' (in Blanc) and 'Danton' (in Michelet): the defenders of the Revolutionary achievements and heralds of its future, whose programmes and hopes provide the ground against which any new occurrences are to be evaluated.[5]

[4] A similar configuration of the roles of Robespierre and Danton is also to be found in Lamartine (whose negative account of 10 August we have seen in chapter 2). On the one hand, Lamartine insists on Danton's role as instigator and accomplice of the insurrection: 'Having conceived the plan and set it in motion, he handed over the execution of it to the men of violence, abandoning the fate of his idea to the energy or cowardice of the *peuple*' (I:602). On the other hand, he insists on Robespierre's non-participation in the insurrection and on the fact that he would have been content with the Constitution of 1791 if this had been properly brought into effect (I:559). In his account of September, Lamartine attributes the impulsion behind the massacres to Danton (I:683, 687), while, in a scenic representation of a conversation with Saint-Just, he presents Robespierre's horror at the massacres which he did not have the power to prevent (I:688–9).

[5] The privileged figure may not only provide a point of view from which events are regularly approached and assessed; but he is often also endowed with 'foresight' or prescience with respect to later developments in the Revolution or to those which were to follow it (see Blanc on Robespierre, II:68, and Michelet on Danton, I:1011). The fact of having superior insight into current and future developments shows the figure to be capable of initiating and anticipating changes, and endows him with a certain 'historiographical' authority which allies him with the historian who retrospectively shares his knowledge. Michelet makes this connection explicit in describing Danton's actions in the winter of 1792–3: 'Danton did not know much about the past. His genius made up for this lack: he felt, he penetrated things, and the whole of history lay within him. We have no doubt but that, at this time, he had already scented the Vendée' (II:161).

Revolutionary careers

The assignment of roles and the distribution of symbolic property in the representations of August-September 1792 are typical of the two narratives as a whole: on the one hand, the procedures of amalgamation, concentration, and transference provide a model of those used in the later episodes; on the other hand, the particular roles played by Michelet's Danton and by Blanc's Robespierre in September provide an index to their roles in the events of 1793 and 1794 – which I can only schematically outline here.

Blanc's Robespierre, who sought in 1792 to ensure the full participation of all citizens in government, subsequently figures in the narrative in association with specific institutional reforms and with projects for future changes which are explicitly endorsed by the narrator: his proposal for popular education (II:568f), for example, or his draft constitution of 1793, which is presented as being ahead of its time in its concern that the right to enjoy property be limited by the right of others to life and liberty (II:452–3).

On the other hand, Blanc's Robespierre is also shown as engaged in an ongoing struggle to steer a precarious course for the Revolution between the Scylla of the Terrorists and the Charybdis of the counter-revolutionaries (an amalgam of reactionaries, royalists, and in the end 'indulgents' like Desmoulins and Danton). Blanc claims, for example, that it was not Robespierre, but other elements within the *Comité de salut public* who were responsible for organising the *Terreur* (II:519); that Robespierre's signature is not to be found on some of the most controversial decrees (II:648); that through Saint-Just and Couthon, Robespierre attempted to control the excesses in Strasbourg and Lyon, and was personally responsible for recalling the infamous Carrier from Nantes; that he openly or privately opposed certain moves (II:566, 721, 733, 736); that in the privacy of his home, he grieved for those whom he had been forced, by political necessity and his commitment to the Revolution, to sacrifice (II:708, 722). In Blanc's representation, then, Robespierre struggles against the *Terreur*, while the 'real' Terrorists are the 'others' – a position which is occupied by various figures at different stages, from the Girondins (who first introduced the ominous concept of 'Suspects', II:404) to the 'Thermidoreans' (who unleashed an intensified *Terreur* as soon as they had succeeded in removing the moderating influence of Robespierre).[6] The very number as well as the heterogeneity

[6] II:646f. In Michelet's account, Robespierre, as the symbolic *maître en titre* of the Revolution, plays the role of Danton's antagonist. In Blanc's account, the

of the arguments used to dissociate Robespierre's name from the *Terreur* is a measure both of the resistance which Robespierre's reputation opposes to such a reading, and of the nearly obsessive extent to which this particular narrator is committed to remaking Robespierre's name in his re-presentation of the events.

Michelet's 'Danton', who had sought to keep the violent elements in the Commune in check in 1792, while at the same time furthering the Revolution and 'saving the *Patrie*', figures in 1794 as the spearhead – or rather, the nominal figurehead – of the movement to halt the *Terreur* which is kept inexorably in motion by the dictatorial Robespierre. As he did in 1792, Danton acts as a spokesman for the national groundswell, which is now clamouring for an end to the killing. He dares to speak of 'mercy', and makes a tentative move towards ousting the Jacobins from power (II:775–6). Most importantly, Danton's name is linked by proxy with the movement to inaugurate a new reign of clemency which was manifested in Camille Desmoulins' articles in the *Vieux Cordelier* (II:761). Yet, if Danton's name is thus directly and indirectly associated in the representation with the general will to bring the Revolution forward out of the *Terreur* and the Jacobin dictatorship, Michelet admits that the actual performance of the man himself reflected his personal failure to confront the situation and to persist in his programme for clemency in face of the power of Robespierre. The fact that Michelet, despite Danton's relative inaction, should nevertheless make him the figurehead of the movement for clemency points to the *symbolic* value which the name 'Danton' has acquired within the narrative. In the end, as Michelet puts it, 'the Dantonists were more audacious than Danton' (II:728), while the *ci-devant* 'audacious' Danton has himself become 'robespierrised':

> La Convention, étonnée, vit, le 26 novembre, un nouveau Danton, robespierrisé, qui parlait de l'*Etre suprême*... Au milieu, toutefois, de ce discours, sa nature perçant les mensonges, il ouvrit son coeur, parla de *clémence*...(II:664)
>
> [On 26 November, the Convention was astonished to see a new, robespierrised Danton, talking of the Supreme Being... In the middle of his speech, however, his own nature penetrated through the lies and, opening his heart, he spoke of *clemency*...]

If 'Robespierre' is the 'last word' of the Revolution, to recall Lamartine's phrase, we can see now the great lengths to which Blanc and Michelet have gone in order to rewrite that last word in such a way as to dissociate the Revolution from the *Terreur*. Michelet brings into relief the essential

'antagonist'/scapegoat role is occupied by a variety of different figures, Danton being but one of them.

difference between the Revolution as such and the figure of Robespierre by associating the actual, above all patriotic, achievements of the Revolution with the figure of Danton (leaving the *Terreur* to Robespierre), and by establishing the same 'Danton' as the symbolic figurehead of the movement towards 'indulgence'. For his part, Blanc rewrites Robespierre's personal record so that it is 'the others' who were responsible for the *Terreur*, while the *Incorruptible* from Arras signifies – or, what would seem a more accurate term in this case, 'personifies' – the Revolutionary tradition, its institutional achievements, and its aspirations for the future. By opting to pursue his narrative beyond Thermidor to Vendémiaire, moreover, Blanc underscores the continuity in the *Terreur* before and after the 'denouement', as he explicitly terms Robespierre's death.[7]

In both histories, the defeat and death of the valorised figure is explicitly presented as representing the premature, abortive end of the Revolution – though in neither case does this symbolic death of the Revolution coincide with the end of the historical narrative. 'He had been ... the life of the Revolution, the heart of the Republic, and it died with him,' writes Michelet in his account of the execution of Danton (II:808): since losing out to Robespierre also meant losing out to the counter-revolution, Danton's death represents the end of the Revolution itself and of the power of the collective spirit which had engendered it. In a similar way, although with somewhat different timing, the defeat and death of Blanc's Robespierre at the hands of the Thermidoreans represents the end of the Revolution and the victory of the counter-revolution which he had long been struggling to keep at bay; although Blanc's narrative of the history of the Revolution is to continue on for another 250 pages, Robespierre's death is again presented as the last word of the Revolution itself: 'Le couperet s'abaissa et, pour longtemps, tout fut dit' ('The blade dropped down and, for a long time, there was nothing more to say,' III:33).

[7] Lamartine also rewrites Robespierre's name, but in a somewhat different way: by disengaging his *ideals* from his implication in the *Terreur*, which is not denied. Robespierre's ideals had opened up 'perspectives for human happiness' (II:289): he combined a concern for the underprivileged with a respect for property, the family, and religion (II:281); he dreamt of the 'calm and regular reign of the *peuple* personified in its representatives' (II:469); and, it is implied, he inspired the great institutional achievements of the Revolution (II:835–6). The impetus towards the *Terreur*, the desire for bloodshed, came from the revolutionary masses themselves, aided and abetted, for their own ends, by figures like Danton ('Being without any fixed principles, he only loved democracy for its turbulence,' I:156). But the idealist Robespierre became fatally implicated in the *Terreur*: he wanted to go too far, too fast, and made the mistake of believing that he could achieve his democratic goals by giving in to the people's will: 'He wooed the *peuple* by appealing to its ignoble parts' (II:921); the *Terreur* 'was assassination put on as a spectacle for the pleasure of an entire people' (II:786).

In spite of their failure to achieve their aims, indeed because of their very failure, the careers of Danton (Michelet) and Robespierre (Blanc) become a sign of what the Revolution *might have* become had it been allowed to develop freely: 'If Danton (or Robespierre) had had his way...' The symbolic investment of these figures as representatives of the Revolution thus serves to mark out an alternative programme of events against the background of what actually happened – a programme which was only partially fulfilled or realised, but which embodied the authentic essence of the Revolution (on the one hand, the coming to power of the national spirit of France with its natural sense of justice and law; on the other hand, the movement from bourgeois individualism to a fraternal regime with the active participation of all people). This bringing into relief of the essence of the Revolution against the background of the actual events of 1789–94 is something which we have already encountered, from a different perspective, in the representations of 10 August.

Danton's role both as a sign of the actual Revolution's failure (he is defeated) and as a sign of the Revolution as an idea or programme (what he actually realised, what he wanted to realise) is not merely written into the narrative structure of Michelet's account. It is also reiterated and made explicit at the level of the discourse, where Danton's name is invoked as an allegory of the denaturing of the nascent Revolution. A close study of Danton's character, writes Michelet, has authorised him to assert that Danton's sole desire was to be himself: 'Danton wanted nothing more than to be Danton, that is to say, to exercise the great force that was in him' (I:1283). One of the principal reasons for his failure to save the Revolution was the fact that the bourgeois Girondins misunderstood his nature and refused to trust him; they should have allowed him 'to be and to appear in accordance with what his nature and his politics demanded he be' (I:1201). Danton, however, was not allowed to *be* Danton: 'il lui était impossible de mettre d'accord Danton et Danton' ('he found it impossible to reconcile Danton with Danton', I:1289). And, like the Revolution itself, he became 'robespierrised'.

Personal effects

The persons

In the Introduction, I showed the importance for the early nineteenth-century historians of vividly representing men like ourselves, of providing what Barante called 'that intimate knowledge which comes from seeing and hearing living beings' (above, p.2). As Carlyle summed up this poetics in his 1838 essay on Walter Scott, one of the goals of the history-writer must be to show that former ages were not just filled by protocols, state papers, controversies, but by 'living men': 'men, in buff or other coats and breeches, with colour in their cheeks, with passions in their stomach, and the idioms, features and vitalities of very men' (1895, VI:71–2). As we have already seen with respect to the various portraits of the king on 10 August, the description of 'living men' in their ethical and physical aspects, and in their social and physical settings, provides an important, ongoing supplement to the narrative discourse. Danton and Robespierre, like Louis XVI, do not figure in the narrative as mere names or merely in their actorial capacity with respect to the historical action or as agents of certain socio-historical forces. As individuals, they may in addition be presented in their private capacity; and their persons may be described either through brief qualifying descriptions or through extended portraits, which can be freely located in the narrative discourse. What are the particular personal qualities associated with 'Robespierre' and 'Danton' in the three narratives? And how do these personal qualities relate to their historical role?

Michelet writes that Danton, in the months preceding his final defeat in 1794, would withdraw as often as possible to his house in the country: 'The people of Arcis recall how, during his stays in the country, they used to see him standing for hours at the window with his nightcap on, without moving, lost in thought' (II:774–5). Blanc, on the other hand, relates how Robespierre, in the days preceding Thermidor, took long, solitary walks ('promenades solitaires') through the Marbeuf gardens or to the forest of Montmorency and Rousseau's Ermitage (III:57).[8] Similarly, Lamartine relates how Robespierre would go off to the woods of Meudon, Saint-Cloud or Viroflay and how, on 7 Thermidor, he spent the whole day in meditation at the Ermitage (like Danton at the window): 'It is said that he used to spend hours on end, his head in his hands, leaning against the rustic fence which enclosed the little garden.'[9]

[8] The setting or company in which a particular figure is situated serves an important function in marking the figure: Blanc's Robespierre is not merely set in the landscape, but he is accompanied by his faithful dog and, occasionally, stops to listen to the *petits savoyards* (connoting 'childlike innocence') as they sing their songs from the mountains (reiterating the seme of 'nature'). Again: Lamartine portrays Madame Roland in prison, weeping over the potted plants she had had installed in her cell (II:633); and the first edition of his work includes an advertisement for a proposed illustrated edition, which takes the form of a group portrait in which Robespierre is shown holding a bunch of flowers (1847, I).

[9] II:870. The significance of Robespierre's retreat to the Ermitage is heightened by the intertextual models which Lamartine brings into play in relating it: on the one hand, the model of Rousseau himself and his solitary walks and, on the other

These representations of the Revolutionary leaders in their intimate, meditative moments, against the background of a natural setting, must be counted among the strategies used by the historians to remove the 'barrier of horror' surrounding the Revolution; as part of what the legitimist Nettement saw as the attempt to present the revolutionaries as 'men' rather than as the unnatural 'monsters' he considered them to be (1848:587). The fact that the individual, pensive figure is portrayed in a landscape (or contemplating one) patently associates him with 'Nature', and indicates his distance – physical and moral – from the violence which is associated above all with the city. Since 'Nature' is the Romantic location *par excellence* for sentimental moments, the actor's being in nature signifies further his native capacity for feeling. The solitary presence of the particular actor in a landscape is used, then, to make manifest his interior dimension, his naturalness, and his capacity for suffering – to which the reader is made a privileged, and presumably compassionate, witness. (Robespierre is alone at the Ermitage, Danton stands alone at the window, neither knowing that he is being watched and hence neither of them playing to a public.)

The manner in which Danton or Robespierre is represented in each case suggests that the figure of the unique, suffering subject is produced from a combination of historical fact (Robespierre went for solitary walks) and the invocation of certain cultural commonplaces of the early nineteenth century which invest those facts with a particular meaning: the significance of a 'solitary *rêveur*' is independent of the fact whether the individual in question is called Robespierre or Danton. The comparison of the different texts suggests that both Robespierre and Danton engaged in some such private meditation. As it happens, however, Danton is not seen in solitary reverie in the histories of Blanc and Lamartine;[10] nor do Robespierre's 'promenades solitaires' figure as such in Michelet. Though the latter does relate how Robespierre regularly went out walking, his account downplays the naturalness of the setting (the parks are mentioned by name only and

hand, the model of Christ, with the Ermitage as another Gethsemane. Lamartine frequently invokes the Christian analogy in his portrayal of Robespierre: on 10 Thermidor, for example, as Robespierre lay wounded at the Convention, a cup of vinegar and a sponge were set out beside him (II:917); the analogy of Christ's passion is also one which he uses lavishly in describing the trial and death of Louis XVI, above, p.54). It is worth recalling how Michelet's portrait of Louis XVI with his flattened wig and vacant eyes uses the Gethsemane intertext so as to show instead the king's non-conformity to the heroic model (above, p.98).

[10] Blanc does refer indirectly to Danton's frequent retreats to the countryside in the final months of his life; but he presents the love 'for flowers and trees' with which Danton justified his frequent absences as a mere excuse: the true reason for his retreats to the country lay simply in his fatigue and lack of staying power (II:703).

references are made to shops, buildings, encounters); moreover, it stresses Robespierre's relentless need for movement and work (the very opposite of a *rêveur*), and his relentless playing of the role of Rousseau.[11] Thus, rather than give us an intimate glimpse of the man himself (or, as Michelet puts it, 'Catch out this pale character doing something human, in a state resembling happiness'), his frenetic daily walks only reinforce his impenetrability for the onlooker: 'No other relaxation. A closed, sombre interior' (II:885).

Michelet's contrastive application of the *topos* of the solitary leader, his contrasting presentation of Danton and Robespierre in their private moments, points to the fact that the personal attributes of the individual actors may be defined, not on their own terms, but in relation to, or in their significant difference from, the other figures in the narrative.

Personal properties

Robespierre's sartorial sense

The legend defining the names of Danton and Robespierre is not limited to their personal records, but is also made up of the cluster of commonplaces which, through the historiographical and iconographical traditions, have come to mark their persons. Whereas both Robespierre and Danton may potentially be set down in a landscape or represented in their private moments, Danton's enormous stature and booming voice are his personal property, are part of the 'Danton-effect', and cannot be simply transferred to the pale, thin, intense Robespierre.[12] But even though Robespierre can never change his size or become expansive without ceasing to be recognisable as 'Robespierre', neither the relative importance nor the significance of his distinguishing features (or those of Danton) is fixed once and for all; even within the constraints imposed by

[11] Michelet also dismisses the 'novelistic stories' concerning the time spent by Robespierre 'meditating upon nature' at the Ermitage in the days preceding Thermidor; he went there to work, Michelet claims, Penelope-like writing and rewriting his final speech: 'He took it with him to the country, shut himself up in a safe place, and became lost in his literary work, erasing and remaking, polishing, refining, and elaborating his sentences' (II:938–9).

[12] Within the limits of the *vraisemblable* an attempt may be made, however, either to neutralise Danton's potential attractions or to transfer them to Robespierre (following a procedure parallel to the one which we have already considered at the level of the assignment of deeds). In his biography of Robespierre, Rudé points out two different portraits of the *Incorruptible*: one is in profile and accentuates the angular harsh features of his face, while the other is, he suggests, 'Dantonised' – it is frontal rather then in profile, the lines are softened, the lips are curling, and the face fleshed out (1975: opposite p. 41).

the actor's physical and intellectual trademarks, his distinguishing features may undergo rewriting and re-valuation within the economy of each representation.

Danton's clothes apparently do not belong to the set of commonplaces associated with his name in the historical tradition, since none of the writers remarks upon his dress sense. But all writers are agreed that one of Robespierre's hallmarks was his dress; as Lamartine put it, his clothes were his 'drapeau vivant' or 'living flag' (II:873), for he was always dressed with care and always in the same, old-fashioned or *ancien régime* way. In their description of Robespierre's costume, each writer takes into account, somewhere along the way, its three distinguishing features (care, style, consistency); but foregrounds one or other of these and invests it with a particular semantic value.

Characterising it above all by its 'sobriety' and 'decency', Blanc introduces Robespierre's costume in relating the latter's opposition to the fashion of the *bonnet rouge* promoted by the Girondins:

> Sa tenue décente annonça toujours qu'il se respectait lui-même; et dans son langage ... jamais il ne sacrifia le fond au luxe de la forme ... Il pensait que la liberté doit avoir des moeurs simples, des allures dignes, et se montrer sobre dans l'adoption d'emblèmes qui ne servent trop souvent qu'à dissimuler l'idée quand ils n'en tiennent pas lieu ... Il se défiait, en véritable observateur qu'il était, de cette impétueuse tendance à se contenter des dehors. (II:85)
>
> [His decent appearance already announced that this was a man with self-respect; and in his use of language ... he never sacrificed substance to the pleasures of form ... He believed that liberty should always have simple manners and a dignified air, and should be restrained in adopting emblems which too often only serve to conceal an idea or even to take its place ... True observer that he was, he mistrusted any impetuous tendency to be satisfied with appearances.]

Blanc's reader is invited to look at Robespierre and listen to him and, in doing so, to interpret both his 'sober' appearance and his way of expressing himself as mutually reinforcing signs of his preference for substance over mere appearances. The truth status of Robespierre's own costume-as-sign ('his appearance can be trusted') is simultaneously reinforced by the argument of Robespierre's sincerity and trustworthiness which accompanies the description. Robespierre's costume is thus the visible proof of his 'trustworthiness' – a quality which, in turn, legitimises and justifies the role which we have seen accorded to him in the narrative as watchdog for the people's interest.

In Lamartine's account, the *Incorruptible*'s clothes figure in the context of a lengthy portrait of Robespierre in his private capacity *chez* Duplay, that haven of peace on the rue Saint-Honoré which Lamartine likens to Rousseau's Charmettes and characterises by its familiality, domestic order, industry, decency, and 'meritorious poverty' (I:790). Before proceeding to give a detailed catalogue of Robespierre's dress (in which he emphasises above all the care with which the *ensemble* was composed), Lamartine provides the interpretative framework in which its significance is to be decoded:

> Son costume, même à l'époque où les démagogues affectaient de flatter le peuple en imitant le cynisme et le débraillement de l'indigence, était propre, décent, correct comme celui d'un homme qui se respecte dans le regard d'autrui. (I:793)
>
> [Even at a time when the demagogues were taking care to flatter the people by imitating the cynicism and slovenliness of poverty, his clothes were clean, decent, and correct like those of a man who respects himself in the eyes of others.]

If Robespierre's clothes are 'sober' and 'decent' in Blanc's account, they are decent and 'clean' in Lamartine, qualities which reflect the values of the modest, well-organised household in which Robespierre had chosen to settle. In this way, Robespierre's invariable public image (I:793) is presented and made legible as an expression of his irreproachable, model private life: the external sign of the 'decent' domestic values which he also upholds in practice.

Michelet describes and invokes Robespierre's dress on a number of different occasions, each time in combination with a different aspect of his physical, intellectual, or social being. Using physical appearance and demeanour as an index to ideological affiliations, for example, he picks out the fact that Robespierre's taste was distinctly *ancien régime* (II:60): the stiffness of his posture and 'sa tenue sèche, mais soignée' ('his austere, but well-groomed appearance') gave him the appearance of a parliamentary aristocrat (II:55). However, it is above all the uniformity of Robespierre's appearance which Michelet foregrounds: the fact that he always looked the same in 'his invariable green costume (always the same one, austere [*sec*] and severely brushed)' (I:476). What signifies 'consistency' in Blanc's narrative, signifies 'monotony' in Michelet's:

> L'unité de ton, la *monotonie* au sens propre... fut pourtant, il faut l'avouer, pour Robespierre, un très bon moyen politique... Il en usa en toutes choses, non dans la parole seulement, mais dans la vie, la démarche, le costume, de sorte qu'en cet homme identique, en cet invariable habit, en cette coiffure toujours la même, en ce gilet proverbial, on lut toujours les mêmes idées, on trouva la même formule, ou plutôt que la personne tout entière apparut comme une formule qui parlait et qui marchait. (I:870)

> [Unity of tone, *monotony* in its literal sense... was, one must admit, a very good political tool for Robespierre... He used it in everything, not merely in his speech, but in his life, his movements, his dress, with the result that in this identical man, with his invariable costume, invariable hairstyle, and proverbial waistcoat, one always read the same ideas and saw the same formula; or rather, the man himself appeared to be a walking and talking formula.]

Robespierre's 'proverbial' green coat is combined in Michelet's account both with a variety of features relating to other aspects of Robespierre's physical appearance (stiffness, dryness, severity) and with the many other instances of 'invariability' which characterise his person. In this way, through Michelet's selection and combination of descriptive details, together with his own discursive, interpretative interventions, 'Robespierre' comes to be seen as all of a piece, composed through and through of signs of the same monotony. Furthermore, within the semantic web woven in Michelet's representation, Robespierre's overwhelming monotony in turn functions as a sign both of his general sterility (all his academic labours only produce mere 'monotonous generalisations' copied from Rousseau, I:865) and of his unnatural death-in-life – a connotation determined by the sheer accumulation of semes indicating 'dryness', 'pallor', 'rigidity', 'coldness' in other descriptions of Robespierre's appearance.[13]

The foregoing representations of Robespierre's costume illustrate the importance of his physical image as a signifying supplement to the narrative, as well as the historians' didactic concern with ensuring that this image be interpreted in one way rather than another. As it is represented in each case, Robespierre's costume is constituted as a sign and a key is provided for its interpretation: through the discursive intervention of the narrator who attributes a meaning to it; through its being repeatedly referred to in the narrative (as Michelet repeatedly comes back to the invariability of the overcoat); or through the recurrence of the

[13] Robespierre's pallor: I:90, 622, 476, 865; II:59, 1005. His coldness: I:868, 1268. His dryness: I:476, 622; II:59, 870. These attributes tend to be conjoined in the discourse in various different combinations (e.g. cold and pale, pale and thin, cold and thin etc.), and are used, literally and/or figuratively, with reference to all different aspects of his person (e.g. he throws cold water on passionate proposals, I:868). What characterises Michelet's text in particular is the constant interplay between physical and moral attributes: 'rigidity', for example, being characteristic both of Robespierre's posture and his political inflexibility. See Barthes 1954 for a study of the recurrent semantic oppositions in Michelet's work at large. What is of interest in the present context is the way in which Michelet succeeds in setting up these semantic oppositions in his text through reworking historical particulars (e.g. the fact that Robespierre wore the same clothes and had a pale complexion).

foregrounded quality in a different form in some other aspect of the actorial figure (Robespierre's overcoat is decent/clean and he lives with decent/hardworking people; his overcoat is sober, he avoids mere rhetoric, and he rejects the imposition of the *bonnet rouge*).

In each case, the description of the *Incorruptible*'s clothes is inserted in a different context and, since the context functions as an interpretative framework, the same aspect of Robespierre's costume may be foregrounded in two different texts and yet be invested with a radically different significance. We have seen how Robespierre's deliberate care and effort in keeping up his appearance is a significant element both in Michelet's account and in Lamartine's. In the former, however, it figures as part of an isotopic pattern which includes lack of inspiration, lack of spontaneity, physical and moral rigidity, and laboured rhetoric ('l'effet laborieux de cette mâchoire pesante, qui mâchait et remâchait éternellement la même chose' ('the laborious effect of that heavy jaw, eternally chewing and rechewing on the same thing', I:868)). In Lamartine's account, in contrast, Robespierre's sartorial effort is linked, on the one hand, with the exemplary 'laboriousness' of the Duplays and, on the other hand, with his own labours and achievements: in spite of the natural handicap of his meagre and unattractive physique, he had managed to turn himself, through sheer hard work, into a passionate and impassioning orator – 'he had worked on himself for so long, he had reflected so much, written and erased so much ... that he had finally succeeded in making his language warmer and more flexible' (I:788). (In thus acknowledging Robespierre's personal unattractiveness, Lamartine makes him recognisable as 'Robespierre', while at the same time transforming him or, rather, showing him in the process of transforming himself, into something different.)[14] 'Laboriousness' and 'work', then, constitute the pejorative and meliorative versions or rewritings of the same commonplace concerning Robespierre: what in one text signifies lack of genius/instinct (a 'laborious effect') signifies productive work and the overcoming of nature in the other; what in one text is implicitly opposed to creative energies is implicitly opposed to indolence in the other.

But the context in which Robespierre's 'industriousness' or 'monotony' features is not limited simply to the other aspects of his portrait or way of

[14] Blanc follows a similar procedure, while moving towards a different conclusion: having recognised the meagreness and unattractiveness of Robespierre's person, he suggests that he was not always like this, but that the Revolution had moulded him that way. His austere appearance is thus constituted as a sign, not of his nature, but of the great self-abnegating sacrifice he had made to the Revolutionary cause: 'But the Revolution had moved forward, seized him, and fashioned him for her own needs' (I:667).

life, but extends to the representation as a whole. And, as it happens, the significance and value of the different qualities which mark one figure are highlighted by the fact that, within the larger context of the narrative, some other figure is negatively marked with respect to that particular attribute, or marked by its contrary. The attributes of the many individual actors who figure in the representation tend to be described, as we shall see, according to a limited number of common semantic axes, that is to say, on a comparative basis: in relation to each other and in their differences from each other.

Thus, if Lamartine's Robespierre is decently dressed, sober, industrious, and honest, it happens that his Marat's 'uniform' is slovenly, dirty, torn (II:236); and that his Danton is not merely less industrious or less sober, but is downright lazy (I:464), venal (I:157), and given to indulging in expensive, voluptuous tastes (II:236). Similarly, if Michelet's Robespierre is marked by his aristocratic air, sterility, 'scribehood', academic *belletrisme* (I:872), femininity (II:55), and by a whole series of features indicating his 'non-life', it happens that Danton is marked as a peasant-type (I:1284); a 'powerfully productive being' (I:1024); a master of spontaneous eloquence and the spoken word (I:1025); the 'great artist of the Revolution' (I:908); a male (I:1024; 1178); the source of a powerful instinctual life (I:1284) and of great vitality: 'Danton en qui était une vie si puissante, à qui vibrait toute vie...' ('Danton, in whom there was such a powerful life, with whom all life vibrated', I:907).

As the above examples illustrate, the difference between the actors is not one between equal parties. Rather, the attributes of one 'dominant' figure determine the aspects under which his opponents are described, and set the standard against which their personal traits are to be evaluated. Whereas the corrupt Danton clearly occupies a negatively valorised position with respect to the incorruptible Robespierre in Lamartine's text, a different standard is applied in Michelet's, where Danton's creativity, masculinity, and so on, is the norm and Robespierre's sterility the deviation from it.[15]

Through the lengthy portraits and through the repeated descriptions in the course of the narrative, an actorial figure becomes 'a normative crossroads' (Hamon 1983:320n): the meeting ground or point of convergence of a variety of different properties and values; the symbolic locus where 'the feminine' can be connected to 'sterile academic labours', as in Michelet's Robespierre, or where 'luxurious tastes' can be combined, as if naturally, with 'indolence', 'subversiveness', and 'love of riot', as in

[15] For a discussion of the way in which hierarchies of values are created within the economy of particular narratives, see Hamon 1984:1–41.

Lamartine's portrait of Danton (I:156). The apparent 'naturalness' with which these attributes are combined is further reinforced by the fact that the oppositions set up between certain figures with respect to one feature tend to be reproduced with respect to all other features: where Michelet's Robespierre is 'rigid', 'feminine', belletrist and so on, his Danton is 'passionate', 'virile', and 'creative'...

As they are defined in each case, then, the personal properties of 'Danton' and 'Robespierre' reinforce the oppositions drawn up between them at the level of the action and, in a variety of ways, serve to justify the particular roles which are ascribed to them. The actor who plays the privileged role in Michelet's narrative as spokesman for the patriotic movement in 1792 is also the actor who is marked by the positive values of being 'creative' and 'virile'; and, on both counts, he is opposed to Robespierre, the actor who is assigned the negatively valorised role of would-be dictator in 1792 and who is also negatively marked as academic, sterile, and of a meagre physique. Blanc's 'honest' Robespierre, who is given the privileged role as defender of the people's rights, is opposed both in action and by virtue of his character to the artistic Girondins (II:84–85) and the double-dealing Danton (I:698).

The amalgam of personal properties by which 'Robespierre' and 'Danton' are defined in each instance does not merely serve to underscore or explain the oppositions between these two individual actors at the level of the action. Particularly in Michelet and Lamartine, they also contribute to revealing or to reinforcing their connections with the other collective and individual figures in the narrative. As we have already seen in the treatment of the crowd on 5–6 October, or in Lamartine's treatment of 'familiality' on 10 August, the fact of sharing one or more qualities points to the kinship between two figures and/or reinforces an association which may already be evident at the level of the action. One of the most remarkable features of Lamartine's history is that the figures kindred with his virtuous, hard-working, familial-minded Robespierre – the 'last word' of the Revolution – are not to be found on the side of the revolutionary masses. (The congener of the crowd is the turbulent, indolent Danton whose famous voice 'resembled the roaring of a riot', I:156). The values which characterise Robespierre are to be found, instead, in the Duplay family and their friends, who look to the *Incorruptible* as a model and whom Lamartine presents as representatives of 'la masse révolutionnaire, mais probe, du peuple de Paris' ('the revolutionary, but honest, mass of the people of Paris', I:795). Robespierre's values are also to be found in part on the side of the crowd's victims, who are regularly described in familial terms[16] – in particular, the royal family whom Lamartine, in the extensive portrait which he gives of their lives as captives in the *Temple*, contrives to represent as a poor, working family.[17]

The different hallmarks of the Robespierre-effect in Michelet's text are to be found widely distributed among Robespierre's friends (Saint-Just is 'aristocratic', 'feminine' and superlatively stiff, II:74–5), as well as among those with whom his association is less evident, indirect, or indeed, secret: his 'dryness' suggests that his association with the furious fanatic elements in the Commune is the result of a natural kinship with these 'base natures... superficial, dry, empty, without consistency' (I:1003); while his 'rigidity' (as much as his aristocratic taste both in clothes and literature, II:50) suggests his kinship with the forces of royalism and the *ancien régime*.[18] In this way, the *Incorruptible*'s appearance reveals his natural links with a number of apparently unrelated ideological forces: the counter-revolution and revolutionary fanaticism meet, in a seemingly natural association, in the figure of 'Robespierre'. These signs of his natural kinship with the Reaction and the *terroristes* serve to reinforce the role which Michelet assigns to Robespierre at the level of the action as the inspiration behind the ultimately counter-revolutionary *Terreur*.

Moreover, if some of Robespierre's personal properties naturally link him to the aristocracy and the Church, other ones (such as his coldness and sterility) serve to dissociate him from the 'féconde et chaleureuse vie qui est dans l'instinct du peuple' ('the warm, fecund life which is instinctive to the *peuple*', I:869). In this way, his personal qualities

[16] As, one after the other, the condemned make their way to the guillotine (and frequently entire families go together – 'husband and wife, father and son, mother and daughters'), the attendant public jeers, cheers and calls for more (II:786).

[17] Doing the Cinderella in reverse as it were, Lamartine presents the queen and her sister-in-law as spending their days 'like poor working women' who must patch up their clothes (II:24); the queen sweeps the floor; the king uses his skills as a locksmith, like 'a true artisan' (II:39). It is interesting to note here that, although Robespierre had been living at the Duplays since 1791, the description of his exemplary domestic life only features in the narrative after the fall of the monarchy on 10 August 1792. This structure suggests that Lamartine is engaged in a transfer of symbolic power from the image of the 'king' as the symbolic linchpin of the state to the 'democratic' image of the industrious working family, exemplified in the figure of Robespierre.

[18] Gaspard (1985) offers a close study of the sustained metaphoric association which Michelet also establishes throughout the text between Robespierre and the Church, the Inquisition, the Jesuits; through these associations, the figure of Robespierre becomes the sign of the virtual action of a much larger actorial group (one which was clearly anathema to the strenuously anti-clerical Michelet). Through this portrait of Robespierre, Michelet can be seen to address one of the central controversies of the mid-nineteenth century, namely the relationship between Christianity and the Revolution (see Furet 1986).

dissociate his person, and hence his deeds, from the *peuple* he claimed to serve ('with all the resources of his academic talent, he worked at becoming part of the *peuple*', writes Michelet, I:868). On the other hand, of course, Danton's vitality and his powerful instinctual life make him naturally akin to Michelet's *peuple*, a kinship which serves to reinforce and justify the representative role which is ascribed to him in the narrative.[19]

Ontological values

We have seen earlier how 'Danton' and 'Robespierre' are invested with a symbolic function in the different narratives as signs of the collective situation, as representatives of the true Revolution which went off course. We have now seen how the description of 'Danton' and 'Robespierre' in their purely private capacity, and in their ethical and physical being, provides an important, ongoing supplement to the narrative configuration: in justifying the roles attributed to the leaders by an appeal to their personal qualities or defects; in reinforcing the oppositions between them at the level of the action; in confirming or establishing their associations with other collective actors and with the *peuple*. But to see the 'personal properties' of Robespierre and Danton solely in terms of their signifying function, that is, in relation to their narrative role as representatives of certain aspirations, would be to ignore the rhetorical function of the portraits given of the 'men themselves'. Representing Robespierre and Danton involves not only investing their appearance or person with significance, but also with *value* – be this ethical (as in the case of Blanc and Lamartine), be this aesthetic (as in the case of Michelet). The fact that the man who is the spokesman for certain aspirations is himself admirable, sympathetic, or attractive has clearly a function in increasing the attractiveness or rhetorical force of the programme which he represents.

The particular values associated with the privileged figures are to a large extent text specific, a product of the system of differences which each historian establishes within the economy of his representation. Nevertheless, as we have seen in the different invocations of nature as a background for the privileged figure, certain properties/values do recur across the different representations; in particular, those which I shall call here 'ontological values'.

In his account of Robespierre's expeditions out of doors, as we have seen, Michelet presents him either as engaged in literary pursuits (literally, writing his speeches) or in an equally literary imitation of Rousseau

19 This natural affiliation with the *peuple* is also written metaphorically into Danton's rough-hewn physique, which Michelet presents as the very image of the French peasantry (I:1284).

(seeking to popularise himself, he would go into carpenter shops 'in memory of *Émile*', II:88). Moreover, when Michelet portrays Robespierre's 'private life' in his description of his household arrangements *chez* Duplay, he does so only to reveal that Robespierre's (famous) private life is in fact a mere public show; also a piece of literature, a calculated, unnatural, *mise en scène* designed to signify his 'popularity' and to fabricate his own legend as the *Incorruptible* and as a man of the people. (In fact, Michelet suggests, a closer look shows that the Duplays belonged to the *petite bourgeoisie*, II:58). In this way, Michelet's formulaic would-be dictator Robespierre is shown not only to be alienated from the true *peuple*, but to be through and through a histrion. Even his private life belongs to a second-order, mediated, 'literary' reality: a second-hand, academic rewriting of Rousseau.

Blanc, in contrast, portrays Robespierre as rejecting mere signs in favour of substance, while he portrays the Girondins as theatrically minded *artistes* whose natural medium is spectacle, and whose words and deeds must be treated, therefore, with suspicion as potentially a 'mere show' or simulacrum. Lamartine, for his part, describes Danton as an inveterate actor: 'His courage needed spectators. His window was his rostrum. He played to the gallery even in his prison cell' (II:733); at his trial, Danton's dignity was 'a bit theatrical' (II:746), while his death scene was a gala performance:

> Ainsi mourut en scène devant le peuple cet homme pour qui l'échafaud était encore un théâtre, et qui avait voulu mourir applaudi à la fin tragique de sa vie, comme il l'avait été au commencement et au milieu. (II:757)
>
> [Thus did this man die, this man for whom the scaffold was still a theatre and who, at the tragic end of his life, wanted to die hearing the applause he had heard at its beginning and half-way through.]

In distributing the quality of theatricality or literarity among the different figures, the historians can be said to chart out a semiotic map for their readers distinguishing what is real from what is not real or rather, from what is less real or of a second-order *mimesis* in the events represented: Robespierre's clothes are what they appear, while Danton's apparently heroic deeds or speeches may only have been done for the effect. In marking these actors or their actions as 'theatrical', the historians can be said to deposit traces of their own re-readings of the personal legends of Danton and Robespierre in their actual representation of these figures. For the marker of 'theatricality' or 'simulation' clearly serves to undermine both the historical status and the potential rhetorical force of the men's legends, including their programme of action: 'don't be deceived by appearances; this is not historical reality or this is not a sincerely held belief, this is only theatre or literature'. (It will be recalled how 'theatricality' is invoked in a similar way by Michelet in his treatment of the Comte d'Hervilly's would-be sublime gesture on 10 August (above, p.98n), and by Blanc in his description of the fear simulated by the royalists at the trial of the king (above, p.56).)

Moreover, following the same 'rhetoric of anti-rhetoric' (Valesio 1980:41f) which we have seen the historians use in relation to each other, the fact that 'theatricality' or 'artifice' is imputed to the 'other' negatively valorised figure serves to highlight the naturalness, the reality, and the truth status of his symbolically dominant opponent. Thus, where Blanc's Danton is marked both as a double-dealer and as an unoriginal imitator,[20] Michelet's Danton is marked by his vitality, energy, naturalness, lack of artifice – all the qualities by which historical truth is to be recognised, according to the historiographical programmes which I considered in my Introduction. Danton shares these qualities, moreover, with the 'living reality' of the nation, as Michelet explicitly calls the object of general allegiance on 10 August (above, pp.98f). In contrast, the person of Robespierre is consistently marked by its non-life (rigidity, dryness etc.), its derivativeness, and its 'literariness'.[21]

In this way, defining 'Robespierre' and 'Danton' goes together with establishing a certain ontological hierarchy between them, which functions as a metahistorical comment on the representation, distinguishing what is 'really historical' from what is not. Distinguishing the 'historical' from the 'literary' or from the 'less real' does not merely serve to legitimise the historian's configuration of events; but it may also work in curious ways

[20] Danton's rhetoric is modelled on that of Isnard (II:181), his speeches were written by Desmoulins (II:181), his ideas and strategies were inspired by Robespierre (II:598, 664, 681), and even his 'famous last words', 'Show my head to the people: it's worth it,' turn out to have been in imitation of Mirabeau's deathbed scene (I:655). In Michelet's narrative, in contrast, it is Robespierre who is the imitator *par excellence*: 'Rousseau's miserable bastard' (I:684); 'An imitator by nature' (II:63). This charge of 'imitation' serves to reduce the ontological value of the figure as an original type or model and, hence, to reduce his status as a potential source for historical change.

[21] It is worth noting here that, in Carlyle's history of the Revolution the principal semantic axis drawn up between Danton and Robespierre is also that of 'Reality' versus 'Formula', with Robespierre as the 'formula' and Danton as the 'real man': 'No hollow Formalist this; but a very Man: with all his dross he was a Man; fiery-real, from the great fire bosom of Nature herself' (1903, II:338); 'with what terror of feminine hatred the poor sea-green Formula looked at the monstrous colossal Reality, and grew greener to behold him' (1903, II:334). Besides Danton, who was not strong enough in practice to defeat Robespierre, the other 'real' men in Carlyle's narrative are Mirabeau ('a Reality and no Simulacrum', 1903, I:349) and Napoleon ('of the genus Reality', 1903, II:366).

towards legitimising or reinforcing the symbolic role accorded to the ontologically superior figure in the representation. Michelet's 'Robespierre', as we have seen, symbolises the actual Revolution as *Terreur* and dictatorship, while his person is marked (like that of Louis XVI in the *mise en spectacle* of 10 August) by its 'non-vitality'. The name 'Danton' comes to symbolise the unrealised Revolution, the Revolution as idea and ideal, while his person is characterised both as being akin to the genius of the people and as an original type, marked by his energy, force, and fecundity. Within Michelet's representation, then, and through the symbolic mediation of the individual figures of Robespierre and Danton, the Revolution as idea and as unfulfilled, patriotic programme is marked as having a greater force and a higher ontological status than the actual event of the *Terreur*.

Epilogue: Robespierre before the public (8 June 1794)

The *Fête de l'Etre suprême* – one of the final core events of the Revolution – was a unique historical event as well as the choreographed performance of an elaborate, highly symbolic score. Both as text and as historical event it is unanimously associated with the name of Robespierre, who not only conceived the Supreme Being and organised the festival to celebrate its existence, but went on to play a leading role in officiating at the actual ceremony in his capacity as president of the Convention. What is of interest here is less the nature of the Supreme Being itself than the fact that the festival around its investiture should finally bring the figure of Robespierre face to face with the public – a crowd of spectators which Michelet, Lamartine, and Blanc refer to as 'the *peuple*' and which they represent by flower-bearing familial figures of various ages.[22]

Having considered the configuration of collective actors in the previous chapter and the representation of individual actors in the present one, I would like to conclude with a brief analysis of the different relationships established between Robespierre and the public in the narrative representations of the ceremony which took place on 8 June 1794.

Michelet describes how Robespierre, for once having replaced his proverbial costume by the official uniform of the Convention – albeit with an overcoat a shade 'paler' than that of his colleagues – appeared before

[22] The organisers of the feast had given the role of 'chorus' to the public, who were to be both spectators and participants in the event; and who were even taken through a rehearsal prior to the feast itself (see Schlanger 1975:272). In this sense, the 'public' which attended the ceremony is already a representation of the *peuple* (young, old, mothers, fathers etc.), a prior representation which the three historians take over into their own narratives.

the Tuileries to initiate the *Fête de l'Etre suprême* and was acclaimed 'blindly' by the assembled crowd: given the festive preparations, the people expect or hope that Robespierre will use his power to end the *Terreur* and introduce a new reign of clemency (II:868–9). Would Robespierre respond to popular opinion, 'la pensée populaire'? No: he did not *dare* to – a word resonant with the ghost of the by now defunct Danton. In the event, the crowd hears nothing at all of the long speech which Robespierre delivers (he speaks from a height, and his voice is lost in the enormous space), except the invariable refrain: 'Death to the tyrants!...Tomorrow we shall take up the fight again etc.' (II:869). The *Incorruptible*'s alienation from the desires of the public is further reinforced by the fact that within the festive familial setting and among all the signs celebrating the natural world, the rigid, 'undead' Robespierre is patently a discordant figure, his very gaiety making him not so much radiant as like a 'chat noyé jadis et ressuscité par le galvanisme' (a 'drowned cat resuscitated by galvanism', II:870).

Blanc describes how, dressed in the uniform of the Convention, Robespierre appeared before the Tuileries and was acclaimed by the joyous multitude (II:742). Like the radiant faces in the crowd, Robespierre's pale face is transfigured by joy, both at the sight of the happiness of the people before him and at the prospect of the new era which the *fête* prefigured: 'for the first time, his face was radiant with joy' (II:741); 'He stood there, lifting up his pale face and smooth brow which shone with a ray of tenderness' (II:742). In this transfigured pose, Robespierre delivers his 'beautiful and pathetic' speech in praise of the 'author of Nature', which the narrator paraphrases in part, but which he then breaks off in order to explain why Robespierre, for all that he shared the people's longings for the new era, should have considered that the time was not yet entirely ripe for it. Even in the midst of the general happiness, there were signs of the existence of a counter-revolutionary plot brewing among the factionary (or 'false' national) representatives, which threatened not only Robespierre himself, but by implication that universal happiness which he ('true' national representative) and the *peuple* desired: hence his warning to the public – today, let us enjoy the celebration, 'tomorrow, we shall take up the fight again against vice and tyranny' (II:742).

Lamartine, finally, describes how Robespierre appeared to the assembled crowd and took his place in the highest row of seats reserved for the Convention, wearing a uniform slightly different in colour from that of his fellow-*conventionnels*, and (a detail which is also in Michelet) carrying a symbolic bouquet which was much bigger than theirs:

> Robespierre parut. Son isolement, son élévation, son panache, son bouquet plus volumineux, lui donnaient l'apparence d'un maître. Le peuple, que son nom dominait comme son trône dominait la Convention, croyait qu'on allait proclamer sa dictature. (II:829)
>
> [Robespierre appeared. His isolation, his elevated position, his panache, his larger bouquet: all these gave him the air of a master. The people, whom his name dominated in the same way that his throne now dominated the Convention, believed that his dictatorship was to be proclaimed.]

The spectator-public then gives a rapturous response to the 'act of faith of the French people' (II:832) which Robespierre goes on to pronounce in praise of the Supreme Being. Indeed, their enthusiasm is such that the day becomes as much the apotheosis of the leader who had 'professed their faith' in the Supreme Being as it is a celebration of the deity itself: 'The *peuple* was intoxicated,' while the Convention contemplated with dismay 'la préséance majestueuse de Robespierre; l'enthousiasme exclusif du peuple pour son représentant' ('the majestic presence of Robespierre; the exclusive enthusiasm of the *peuple* for its representative', II:832).

The different representations of the figure of Robespierre at the *fête* exemplify in a particularly striking manner one of the principal concerns of this study; namely, how the figurative, and more specifically, the scenic representation of events and persons can be used to produce meaning: in each case, the description of Robespierre's mien, the colour of his uniform, and the size of his bouquet, together with the description of his physical proximity to (or distance from) the public and his fellow deputies, are used to *make manifest* the nature of his relationship with these other figures at that time. In each case, the figurative representation of the ceremony (what it looked like to the public) works together with the explicit interventions of the narrator in such a way as to establish a different type of relationship between Robespierre and the public; in such a way as to set him up as one sort of leader rather than another in relation to an implied model of what a 'national representative' should be.

Thus, against the background of the role hitherto ascribed to him in Michelet's narrative, Robespierre's physical isolation at the *Etre suprême*, his alien appearance, and his visible difference from the other uniformed deputies, are all objective manifestations and confirmations of his *de facto* dictatorship: his pronouncements run counter to the people's will rather than representing it, and his nature is alien to theirs (in contrast, the voice of the dead Danton had been 'the energy of France made manifest', 'the very voice of the Revolution and of France', I:1025).

Blanc, on the other hand, does not note any difference between the

Incorruptible's costume and that of his fellow deputies, and he presents his radiant Robespierre as fully sharing the desires of the radiant public. Through Blanc's discursive intervention, however, whereby the event becomes focalised through the speaker rather than through the crowd, Robespierre is presented as possessing an exclusive insight into the obstacles standing in the people's way. His Robespierre is thus a leader whose pronouncements are apparently, but not actually, out of step with the people's will: while his nature may be similar to theirs, his role is not to give direct expression to their will (the implied model in Michelet), but rather, following a pattern we have seen earlier in Blanc's narrative, to use his superior insight, above all his superior knowledge of the enemy, to act selflessly as their protector.

In Lamartine's account, finally, Robespierre is a *de facto* 'dictator'. However, if the difference in his uniform and bouquet are stressed, along with his majestic pre-eminence at the top of the Convention, so too is the public's joyous readiness to endorse his pronouncements as soon as they hear him, and thus to recognise him, in Lamartine's words, as their 'national representative'.

But the message which Lamartine's crowd so enthusiastically endorses is not the same as that heard by the public in the other accounts. The only lines of Robespierre's discourse on the Supreme Being which Michelet quotes (as being the only message actually registered by the crowd) are those indicating that the *Incorruptible* did not in fact intend to use his power and the occasion to dismantle the *Terreur*: 'Death to the tyrants!...' Lamartine, in contrast, skips lightly over the question of whether all or any of Robespierre's speech was actually heard by the crowd and, like Blanc, quotes Robespierre's speech directly and at length. But, while Blanc's paraphrase/quotation of the same speech suggests that it stressed above all the fact that the Supreme Being had decreed innocent people should not be oppressed by tyrants, Lamartine has him praise the Supreme Being for rather different reasons: he had created men for mutual love and for the happiness acquired through virtue ('par la route de la vertu'); for the love of the *patrie* and the joys of family life, rather than for debauchery and perfidy. If the *peuple* are intoxicated with enthusiasm, then, it is in response to hearing this particular 'virtuous' message – not the one heard and rejected by Michelet's crowd on the same occasion.[23]

[23] II:830. The theme of virtue is further accentuated by the fact that Lamartine includes statues of Vice and Crime among the allegorical figures which Robespierre is to destroy symbolically as part of the ceremony: 'Atheism, Egoism, Nothingness,

The comparison of the different 'direct', 'unmediated' quotations from Robespierre's philosophico-exhortatory speech shows how it has in fact been edited by the historians themselves; in each case, through the historian's selective quotation, the *Incorruptible* transmits a different message to the awaiting public in 1794 – and posthumously, through the mediation of the narrative discourse, to the historian's public. Moreover, where Blanc gives his readers an insight into Robespierre's private fears, which were not evident to the original public in 1794, Lamartine and Michelet present the reactions of the spectators themselves. The public's disappointment or, conversely, their endorsement of Robespierre's speech not only guides the historian's public in his approach to the figure of Robespierre, but it also serves to corroborate and legitimise the significance which the historian himself attributes to Robespierre's speech. In Lamartine's account, the values expressed by Robespierre resemble so closely the norms which have been implied throughout the narrative representation that, in dictating a quest for virtue to the public in 1794, Robespierre can be seen to act in turn as a spokesman for Lamartine in 1847: the historian not only 'dictates' retrospectively to the public, but simultaneously represents that public as rapturously accepting his message.

With this, I turn to the figure of the public. The signs in Blanc's account are that the *peuple* protected by Robespierre at the *Fête de l'Etre suprême* is a direct descendant of the crowds who participated in the events of 5 October 1789 and 17 July 1791: like the earlier crowds, it is defined by familial figures and characterised by its innocence, harmony, and its spontaneous enjoyment of natural pleasures (in 1794, as in 1789 and 1791, the crowd is seen in radiant sunshine, II:741, I:405, I:729); and, like the earlier crowds, it plays a role as the actual or potential victim of factional interests or conspiracies.

In Michelet's narrative, the connection between the public who rejects Robespierre's speech on 8 June 1794 and the *peuple* as it has hitherto figured is less direct than in Blanc's; but that such a connection exists is suggested by the familial composition of the crowd and its consistent desire for clemency and reconciliation, and *a contrario* by its alienation from the unnatural, deathlike person of Robespierre.

And the crowd in Lamartine's account? The *peuple* which enthusiastically endorses Robespierre's philosophical exhortations on the joys of virtue and acclaims him as their 'national representative' is akin to the

Crimes and Vices' (II:829). Michelet simply mentions Atheism, Egoism, and Nothingness (II:869), while Blanc significantly adds to these the figures of Ambition and Discord (II:742).

'revolutionary, but honest' *peuple* in the immediate circle of the Duplays, who looked to him as the 'very type of truth and virtue' (I:795). But if it does have associates within a part of the nation, the *peuple* at the *Fête de l'Etre suprême* is clearly not a direct descendant of the revolutionary masses such as they have actually figured in Lamartine's narrative of the events of the Revolution. For there, as we have seen, the crowd is generally shown as the source of outrages against the family and as the bloodthirsty impetus behind the *Terreur*, while positive values tend to be located on the side of minority figures who, more often than not, are victims of the Revolution's violence. In provoking a collective adherence to a life of virtue and probity on 8 June 1794, then, Robespierre does not give expression to, or represent, a collective spirit which the narrative presumes to exist already. Instead, the public endorsement of the king-like Robespierre – spokesman for virtue and a christian society, himself a paragon of virtue and the living proof of what can be achieved through hard work – heralds a collective state which comes into existence in the very act of recognising his leadership and in the very act of taking him as a model.[24]

We have seen earlier how Michelet and Blanc, in representing the actual events of the period 1789–94, seek to correct current misconceptions concerning the Revolution by bringing into relief, against the background of what actually happened, the image of the 'real' or 'authentic' (if failed) Revolution and the alternative history it might have given rise to. Although with very different implications, Lamartine's reconstitution of the *Fête de l'Etre suprême* can also be said to disengage the image of an 'alternative history' for his public. What is involved in his case, however, is an attempt to disengage the true ideals of the Revolution (as represented by Robespierre) from the actual circumstances which caused it to go off course; it is an attempt to distil the model of a 'different Revolution' from the fiasco of what actually happened, from the mistakes which others, including Robespierre, made in trying to realise their ideals. This alternative Revolution was briefly prefigured in the recognition of Robespierre at the *Etre suprême* and the endorsement of his virtuous programme – but not, as we have seen earlier, in the insurrection of 10 August. This Revolution was/would be centred on the role of a virtuous leader and was/would be dependent on the reform of the *peuple* whom he represents – a reform which Lamartine's own representation of the past

[24] The *peuple* who acclaims Robespierre at the *Etre suprême* has been intermittently present or prefigured in the preceding events; in the 'peuple immense', for example, which Lamartine has accompany the forces of order in their crusade against 'the other *peuple*' at the Champ de Mars (above, p.131).

seeks to bring into being, by presenting it with all the prestige of 'having been there' already on 8 June 1794.

The revealing gap in Lamartine's narrative between the 'revolutionary masses' which actually carried out the Revolution and the *peuple* which takes its lead from the majestic, virtuous Robespierre points to the way in which the historian's own political agenda (what he would like to see happen, and perhaps also the role which he himself would like to play) breaks through his re-presentation of past events. In this way, his text brings blatantly to the fore one of the principal concerns of this study: namely, the fact that historical narrative has a double focus in that it is at once a symbolic reconstitution of past realities and a discourse directed by the historian to his own public. At the same time, Lamartine's narrative points to the 'discontinuous' nature of the socio-historical reality which is both the object of the historian's representation and the context in which his discourse is located. Whereas Michelet and Blanc suggest that there is a continuity in the *peuple* between past and present, be this between 1789 and 1794, or between 1794 and 1847, Lamartine's narrative suggests that the relationship between the collective past and present can be at once that of conjunction and disjunction, of continuity and difference.

Conclusion

> ... we beg our readers to keep the following in mind: to narrate the history of the Revolution is not merely to write a book; it is to take action.
>
> Louis Blanc

In the *critique historique* which follows his account of the emergence of the Girondin party in 1791, Louis Blanc, as we have seen (above, p.50), accuses both Michelet and Lamartine of having been biassed in favour of that party. He explains this bias by their natural kinship as 'artists' with the artists of the Revolution and hence, following the logic of his text, by their preference for esthetics and appearances over historical realities and the 'austere duties' of the historian (II:586).

Blanc's representation of his rivals as latter-day crypto-Girondins illustrates both the agonistic element in the representation of the revolutionary past and the historical links between the *dramatis personae* of the Revolution and the historians who constitute it as an object of knowledge. Michelet and Lamartine are not merely biassed towards the *artistes* of the Revolution; the austere (robespierriste) Blanc also implies that, through their distortions of the past, they replay a similarly 'artistic' role whose effects he himself is now seeking to counter.

Blanc's representation of his rivals as being more interested in literary effects than in reality and as being, for that reason, partial to one particular faction, also points to the model of the 'true' historian – embodied, it is implied, in the writer himself. The true historian is, in a double sense, impartial. He faithfully represents the past and, what is inseparable from this, he is spokesman for the history, not of a particular party or class, but of the social body as a whole.

In the foregoing analysis, we have seen how each latter-day representation of the Revolution, while making similar claims to speak with the authority of reality, takes place through the complex mediation of a finite, narrative text – a text in which the discourse of the historian is combined with that of his sources, who are at times delegated to tell their own story; in which the discursive interventions of the latter-day narrator work in complicated ways together with his figurative re-presentation of events and persons in the past; in which the detailed description of actors and circumstances plays an important role in supplementing the narration of events; in which the narrative discourse strategically shifts between summary and scenic representations, presents events in a particular order, and focalises them through one actor rather than another. Through his selection of representative events, and through his representation and combination of those events in his discourse, each historian configures the common past in a different way, investing it – or rather, seeking to invest it – with a different historical significance for his readers. But what sort of significance? And how is it 'historical'?

For convenience sake, I have just defined the task of the history-writer as that of representing historical events. But, in a sense, this is a misrepresentation or, at least, an over-simplification of what we have seen go on in practice. For, as I have shown, representing the Revolution is not simply a question of representing *events* (that is, what happened). It also involves representing and defining the collective subject involved in those events: what happened to whom? The narrative configuration of the Revolution for a latter-day public is inseparable from defining and symbolically conjoining the different actorial figures (groups and individuals) which are taken to represent the collective subject of history across time – and hence to represent the forerunners of the historian's public. (The filiation between the contemporary public and the actors in the past is, as we have seen, reinforced by the fact that the latter are also identified as the locus of certain 'transhistorical' values or norms held by the narrator and presumed shared by his public). It is the actions and aspirations of these actors – these 'men like ourselves', to recall Thierry's phrase – which the historian, through the variety of technical means at his disposal, makes the focus or subject of his narrative and the object of his reader's sympathy.

Within the context of the narrative, then, 'what happened' becomes invested with a particular significance as the fulfillment or – what is ultimately the case in all three histories – as the frustration of the narrative subject's hopes or desires. That these aspirations are thwarted is due to the role of the antagonist 'marginal' figures, into whose hands power ultimately falls and who give the final direction to events. In Michelet: these antagonists are the ultimately counter-revolutionary fanatics/theorists who are out of touch with the *peuple* who gave the original momentum to events and whose natural spirit of justice and harmony was behind the most glorious moments of the Revolution. In Blanc: they are the false national representatives who, under the guise of furthering the

Revolution, work against the *peuple* (p.p. Robespierre) towards their own counter-revolutionary, factional ends. In Lamartine: they are the turbulent crowd (aided and abetted by the unprincipled Danton) who drag Robespierre into the *Terreur* and ultimately sabotage his aspirations for a 'reasonable democracy' (II:921) based on christian principles. I call these figures 'marginal' since – as Lamartine's treatment of the numerically preponderant crowd makes particularly clear – they are in effect marginalised by the representation itself. For if the historians use their narrative and rhetorical strategies to establish certain figures as representatives of the posited social subject, of 'our history', we have seen that they use similar procedures to establish certain other figures as deviant, non-representative: 'men *un*like ourselves'.

In his 'Le Discours de l'histoire', Barthes argues that historical discourse is 'uniformly assertive', that the historian 'narrates that which was, not that which was not, or which was merely doubtful' (1982:18). My study of the intertextual antagonism between Blanc, Michelet, and Lamartine (chapter 1) has shown how, in order to correct their readers' prior misconceptions concerning the Revolution and in order to assert the authority of their own version over the claims of others, they in fact do take into account 'that which was not', for example, by denying the reality of certain events which never existed except in the fictional fabrications of other historians. Moreover, as I showed in subsequent chapters, the historians seek, in the very act of representing 'what was', to *augment* the 'presence' and hence, the significance of certain actions/actors over others (Michelet goes even further by explicitly marking the 'nation', and its representative Danton, as more 'real' and 'vital' than their opponents). Conversely, the historians use a variety of strategies to attenuate the possible significance of certain other actions: by decreasing their presence in the text or, through a complex set of checks and balances, by countering their possible claims to define 'what was'. Through description and through the discursive interventions of the narrators, moreover, certain actions are reduced to a sort of second-class ontological status as being merely 'theatrical' or 'pieces of literature'.

In thus representing 'what was', the three historians can be seen as attempting to distinguish the actual Revolution (the *ensemble* of events 1789–94) from the 'essence' or 'idea' of the Revolution by which it is to be defined for the latter-day public. For all the differences in the way in which the historians define it, the promise of the Revolution, corresponding to the hopes of the narrative subject and of the narrator (and, by implication, of his public), fails to be realised in the actual outcome of events. In different ways, the actual outcome of the events of 1789–94 is shown to be a deviation from what the Revolution was in its origins and from what it might or should have become. But the narrative configuration of 'what actually happened' is itself inseparable from the bringing into relief of 'alternative histories'; that is to say, with revealing against the background of what actually happened the 'paths not taken', the direction in which events might or could have developed had power been located elsewhere, had the desires of the narrative subject been realised. In this way, the logic of the narrative makes us once again recognise the fact that historical discourse may not simply deal with 'what was'. Rather, through its narrative configuration of 'what was', the representation brings into relief what might have been or should have been, what could be; the indicative is not its sole modality.[1]

Although the marginal deviant forces may have actually carried the day and brought the national history off-course, the historians can be said to try to compensate symbolically for this by presenting the programme of their narrative subjects as the most 'vital' or 'natural' one and as the one which was ardently desired by the *peuple* (if only by the 'honest' *peuple*, as in Lamartine) – the one which, by implication, is most desirable for the contemporary public. We have seen how scenes of public consensus – from the spontaneous turning of the national guards away from the figure of the king in Michelet's account of 'Le 10 août' to the spontaneous acclamation of Robespierre in Lamartine's account of the *Etre suprême* – play an important rhetorical role in endorsing certain actions or programmes. In his recent work, Hayden White has argued that historians seek to make the real desirable by giving it the coherence of a story, with a well-marked beginning, middle, and end (1987:21). In the case of the three histories considered here, one can argue, rather, that it is the desirable which is made 'real' and, in the process, constituted as the possible outcome of an, as yet, incompleted story.

Only the superficial, apparently 'terrifying' history of the Revolution has so far been written, remarks Louis Blanc at the beginning of his account of the legal changes brought about by the Revolution:

> Et pourtant, la partie vivante de l'histoire était là… vivante, car c'est celle qui s'est continuée jusqu'à nous, celle qui encadre notre existence, celle qui touche à nos plus chers désirs… (I:526)

[1] As Todorov has written concerning the different modalities of narrative propositions, 'Indicative propositions are perceived as designating actions which actually took place; if another modality is used, it is because the action has not yet been carried out, but exists potentially, virtually… Classical grammarians explained the existence of modal propositions by the fact that language not only serves to describe and refer to reality, but also to express our will' (1971:123).

> [And yet, the living part of history was there... it is 'living' since it is the history which has persisted until now, which frames our existence, which touches our most cherished desires...]

The course of 'real' history or the 'living history which binds the past to the present' has been ruptured or suspended (at the same time as the 'real past' has been obscured through partisan misrepresentations). The 'living history' has been forced underground and can now only be resurrected symbolically by the individual historian in anticipation – or hope – of its actual re-emergence into reality.

My study of the rhetoric of the historians' representation has brought to light the main procedures through which Lamartine, Blanc, and Michelet seek to invest the Revolution with a particular significance for the public in whose name they wrote. It ends up pointing to some of ways in which the figurative representation and commemoration of past actualities can play a symbolic role in the present: the past as an implied negative projection of the present (undesirable) state of affairs; the past as an example of how not to do things; or, finally and most importantly, the past as a symbolic prefigurement or model of future action. For if Lamartine, Blanc, and Michelet are, in the first instance, concerned with representing actual events and with disengaging historical truth from the literary distortions of it, it is clear that they are also concerned with continuing the work begun in the past – by specifically discursive means. In their different ways, they seek to salvage from the shipwreck of the later phases of the Revolution the memory of certain collective states and aspirations which really existed, but which can now only be imagined; collective states which, because they have already existed, may exist again and which, in the meantime, thanks to the historian, can already be imagined *as* real, enjoying all 'the prestige of having really been there'.

Seen in this light, Michelet's description of Danton's power to speak with the 'voix même de la France' in 1792, and to unite people around the patriotic cause, becomes an expression of the historian's own desire, not only to speak with 'the authority of reality' and the voice of the *peuple*, but also to be 'author' of a patriotic reality:

> Qu'on ne dise pas que la parole soit peu de chose en de tels moments. Parole et acte, c'est tout un. La puissante, l'énergique affirmation qui assure les coeurs, c'est une création d'actes; ce qu'elle dit, elle le produit. L'action est ici la servante de la parole; elle vient docilement derrière, comme au premier jour du monde: *Il dit, et le monde fut.* (I:1025)

> [Let it not be said that discourse is of little importance at such moments. Discourse and action, they are all of a piece. In fortifying

> the hearts of others, a powerful, energetic affirmation creates action; what is said is produced. Action is here the servant of discourse; action follows obediently behind, as it did on the first day of creation: *He spoke, and the world was.*]

With Michelet's expression of the performative power of language to create realities and produce action, we reach the limits both of discourse and of a purely textual analysis. 'He spoke, and the world was'? The failure of 1848 had made one thing clear even before Michelet and Blanc had finished the histories which they began to publish in 1847: if historical discourse gives shape and meaning to historical reality and so can inspire or shape collective action, it is also destined to meet the resistance both of events and of other discourses. For words to bring a world immediately into being in the act of pronouncing them, the speaker can indeed only be 'on the first day of creation' – a possible image for the fiction-writer, but the very antithesis of the historian.

References

Agulhon, Maurice. 1973. *1848 ou l'apprentissage de la république 1848–1852.* Nouvelle histoire de la France contemporaine 8. Paris: Seuil.

1979. *Marianne au combat: l'imagerie et la symbolique républicaines de 1789 à 1880.* Paris: Flammarion.

Aulard, Alphonse. 1893. *Études et leçons sur la Révolution française.* 1st series. Paris: Alcan.

Bal, Mieke. 1985. *Narratology: Introduction to the Theory of Narrative.* Translated by Christine van Boheemen. University of Toronto Press.

Balzac, Honoré de. 1976–81. *La Comédie humaine.* Ed. P.-G. Castex. 12 vols. Paris: Gallimard (Bibliothèque de la Pléiade).

Bann, Stephen. 1984. *The Clothing of Clio: A Study of the Representation of History in Nineteenth-century Britain and France.* Cambridge University Press.

Barante, Prosper de. 1838. *Histoire des Ducs de Bourgogne de la maison de Valois 1364–1477.* 2 vols. Brussels: Société Typographique Belge.

Barthes, Roland. 1954. *Michelet par lui-même.* Paris: Seuil.

1968. 'L'Effet de réel.' *Communications* 11: 84–9.

1977. 'Introduction à l'analyse structurale des récits.' In R. Barthes *et al.*, *Poétique du récit*, 7–57. Paris: Seuil.

1982. 'Le Discours de l'histoire.' *Poétique* 49: 13–21.

Baudrillart, Henri. 1850. 'Les Historiens de la Révolution française et la révolution de février.' *Revue des deux mondes* 20th year, no. 4 (new series, vol. 8): 808–31.

Blanc, Louis. 1847–62a. *Histoire de la Révolution française.* 3 vols. Brussels: Meline, Cans (vols. 1–2); Lacroix, Verboeckhoven (vol. 3).

1847–62b. *Histoire de la Révolution française.* 12 vols. Paris: Langlois & Leclercq (vols. 1–9); Langlois & Furne (vol. 10); Pagnerre & Furne (vols. 11–12).

Boer, Pim den. 1987. *Geschiedenis als beroep: de professionalisering van de geschiedbeoefening in Frankrijk (1818–1914).* Nijmegen: SUN.

Braudel, Fernand. 1969. *Écrits sur l'histoire.* Paris: Flammarion.

Brinker, Menachem. 1985. 'Thème et interprétation.' *Poétique* 64: 435–43.

Brooks, Peter. 1985. *The Melodramatic Imagination: Balzac, Henry James, Melodrama, and the Mode of Excess.* Columbia University Press.

Burke, Edmund. 1930. *Reflections on the Revolution in France*. Ed. F.G. Selby. London: Macmillan.

Cabet, Etienne. 1839–40. *Histoire populaire de la Révolution française de 1789 à 1830; précédée d'une introduction contenant le précis de l'histoire des Français depuis leur origine jusqu'aux états généraux*. 4 vols. Paris: Pagnerre.

Canary, Robert H. and Henry Kozicki, eds. 1978. *The Writing of History: Literary Form and Historical Understanding*. University of Wisconsin Press.

Capefigue, Jean-Baptiste 1829. *Histoire de Philippe-Auguste*. 2nd edn. 4 vols. Paris: Dufey.

Carlyle, Thomas. 1895. *Critical and Miscellaneous Essays*. 7 vols. London: Chapman & Hall.

1903. *The French Revolution*. 2 vols. London: Dent (Everyman's Library).

de Certeau, Michel. 1975. *L'Écriture de l'histoire*. Paris: Gallimard.

1982. 'L'Histoire, science et fiction.' In *La Philosophie de l'histoire et la pratique historienne d'aujourd'hui/Philosophy of History and Contemporary Historiography*, 19–39. Ed. D. Carr *et al.* University of Ottawa Press.

Le Charivari. 1847. 'La Révolution française.' 12 April: 2.

Chatman, Seymour. 1978. *Story and Discourse: Narrative Structure in Discourse and Film*. Cornell University Press.

Compagnon, Antoine. 1979. *La Seconde main: ou le travail de la citation*. Paris: Seuil.

Coornaert, Emile. 1977. *Destins de Clio en France depuis 1800: essai*. Paris: Les Editions ouvrières.

Court, Antoine. 1980. 'Lamartine et le neveu de Vergniaud.' *Revue d'histoire littéraire de la France* 80: 764–73.

1985. 'Lamartine – historien.' Dissertation, University of Clermont-Ferrand II.

Danto, Arthur C. 1985. *Narration and Knowledge (Including the Integral Text of 'Analytical Philosophy of History')*. New York: Columbia University Press.

Delon, Michel. 1981. 'La Saint-Barthélémy et la Terreur chez Mme Staël et les historiens de la Révolution au XIXe siècle.' *Romantisme* 31: 49–62.

Dubois, Jacques. 1983. *L'Institution de la littérature: introduction à une sociologie*. Brussels: Éditions Labor.

Duchet, Claude. 1973. 'Une écriture de la socialité.' *Poétique* 16: 446–54.

Ducrot, Oswald, and Tzvetan Todorov. 1972. *Dictionnaire encyclopédique des sciences du langage*. Paris: Seuil.

Dumas, Alexandre. n.d. *Les Blancs et les bleus*. 2 vols. Paris: Calmann-Lévy.

1851. *Ange Pitou*. 8 vols. Paris: Cadot.

Duprat, Pascal. 1847. 'Les Nouveaux historiens de la Révolution française. MM. L. Blanc, Michelet et de Lamartine.' *La Revue indépendante*, 7th year, 2nd series 10: 60–85.

Eco, Umberto. 1979a. *A Theory of Semiotics*. Indiana University Press.

1979b. *The Role of the Reader: Explorations in the Semiotics of Texts*. Indiana University Press.

1984. *Semiotics and the Philosophy of Language*. London: Macmillan.

Edwards, E. 1849. 'Historians of the French Revolution.' *British Quarterly Review* 10: 168–92.

Erlich, Victor. 1981. *Russian Formalism: History – Doctrine*. 3rd edn. Yale University Press.

Esquiros, Alphonse. 1847. *Histoire des Montagnards*. 2 vols. Paris: Victor Lecou.

Febvre, Lucien. 1948. 'Avant-Propos.' In Charles Morazé. *Trois essais sur histoire et culture*, v-vi. Cahiers des Annales. Paris: Armand Colin.

Foucault, Michel. 1969. *L'Archéologie du savoir*. Paris: Gallimard.

Fournel, Victor. 1890. *L'Événement de Varennes*. Paris: Honoré Champion.

Fueter, Eduard. 1911. *Geschichte der neueren Historiographie*. Munich and Berlin: R. Oldenbourg.

Furet, François. 1978. *Penser la Révolution française*. Paris: Gallimard.

1986. *La Gauche et la Révolution française au milieu du XIXe siècle: Edgar Quinet et la question du Jacobinisme (1865–1870)*. Paris: Hachette.

Gaspard, Claire. 1985. 'Michelet et les Jacobins.' Dissertation, University of Paris I.

Gearhart, Suzanne. 1984. *The Open Boundary of History and Fiction: A Critical Approach to the French Enlightenment*. Princeton University Press.

Genette, Gérard. 1969. 'Frontières du récit.' In G. Genette, *Figures 2: essais*, 49–69. Paris: Seuil.

1980. *Narrative Discourse: An Essay in Method*. Translated by Jane Lewin. Cornell University Press.

1983. *Nouveau discours du récit*. Paris: Seuil.

1987. *Seuils*. Paris: Seuil.

Gérard, Alice. 1970. *La Révolution française, mythes et interprétations (1789–1970)*. Paris: Flammarion.

Geyl, Pieter. 1961. 'French Historians For and Against the Revolution.' In P. Geyl, *Encounters in History*, 87–142. Cleveland and New York: Meridian Books.

Ginzburg, Carlo. 1981. *The Cheese and the Worms: The Cosmos of a Sixteenth-Century Miller*. Translated by John and Anne Tedeschi. London: Routledge & Kegan Paul.

Godechot, Jacques. 1974. *Un jury pour la Révolution*. Paris: Robert Laffont.

Gombrich, E.H. 1969. *Art and Illusion: A Study in the Psychology of Pictorial Representation*. Bollingen Series 35.5. Princeton University Press.

Gossman, Lionel. 1976. *Augustin Thierry and Liberal Historiography*. History and Theory, Beiheft 15. Wesleyan University Press.

1978. 'History and Literature: Reproduction or Signification?' In Canary and Kozicki 1978, 3–39.

Graner, Marcel. 1984. '"Un roman tombe dans l'Histoire"; Dumas adaptateur de Michelet dans *Ange Pitou* et *La Comtesse de Charny*.' In *Récit et histoire*, 61–74. Ed. J. Bessière. Paris: Presses universitaires de France.

Greimas, Algirdas Julien. 1973. 'Sur l'histoire événementielle et l'histoire fondamentale.' In Koselleck and Stempel 1973, 139–53.

1983. *Du sens II: Essais sémiotiques*. Paris: Seuil.

Greimas, Algirdas Julien, and Joseph Courtès. 1979. *Sémiotique: dictionnaire raisonné de la théorie du langage*. Paris: Hachette.

Guillemin, Henri. 1946. *Lamartine et la question sociale: documents inédits*. Paris: Plon.

1948. *Lamartine en 1848*. Paris: Presses universitaires de France.

Halkin, Léon E. 1973. *Initiation à la critique historique*. Cahiers des Annales. Paris: Armand Colin.

Hamon, Philippe. 1972. 'Qu'est-ce qu'une description?' *Poétique* 12: 465–85.

1973. 'Un discours contraint.' *Poétique* 16: 411–45.

1977. 'Pour un statut sémiologique du personnage.' In R. Barthes *et al.*, *Poétique du récit*, 115–80. Paris: Seuil.

1981. *Introduction à l'analyse du descriptif*. Paris: Hachette.

1983. *Le Personnel du roman: le système des personnages dans les* Rougon-Macquart *d'Emile Zola*. Geneva: Droz.

1984. *Texte et idéologie: valeurs, hiérarchies et évaluations dans l'oeuvre littéraire*. Paris: Presses universitaires de France.

Hughes, Peter. 1984. 'Narrative, Scene, and the Fictions of History.' In *Contemporary Approaches to Narrative*, 73–87. Ed. A. Mortimer. Tübingen: Gunter Narr.

Hugo, Victor. 1965. *Quatrevingt-treize*. Paris: Garnier.

Hunt, Lynn. 1984. *Politics, Culture, and Class in the French Revolution*. University of California Press.

Iknayan, Marguerite. 1961. *The Idea of the Novel in France: The Critical Reaction 1815–1848*. Geneva: Droz.

Jullian, Camille. 1897. *Extraits des historiens français du XIXe siècle: publiés, annotés et précédés d'une introduction sur l'histoire en France*. Paris: Hachette.

Keylor, William R. 1975. *Academy and Community: The Foundation of the French Historical Profession*. Harvard University Press.

Kocka, Jürgen, and Thomas Nipperdey, eds. 1979. *Theorie und Erzählung in der Geschichte*. Beiträge zur Historik 3. Munich: DTV.

Koselleck, Reinhart, and Wolf-Dieter Stempel, eds. 1973. *Geschichte – Ereignis und Erzählung*. Poetik und Hermeneutik 5. Munich: Wilhelm Fink.

LaCapra, Dominick. 1985. *History and Criticism*. Cornell University Press.

Lamartine, Alphonse de. 1847. *Histoire des Girondins*. 8 vols. Paris: Furne & Coquebert.

1856–69. *Cours familier de littérature: un entretien par mois*. 28 vols. Paris: privately printed.

1983. *Histoire des Girondins*. 2 vols. Paris: Plon.

Langlois, Charles-Victor, and Seignobos, Charles. 1898. *Introduction aux études historiques*. Paris: Hachette.

Lefebvre, Georges. 1951. *La Révolution française*. 3rd edn. Peuples et Civilisations; Histoire générale 13. Paris: Presses universitaires de France.

Lerminier, Eugène. 1847. 'Les Nouveaux historiens de la Révolution française.' *Revue des deux mondes* 17th year, no. 2 (new series, vol. 18): 1048–70.

Macaulay, Thomas Babington. 1906. *Complete Works*. 12 vols. London: Longmans.

Massmann, Klaus. 1972. *Die Rezeption der historischen Romane Sir Walter Scotts in Frankreich (1816–1832)*. Heidelberg: Carl Winter Universitätsverlag.

McManners, J. 1965. 'The Historiography of the French Revolution.' In *The American and French Revolutions (1763–93)*, 618–52. Ed. A. Goodwin. *The New Cambridge Modern History*, vol. 8. Cambridge University Press.

Mellon, Stanley. 1958. *The Political Uses of History: A Study of Historians in the French Restoration*. Stanford University Press.
Mercier, Louis-Sébastien. 1862. *Paris pendant la Révolution (1789–1798) ou le nouveau Paris*. 2 vols. Paris: Poulet-Malassis.
Michelet, Jules. 1952. *Histoire de la Révolution française*. Ed. Gérard Walter. 2 vols. Paris: Gallimard (Bibliothèque de la Pléiade).
1982. *Histoire du dix-neuvième siècle*. Ed. B. Leuillot. *Oeuvres complètes*. Ed. P. Viallaneix. Vol. 21. Paris: Flammarion.
Mink, Louis O. 1978. 'Narrative Form as Cognitive Instrument.' In Canary and Kozicki 1978, 129–49.
Monteil, Amans-Alexis. 1841. *Les Français pour la première fois dans l'histoire de France ou poétique de l'histoire des divers états*. Paris: Coquebert.
1843. *Histoire des Français des divers états*. 5 vols. Brussels: Wouters, Raspoet.
Moreau, Pierre. 1935. *L'Histoire en France au XIXe siècle: état présent des travaux et equisse d'un plan d'études*. Paris: Les Belles Lettres.
Morse, William Marston. 1974. 'Narrative Structure and the Historical Imagination in Michelet's *Histoire de la Révolution française*.' Dissertation, Yale University.
Nettement, Alfred. 1848. *Les Historiens de la Révolution française: M. de Lamartine: Études critiques sur les Girondins*. Paris: De Signy & Dubey.
Orr, Linda. 1976. *Jules Michelet: Nature, History, and Language*. Cornell University Press.
1982. 'L'Autorité "populaire" de l'historiographie romantique.' *Romanic Review* 73: 463–72.
1984. 'The Romantic Historiography of the Revolution and French Society.' *Consortium on Revolutionary Europe 1750–1850: Proceedings* 14: 242–7.
1986. 'The Revenge of Literature: A History of History.' *New Literary History* 18.1: 1–22.
1989. 'French Romantic Histories of the Revolution: Michelet, Blanc, Tocqueville – A Narrative.' In *The French Revolution 1789–1989: Two Hundred Years of Rethinking*, 123–42. Ed. Sandy Petrey. Special issue of *The Eighteenth Century: Theory and Interpretation*. Texas Tech University Press.
Ory, Pascal. 1984. 'Le Centenaire de la Révolution française: la preuve par 89.' In *Les Lieux de mémoire*. Ed. Pierre Nora. Paris: Gallimard. I. *La République*: 523–60.
Ozouf, Mona. 1970. 'De thermidor à brumaire: les discours de la Révolution sur elle-même.' *Revue historique* 243: 31–66.
Paulson, Ronald. 1983. *Representations of Revolution (1789–1820)*. Yale University Press.
Perelman, Chaim, and Lucie Olbrechts-Tyteca. 1969. *The New Rhetoric: A Treatise on Argumentation*. Translated by John Wilkinson and Purcell Weaver. University of Notre Dame Press.
Perry, Menachem. 1979. 'Literary Dynamics: How the Order of a Text Creates its Meanings (with an Analysis of Faulkner's "A Rose for Emily").' *Poetics Today* 1.1: 35–64, 311–61.
Reboul, Fabienne. 1980. 'Histoire ou feuilleton? La Révolution française vue par Lamartine.' *Romantisme* 52: 19–33.

Reinhard, Marcel. 1969. *La Chute de la royauté: 10 août 1792*. Paris: Gallimard.
Reizov, Boris. c.1962. *L'Historiographie romantique française 1815–1830*. Authorised translation. Moscow: Éditions en langues étrangères.
Ricoeur, Paul. 1983–5. *Temps et récit*. 3 vols. Paris: Seuil.
Rigney, Ann. 1986. 'Toward Varennes.' *New Literary History* 18.1: 77–98.
1988. 'Du récit historique: la Prise de la Bastille selon Michelet (1847).' *Poétique* 75: 267–78.
1989. 'Narrative Representation and National Identity: On the "Frenchness" of the Revolution.' *Yearbook of European Studies* 2: 53–69.
Rudé, George. 1975. *Robespierre: Portrait of a Revolutionary Democrat*. London: Collins.
Sarazin, J. 1835. *Du progrès des études historiques en France au XIXe siècle*. Strasburg: F.G. Levrault.
Schlanger, Judith E. 1975. 'Théâtre révolutionnaire et représentation du bien.' *Poétique* 22: 268–83.
Schmid, Georg, ed. 1986. *Die Zeichen der Historie: Beiträge zu einer semiologischen Geschichtswissenschaft*. Vienna: Hermann Böhlau.
Searle, John. 1958. 'Proper Names.' *Mind* 67: 166–73.
Sismondi, J.C.L. Simonde de. 1821–44. *Histoire des Français*. 31 vols. Paris: Treuttel & Wurtz.
Smithson, Rulon Nephi. 1973. *Augustin Thierry: Social and Political Consciousness in the Evolution of a Historical Method*. Geneva: Droz.
Soboul, Albert. 1966. *Le Procès de Louis XVI*. n.p.: René Julliard.
Stadler, Pieter. 1958. *Geschichtschreibung und historisches Denken in Frankreich 1789–1871*. Zürich: Berichthaus.
Staël, Germaine de. 1820. *De la littérature considérée dans ses rapports avec les institutions sociales*. In *Oeuvres complètes*. Vol.2. (facs. repr. Geneva: Slatkine, 1967).
Struever, Nancy S. 1985. 'Historical Discourse.' In *Handbook of Discourse Analysis*. Ed. T. van Dijk. London: Academic Press. I. *Disciplines of Discourse*: 249–71.
Suleiman, Susan Rubin. 1983. *Authoritarian Fictions: The Ideological Novel as a Literary Genre*. Columbia University Press.
Thierry, Augustin. 1851. *Oeuvres complètes*. 8 vols. Paris: Furne.
Thiers, Louis Adolphe. 1865. *Histoire de la Révolution française*. 2 vols. Paris: Furne.
Thiesse, Anne-Marie. 1980. 'L'Éducation sociale d'un romancier: le cas d'Eugène Süe.' *Actes de la recherche en sciences sociales* 32–3: 51–63.
Todorov, Tzvetan. 1971. *Poétique de la prose*. Paris: Seuil.
Valesio, Paolo. 1980. *Novantiqua: Rhetorics as a Contemporary Theory*. Indiana University Press.
Veyne, Paul. 1978. *Comment on écrit l'histoire; suivi de 'Foucault revolutionne l'histoire'*. Paris: Seuil.
Viallaneix, Paul. 1973. 'A l'école buissonière.' *L'Arc* 52: 59–67.
Weinrich, Harald. 1973. 'Narrative Strukturen in der Geschichtschreibung.' In Koselleck and Stempel 1973, 519–23.
White, Hayden. 1973. *Metahistory: The Historical Imagination in Nineteenth-century Europe*. Johns Hopkins University Press.

1976. 'The Fictions of Factual Representation.' In *The Literature of Fact: Selected Papers from the English Institute*, 21–44. Ed. Angus Fletcher. Columbia University Press.
1978. 'The Historical Text as Literary Artifact.' In Canary and Kozicki 1978, 41–62.
1987. *The Content of the Form: Narrative Discourse and Historical Representation*. Johns Hopkins University Press.

Index